D1555261

From Recovery to Catastrophe

MONOGRAPHS IN GERMAN HISTORY

FROM RECOVERY TO CATASTROPHE
Municipal Stabilization and Political Crisis
in Weimar Germany

Ben Lieberman

Berghahn Books
NEW YORK · OXFORD

First published in 1998 by
Berghahn Books

Library of Congress Cataloging-in-Publication Data

Lieberman, Benjamin David, 1962-
From recovery to catastrophe : municipal recovery and political
crisis in Weimar, Germany / Ben Lieberman.
   p.   cm. — (Monographs in German history ; v. 3)
Includes bibliographical references and index.
ISBN 1-57181-104-4 (alk. paper)
1. Municipal government—Germany.   1. Municipal finance—Germany.
3. Germany—Economic conditions—1918-1945.   4. Germany—Social
conditions—1918-1933.   I. Title.   II. Series
JS5431.L53   1998
338.943'009042—dc21   97-19436
                                                                CIP

British Library Cataloguing in Publication Data

A catalogue record for this book is available from the British Library.

Printed in the United States on acid-free paper.

Contents

LIST OF TABLES

LIST OF ABBREVIATIONS

BA	Bundesarchiv
BVK	Bürgervorsteher-Kollegium
BVP	Bayerischen Volkspartei (Bavarian People's Party)
DDP	Deutsche Demokratische Partei (German Democratic Party)
DINTA	Deutsches Institut für technische Arbeitsschulung
DNVP	Deutschnationale Volkspartei (German National People's Party)
DVP	Deutsche Volkspartei (German People's Party)
HZS	Hauszinssteuer
KPD	Kommunistische Partei Deutschlands (German Communist Party)
LA	Landesarchiv
NSDAP	National Socialist Party
NWHStA	Nordrhein-Westfälisches Hauptstaatsarchiv Düsseldorf
StA	Stadtarchiv
StVV	Stadtveordnetenversammlung
RM	Reichsmark
RWE	Rheinisch-Westfälisches Elektrizitätswerk
SPD	Sozialdemokratische Partei Deutschlands (German Social Democratic Party)
USPD	Unabhängige Sozialdemokratische Partei Deutschlands (Independent German Social Democratic Party)

PREFACE

While carrying out preliminary research on German cities, I one day came across Reichsbank President Hjalmar Schacht's highly publicized 1927 attack against municipal luxury expenditures. I soon discovered, however, that the same city governments condemned by powerful financial authorities simultaneously won acclaim for their programs of recovery. I then began to investigate the paradoxes of the politics and policies of Weimar municipal recovery. In broader terms, I have aimed to reconcile the considerable evidence of success at the municipal level with depictions of Weimar history as a sequence of catastrophes.

This work owes an initial debt to my dissertation committee of John Boyer, Michael Geyer, and George Steinmetz. John Boyer directed me toward the world of Central European Cities. Michael Geyer provided invaluable guidance. My research was supported by the Friedrich Ebert Stiftung. I wish to thank the staffs of the Düsseldorf Stadtarchiv, Stadtarchiv Frankfurt am Main, and Hanover Stadtarchiv. I would like to thank Dieter Rebentisch, Jürgen Reulecke, Adelheid von Saldern, and the late Peter Hüttenberger for sharing their vast knowledge about municipal and urban history with me. I also thank the Interlibrary Loan Office at the Fitchburg State College Library. Volker Berghahn and Christoph Conrad also provided valuable suggestions.

Unless otherwise noted, all translations are my own.

Marcia and Philip Lieberman helped my works in many ways, and I therefore dedicate this book to them.

I would also like to thank Nancy Waters for advice, support, and much more.

For Marcia and Philip Lieberman

RECOVERING WEIMAR RECOVERY

The Weimar Republic is understandably remembered for failure rather than for success. The revolution that ended the German Empire and began the Weimar Republic in 1918 left few groups within German society satisfied. Assassinations, attempted coups, economic turmoil, and social deprivation plagued the Republic's early years. Even as Germans confronted an imposing bill for reparations, inflation left German currency virtually worthless. By 1923, the Weimar Republic, suffering from hyperinflation and the occupation of the industrial region of the Ruhr by France and Belgium, appeared on the verge of collapse. Shaken by political, economic, and social crisis, these early years together with the First World War have been recently described as the "Great Disorder."[1]

If the early years of the Republic were dreadful, the last years were worse. The late 1920s and the early 1930s saw the breakdown of democracy, mass unemployment, social trauma, National Socialist electoral gains, and the Republic's end with the appointment of Adolf Hitler as German Chancellor in January 1933. Looking back on this record of disasters after the Second World War, it was entirely reasonable for observers of the Federal Republic of Germany to stress that "Bonn was not Weimar."[2]

Because of these traumatic events in the first and last years of Weimar Germany, historical narratives have depicted the Republic as a sequence of disasters. The familiar historical narrative of Weimar disappointments and setbacks begins with the revolution, which marked the end of the German Empire and the start of the new German Republic. Despite disputes about such issues as the range of options during the revolution and the political role of workers' and soldiers' councils, the extensive historiography of the German revolution written in the 1960s and 1970s generally described the revolutionary transition of 1918-1920 as a disappointment to most Germans.[3] Summarizing these debates, Wolfgang J. Mommsen concluded that the stabilization of the Weimar Republic in 1919 and 1920 was "paid for … with a continuous political polarization of German society."[4] In more recent work, Richard Bessel stressed that broad sectors of Weimar society resented the postwar political and social order despite the short-term successes of economic demobilization.[5]

Scholarship on the inflationary era, one of the true growth areas of Weimar historiography since the late 1970s, continued the narrative of Weimar calamities past the revolution.[6] In *The Great Disorder*, the authoritative account of the infamous German inflation of the early 1920s, Gerald D. Feldman depicted the traumatic impact of successive waves of inflation on German society and politics. Sending prices soaring and living standards into steep decline, hyperinflation unquestionably brought new shocks for many Germans. Feldman noted in a particularly telling observation that "the sale of personal valuables and household possessions by … persons from the *Mittelstand* [middle class] … became so ubiquitous in 1922 that housewives' associations … undertook the painful task." Economic misery grew with the collapse of the passive resistance policy to the French occupation of the Ruhr in 1923, and "one-quarter of all Germans were in need of some support at the turn of 1923-1924."[7]

Beginning with accounts of revolutionary disappointment, inflationary trauma, and social discontent, the historical narrative of Weimar disasters culminates between 1929 and 1933 with economic catastrophe, the collapse of democracy, and the rise of the National Socialists to power. In one of the most widely discussed contributions to the literature of economic collapse, Knut Borchardt argued that political leaders had little alternative other than to pursue deflationary policies as the German economy collapsed in the early 1930s.[8] Explaining how the National Socialists capitalized on the Republic's final crisis, the vast historiography of Weimar's political collapse has concentrated on such topics as the improving fortunes of the National Socialist Party (NSDAP) in elections, National Socialist mobilization in individual towns, and political violence.[9] The paralysis of democratic institutions and the transition toward increasingly authoritarian cabinets have also received extensive attention.[10]

The early and late catastrophes of the Weimar Republic have understandably dominated Weimar historiography, but any historical narrative of the Republic as a sequence of disasters breaks down for the middle years of the Weimar Republic between the end of hyperinflation in 1923-1924 and the onset of depression in 1929. The Weimar Republic did not collapse immediately after hyperinflation. Instead, it experienced a period of comparative political and economic stability, which would seem to interrupt the prevailing catastrophic narrative of Weimar history. How, indeed, is it even possible to account for stability in an historical epoch now synonymous with instability? Confronting the peculiarity of Weimar stability, historians sought over several decades to place the period of stabilization back into the standard narrative of crises and catastrophes by stressing the fragility of Weimar stability.

The first major re-evaluation of Weimar's middle years of stabilization concentrated on national politics. Analyzing parliamentary coalitions in the Reichstag between 1924 and 1928, Michael Stürmer concluded in a study published in 1967 that disagreements over domestic and foreign policy undermined all parliamentary majorities. The absence of any durable coalitions produced political improvisation.[11] Chronic political instability was evident in frequent changes in government and disputes over issues such as the flag, the expropriation of princely houses, the school law, and the reform of unemployment insurance. M. Rainer Lepsius first suggested in the 1960s that this pattern of conflict reflected the persistent division of the German party system by social and cultural cleavages into several distinct political groupings, which he termed "sociocultural milieus."[12] Subsequent research on the decline of liberalism has also confirmed the instability of Weimar politics during the period of stabilization.[13]

Pioneering cultural history of the Weimar Republic during the late 1960s and 1970s also came to stress the fragility of Weimar stabilization. Revival of interest in Weimar culture in the 1960s brought new attention to the Republic's "golden" years of innovation in architecture, art, and drama.[14] However, historians simultaneously emphasized Weimar's cultural pessimism. Acknowledging the excitement of Berlin's cultural scene in the mid-1920s, Peter Gay also noted signs of imminent decay in the same period. "But Weimar of those years," Gay suggested, "was like the society on the magic mountain: ruddy cheeks concealed insidious symptoms." Gay also found evidence of morbidity in contemporary fascination with themes such as suicide. "There was a whole genre of novels dealing with the suicides of young high-school students."[15] Continuing to explore Weimar culture, historians outlined a sharp backlash against cultural innovation. Walter Laqueur detected a "fin-de-siè-cle mood" on both sides of the political spectrum. The extreme Right "loathed" Weimar culture, and "some spokesmen of the extreme Left attacked the Republic and all it stood for as something that was rotten through and through."[16] Subsequent research on interwar culture has also described National Socialist reaction against the legacy of Weimar culture.[17]

By the 1970s, detailed research on varied economic and indus-trial interest groups underscored the fragility of Weimar stabiliza-tion. Building on prior studies from the 1960s of reaction against the Weimar Republic among farmers and peasants, papers pre-sented at a major conference held in 1973 on the "Industrial System and Political Development in the Weimar Republic" revealed wide-spread dissatisfaction among industrialists, the old middle class, and white collar workers even during the Republic's middle years.[18] Additional studies of economic and social interest groups almost invariably confirmed mounting dissatisfaction with the Weimar Republic. Despite bitter debates over how best to analyze German industry, historians as diverse as Henry Ashby Turner and David Abraham described deep-seated discontent among industrialists with the Weimar social and economic policies.[19] Historians study-ing the old Mittelstand similarly documented dissatisfaction with social and economic policy as well as with big business.[20] Further studies of agriculture showed, if anything, even more consistent and vehement antagonism by farmers and peasants against the Weimar Republic.[21] Histories of German workers, meanwhile, also pointed to the limits of Weimar stability. Thus, the very title of Hein-rich August Winkler's comprehensive study on labor in Weimar's middle years, "*The Appearance of Normality*," stressed the provisional nature of Weimar stabilization.[22]

Reinforcing skeptical reassessment of Weimar stability, economic historians from the late 1970s onward stressed the short duration and sharp limits of economic stabilization during Weimar's middle years. Knut Borchardt depicted the years between 1924 and 1929 as a period of economic crisis in which businesses faced an excessive wage push and falling profits. In this account of Weimar economic history, intense distributional conflict slowed growth and provoked political conflict well before the onset of depression.[23] In a compre-hensive study of the interwar German economy published in 1986, Harold James outlined the limits of German rationalization, the mounting debts of German agriculture, and the burden of rising government spending during the Weimar Republic. Such spending, William McNeil noted, provoked a sharp backlash by Reparations Agent Parker Gilbert and Reichsbank President Hjalmar Schacht against government waste.[24]

As economic historians traced the many causes of Weimar Germany's economic collapse back to the structural weaknesses of the Republic's middle years, historians studying Weimar inflation simultaneously followed the destructive consequences of hyperinflation after 1923 into the period of stabilization. Histories of inflation, carried out in part under the auspices of an international research project entitled "Inflation and Reconstruction in Germany and Europe, 1914-1924," argued that monetary stabilization inflicted grievous injuries on the Republic that did not heal after 1924, despite the outer appearance of improving economic health. Revaluation enraged creditors who saw their assets erased, and resentment against monetary stabilization subsequently boosted the fortunes of splinter political parties and weakened moderate parties.[25] Though more cautious than other historians in attributing Weimar's final collapse to the consequences of inflation, Gerald Feldman concluded that "many of the conditions that had given rise to the inflation and had driven it to its disastrous hyperinflationary conclusion persisted through the stabilization and depression and played an important role in the destruction of the Republic." Inflation left a legacy of scandals, bankruptcy, structural weakness in the credit and banking system, and budget deficits.[26]

From the 1960s through the 1980s, political, cultural, and economic historians placed the Weimar period of stabilization back into a narrative of Weimar disasters by stressing the Republic's underlying frailty even during its middle years. Recent social history, however, has outlined the successes of Weimar stabilization. Though difficult to incorporate into the standard narrative of Weimar history, the theme of social stabilization emerged in studies of social policy by such historians as Christoph Sachße and Detlev Peukert. Although they discussed the shortcomings of social policies, these studies still drew a picture of ambitious and at times partially successful programs of social provision. As Peukert noted in 1987, the Weimar Republic marked "a qualitative jump in the development of the social state in Germany – and not only in Germany." Recognizing the achievements of Weimar social policy, Peter Stachura, in a study of the younger proletariat, concluded that "the mid-1920s witnessed, therefore, undeniable victories for *Sozialpolitik* [social policy] … all to the substantial material advantage of large sections of the industrial proletariat."[27]

The work of Peukert and other social historians challenges prevailing interpretations of the Weimar Republic's middle years by stressing both the successes and shortcomings of Weimar stabilization. Stabilization ultimately failed, yet Weimar's achievements extended well beyond high culture to encompass social policy, urban innovation, and an emerging mass culture.[28]

A reassessment of Weimar's middle years after Peukert's work reveals multiple unexplained contradictions of Weimar stabilization. First, recovery programs possessed considerable popular appeal despite the anger of those Germans who saw their interests damaged by monetary stabilization. Although stabilization brought the shock of revaluation, it also provided Weimar's institutions the chance to carry out recovery projects that stood to win the support of many Germans after years of deprivation. For several years after 1924, recovery programs won widespread backing despite the opposition of powerful financial authorities. Charges of wasteful public spending by Reparations Agent Parker Gilbert did not erode political enthusiasm for pursuing recovery. Historians including Harold James and William McNeil described the skepticism of contemporary financial authorities about the utility of Weimar public spending, but did not fully explain how Weimar political institutions managed to acquire considerable support for their recovery programs.[29]

Weimar political institutions created these elaborate recovery programs despite deep political divisions. The development of social policies, as outlined by Peukert and others, suggests that Weimar political institutions could create consensus in favor of ambitious social programs, yet the chief studies of national politics have stressed endemic political rifts and conflicts. The leading recent account of Prussia by Dietrich Orlow, in contrast, suggested that Weimar's largest state provided the Republic with some measure of stability, but similarly devoted little attention to explaining the consensus in favor of recovery policy.[30]

How did the Weimar Republic produce programs of social stabilization despite the deep-seated resentment against monetary stabilization, the opposition from powerful financial authorities, and the divided political institutions that have been outlined in three decades of historical reassessments of Weimar's middle years? An explanation can be found in part by shifting from national to local history. Historians of imperial Germany revised a standard historical narrative by focusing on local politics, and a similar strategy is also useful for the Weimar Republic.[31] The Reichstag, though deeply divided, was far from the only important elected assembly in Weimar Germany. Along with state parliaments, cities created an additional arena for state activity and for democracy at the local level.

The extreme difficulty of accounting for recovery and social stabilization in standard narratives of Weimar disasters stems in large part from neglect of local history. Although often absent from accounts of Weimar-era national and Prussian politics, recovery has surfaced as a major theme in monographs on individual mayors and cities. Municipal histories and studies of local politics in such cities as Berlin, Frankfurt, Hamburg, Munich, and Nuremberg present a very different narrative of the period of stabilization from that common to accounts of affairs at the national level. Conflict and instability, the themes of choice for most Weimar histories, were not absent from local history, but municipal histories invariably reveal ongoing and sometimes successful initiatives to promote stabilization up until 1929.[32] From this perspective, stabilization was neither doomed by the legacy of inflation, nor predestined to failure by early traces of future economic crisis. Instead, local democracy created an impressive record of government activity during Weimar's middle years. Challenging the trend toward describing an ever shorter and shakier period of Weimar stability, municipal history offers the opportunity to explain the achievements of stabilization and to investigate the contradictions of recovery.

A Municipal Narrative of Weimar History: Crisis and Activism

A municipal analysis of Weimar history indicates both the considerable problems of recovery and the development of civic activism. At least until 1923, municipal history yields a narrative of crisis that closely follows the familiar national narrative of Weimar history. The remarkable civic activism of the middle years of the Weimar Republic did not emerge instantaneously. The revolution that created tensions throughout Germany also brought political, social, and economic upheavals to many cities. Revolutionary conflict brought political violence to Berlin, Bremen, Munich, and the cities of the Ruhr, and unemployment severely taxed the resources of Berlin.[33]

Hyperinflation, in turn, brought misery to much of Germany's urban population. Germans suffered from poverty, poor nourishment, disease, and lack of access to good housing. Hyperinflation subjected pensioners and even the employed to burdens usually associated with unemployment. Unemployment rose sharply in the cities of the Ruhr during the passive resistance of spring and summer 1923. Basic food provisions fell into short supply leading to protests and plundering in occupied areas.[34]

Hyperinflation decimated municipal finances. City governments struggled to cover soaring salaries and social service costs. In addition, cities lost control over an important source of revenue when Finance Minister Erzberger's financial reforms of 1919 ended the ability of municipalities to levy a surcharge to the income tax. Unable to use their chief prewar tax, city governments relied instead on surcharges to the property and trade taxes. Despite frequently raising these surcharges, municipal authorities found themselves unable to keep pace with inflation by late 1922.[35] Inflation rapidly made large increases in expenditures for any item meaningless and undermined efforts to tend to the needy or to undertake other programs. By 1923, municipal officials invariably presented a grim picture of municipal finance.[36]

By the time monetary stabilization took hold in 1924, civic leaders still confronted a long list of problems. The years of war and inflation had damaged both the urban population and civic institutions. Even well-established civic institutions such as water, gas, and electrical utilities – the core firms of the communal economy – which most city governments had acquired before 1914, had suffered from neglect during the First World War and the immediate postwar years when city governments could not devote substantial resources to maintaining, let alone expanding, infrastructure. The effects of this failure to modernize were most obvious for municipal electrical power plants which could barely meet rising demand for electricity when economic activity began to rebound. In Düsseldorf, for example, use of electricity rose from 4.7 million kilowatt-hours in 1910 to 9.7 million kilowatt-hours in 1924, and 13.5 million kilowatt-hours in 1925.[37] A considerable portion of existing electrical generating capacity also had yet to be converted from direct to alternating current.

The impact of years of war and inflation also damaged less economically important civic institutions. Institutions of bourgeois (*bürgerliche*) culture, zoos, botanical gardens, and theaters founded by the Bürgertum in the second half of the nineteenth century – those elements that David Blackbourn termed "a silent bourgeois revolution" – survived war and inflation in shaky condition.[38] In Hanover, the city's zoo managed to preserve only one-third of the animals from its prewar collection, and the directors of Frankfurt's Palm Garden lamented in 1925 that "we have … only escaped with the bare life. We have preserved our body; but our health … has suffered."[39]

The financial problems of public and private institutions exemplified the economic damage that war and inflation had inflicted on many urban residents, not only those living on the social margins, but also millions of people who had formerly been self-sufficient. Municipal leaders from all political parties were struck by the social expansion of poverty beyond the borders of the laboring poor. Hanover's former Stadtdirektor (the prewar equivalent of mayor in Hanover), Heinrich Tramm, asserted that it was not the "working masses," but the "educated Mittelstand" that was most needy. Such claims of bourgeois suffering could be perceived as a political strategy to justify state aid for groups that had once prided themselves on their independence, but prominent Social Democrats conceded that poverty had become more common outside of the working class. Max Brauer, the Social Democratic Mayor of Altona, stated that "the impoverishment of the middle classes through inflation brought millions to public support."[40]

Swelling the numbers of the poor, war and inflation also created a housing shortage that left many urban residents scrambling for apartments. Housing construction came to a near-halt during the First World War, and a postwar rise in marriages and surge in construction prices aggravated the shortage. No city escaped the housing crisis. By 1923, a conservative estimate placed the total shortage at 600,000 housing units.[41] The housing shortage was widely perceived as one of the chief problems of recovery. Frankfurt's Mayor Ludwig Landmann took an uncontroversial stance when he said: "Of all the problems of war and postwar consequences, the housing shortage presses most painfully on the communities; it is the millstone which hangs around the necks of the large communities."[42]

Mayors, city councilors, and planning professionals worried that poor housing conditions threatened public health. Members of Düsseldorf's city parliament, for example, feared that the housing shortage threatened to create a medical and hygienic catastrophe. A Communist city councilor read his fellow councilors accounts from a medical journal of the consequences of poor housing: tuberculosis, gonorrhea, and syphilis. There was little, on this occasion, to distinguish between the positions of groups as different as the German Communist Party (KPD) and bourgeois parties. A city councilor of the German People's Party (DVP) asserted that many of the maladies of patients at city hospitals came from living in substandard housing.[43]

Making matters worse, the housing shortage was thought to aggravate injuries to public health already caused by war and inflation. For many municipal leaders, damage to public health and vigor was a fundamental social problem of recovery. Detailing postwar deprivation, Councilor Feldmann, a leader of Hanover's Social Democrats, told colleagues in Hanover's city parliament that "we have become not only a poor but also a sick people," and Councilor Liertz of Düsseldorf's Center Party referred to a population "worn down from want and deprivation ... sick in body and soul." Could such a population bear the burdens of recovery? Gustav Reuter, Düsseldorf's councilor for welfare, asked, "How can the modern man who comes from the horrors of war and postwar experiences become healthy and remain healthy? How can he ... commit himself with raised intensity to the great tasks of the near future?"[44]

Such grim diagnoses reinforced the conviction that municipal authorities should strive to protect and develop the capacity to work (Arbeitskraft) of urban residents. A city councilor from the Deutsch Hannoveraner (a regionalist party in Hanover) identified "the preservation and maintenance of capacity for work" as important duties for the Reich, states, and communities.[45] Among German cities, Düsseldorf became widely known for plans for revitalizing Germans when it sponsored the Gesolei, a 1926 exhibition devoted to health, social welfare, and physical exercise. Dr. Arthur Schloßmann of the exhibition's organizing committee saw the preservation of people's capacity for work as a task of utmost national importance. Noting the magnitude of the economic and political tasks confronting Germany and the "almost superhuman feats" that would be required of the German people, Schloßmann perceived a "duty to take into consideration ... that no man becomes incapable of work whose capacity for work can still be used."[46]

Preoccupation with the population's capacity to work heightened concern for social reproduction, a term that can be defined as the reproduction of the labor force and its capacity to work as well as the reproduction of children, wives, and mothers.[47] After reaching a first peak in Germany in the late nineteenth century when social biologists and social reformers charted the deterioration of labor power, anxiety about social reproduction increased again during and after the First World War.[48] Such concern raised enthusiasm for improving housing and leisure during the Weimar period of stabilization.

A municipal narrative of Weimar history diverges from the more established national model, not in assessing the difficult legacy of war and inflation, but in emphasizing the vigorous responses to challenges of recovery. Though dismayed by social and economic damage created by war and inflation, civic leaders were confident in their ability to promote recovery, and a municipal narrative of the Weimar period of stabilization yields striking evidence of civic activism and achievement. A recent study of Konrad Adenauer, for example, noted that "visitors returning to Cologne after a prolonged absence maintained that the city was not only smarter than before and equally as lively, but also offered a better quality of life."[49]

Weimar municipal leaders gained confidence, in part, from their own prewar record of self-government and civic improvement. Cities in Prussia and in other German states had gained substantial powers of self-government in the early nineteenth century, and municipal leaders fulfilled the promise of self-government through their responses to rapid urbanization in the late nineteenth century.[50] As noted by historians including Jürgen Reulecke and Brian Ladd, German municipal governments took the lead in creating a new urban infrastructure of sanitation, utilities, and transportation to preserve public health and provide for continued growth. Such municipal activity offered impressive evidence of the achievements of bourgeois civic culture of the late nineteenth century.[51] By the early twentieth century, German solutions to the problems of urbanization won international recognition. Thus in 1914, Frederic Howe, an American social reformer wrote, "I know of no cities in the modern world which compare with those which have arisen in Germany during the past twenty years."[52]

The Weimar Republic brought a new phase of German municipal activism. With the end of inflation, city governments across Germany undertook numerous programs to encourage social and economic recovery. If the delegation of tasks by national and state authorities expanded municipal activity, so too did local initiative. Civic leaders themselves drew attention to the vast range of municipal activity during the period of Weimar stabilization. Berlin's Mayor Gustav Böß, for example, asserted in 1928 that communal social policy covers "housing construction, transportation policy, social welfare, care for public health and cultural policy."[53] In a similar statement of pride in the breadth of municipal activity, Mannheim's Mayor Hermann Heimrich noted Mannheim's economic activity, industrial policy, and cultivation of culture.[54]

Municipal recovery programs gave rise to a distinctive genre of civic promotion in which city governments celebrated their accomplishments in special magazines and books. Frankfurt and Mannheim celebrated civic achievements in the magazines *Das neue Frankfurt* (The New Frankfurt) and *Die lebendige Stadt* (The Living City). Berlin and Altona did the same with *Das neue Berlin* (New Berlin) and *Neues Altona* (New Altona).[55]

According this civic activism a place in Weimar historiography complicates historical accounts of political mobilization. While a municipal narrative reveals the emergence of civic activism in support of recovery, historians, including Peter Fritzsche and Rudy Koshar, have documented substantial populist mobilization against the Weimar Republic.[56] Even as municipalities won acclaim for recovery programs, they attracted the anger of local activists from the old Mittelstand who charged that civic leaders squandered scarce funds and overburdened small business and house owners. A complete account of the politics of stabilization must therefore account for the simultaneous emergence of civic activism in favor of recovery programs and the populist reaction against an interventionist state at both the national and local levels.

Democratization and Recovery

A strong legacy of administrative initiative and political responses to the pressures exerted by universal equal suffrage were dual sources for Weimar Germany's striking municipal activism. Weimar municipal government displayed significant administrative continuity with the imperial era, for German cities retained their basic prewar government structures. The Magistratsverfassung, the form of government most widely used in Prussia, provided two chambers of local government: an elected city parliament and a Magistrat or administrative board elected by the city parliament, which acted as the chief executive of the city. The approval of both the city parliament and the Magistrat was necessary to pass measures. The Bürgermeisterverfassung, a form of municipal government most common in the Rhineland, had a city parliament and a mayor who acted as chief executive.[57]

As in the prewar era, mayors provided administrative leadership in Weimar city governments. German mayors had already won a reputation for skillful administration during the German Empire, and respect for their expertise extended to the national level at least until the middle years of the Weimar Republic. Mayors of the Weimar Republic served in the highest levels of government. Hans Luther, the former mayor of Essen, served as Reich Chancellor, and

Cologne's Mayor Konrad Adenauer also received serious consideration for the post.

Shaped in part by ambitious mayors, the growth of municipal
activity during the Weimar Republic also had roots in a rapid democratic transition. Whereas municipal administration drew closely on
prewar structures and practices, municipal politics experienced
sharp discontinuity arising from the introduction of universal equal
suffrage in 1919. Although the Social Democratic Party (SPD) at the
national level had eclipsed Liberal parties in the Reichstag by 1912,
a host of voting restrictions and preferences had propped up urban
Liberal political power until the First World War. Liberal control of
municipal assemblies in imperial Germany had rested upon a variety of restrictions including citizenship fees, requirements that voters possess property, and the division of the electorate into three
classes set by income. Such restrictions had slowed the growth of
Social Democratic and Catholic political influence in elected municipal bodies. Insulated from full-scale political competition, local
interest groups such as the property owners' associations had
resisted reforms that might raise taxes. Mayor Richard Rive of Halle,
for example, recalled in his memoirs how house and property owners had fought for municipal thrift. As late as 1911 and 1912, Halle's
city parliament turned down his proposals to build sports fields and
playgrounds.[58] The first decade of the twentieth century did see
some increased Social Democratic participation in civic affairs, but
Liberal notables (*Honoratioren*) and varied Mittelstand interest
groups managed to retain command over city parliaments up until
the First World War.[59]

After recovery, suffrage reform formed the second major challenge for Weimar municipal leaders. Though mayors retained great
influence in civic affairs, the abolition of three-class voting and other
restrictions on suffrage gave a much wider variety of political groups
the opportunity to influence municipal policy by electing representatives to city parliaments. The SPD, which had previously competed with bourgeois parties on highly unequal terms, significantly
increased its share of the seats in city parliaments, although the
party itself soon faced a new challenge from the KPD in cities with
a prewar tradition of radicalism. The Center Party won increased
power in cities with large Catholic populations, and new bourgeois
electoral lists also emerged in many cities.

Universal equal suffrage and the changing composition of city
parliaments encouraged competition by parties across the political
spectrum to represent the interests of the civic public. In debates in

city parliaments and in election campaigns, municipal politicians stressed their understanding of the pressing social, economic, and cultural needs of the urban population. As Social Democrats and deputies of the Center Party demanded improved social provision, bourgeois city councilors also stressed their commitment to improving living conditions for the entire urban population. Even mayors, many of whom decried the democratic transition as politicization of administration, joined in the intense competition to represent the needs of diverse constituencies by vigorously supporting more affordable housing and broader access to leisure and recreation. In an era in which common complaints about the political "system" depicted a remote and arrogant political elite, Weimar's democratic transition created local governments highly attuned to public need.

The Weimar democratic transition also magnified the force of local concerns at the national level. Whatever their views on national and international politics, civic leaders in the Weimar Republic had more reason than ever to take account of demands for municipal assistance. Their responses to civic needs in turn made city governments participants in distributional struggles at the national level, particularly as municipalities competed with other public and private institutions to obtain revenue to fund recovery programs. German mayors invariably insisted that city governments had just as much right to borrow as private industry. Over a period of three decades, politicization and democratization encouraged closer connections between national and local politics. In the 1890s and early 1900s, newly active interest groups brought a national perspective to local politics.[60] By the Weimar Republic, the municipal democratic transition gave civic leaders added reason to fight for local interests at the national level.

In the longer-term context of nineteenth and early twentieth century German history, the democratic transition that shaped Weimar municipal politics was an important stage in the much-disputed development of modern German politics. Accounts of a German *Sonderweg*, or special historical path, written in the 1960s described a process of uneven modernization in which German political modernization lagged far behind rapid economic modernization during the nineteenth and early twentieth centuries. In this Sonderweg, Germany experienced economic modernization without fully developing into a modern democracy.[61] In the 1980s, this model of uneven modernization met with sustained criticism, most notably from David Blackbourn and Geoff Eley who questioned assumptions about the pace of democratic development in Western Europe and depicted "a silent bourgeois revolution" of an emerging civil society in place of a missing political bourgeois revolution, which the Sonderweg's exponents described. Along with other critics of the Sonderweg, Blackbourn and Eley emphasized the politicization of German society in the 1890s and early 1900s.[62]

Although comparing a German Sonderweg with the modernization of other countries may present difficulties, the democratic transition in Weimar cities fits Detlev Peukert's definition of "classical modernity." Declining to search for any single, normative definition of modernization, Peukert instead adopted an additive definition. The social, cultural, economic, and scientific trends that shape life in advanced industrial society together made up "classical modernity." First emerging in the late nineteenth century, the major elements of "classical modernity" such as mass culture and the social state developed more fully during the Weimar Republic.[63] This same pattern of rapid further development of trends dating back to the imperial era is also evident in politics, especially at the municipal level. Prolonged struggles over municipal suffrage produced only limited challenges to local liberal power before the First World War, but rapid suffrage reform created intense political competition during the Weimar Republic.

Applying Peukert's model of "classical modernity" to politics closes much of the gap between historians of the Sonderweg and their critics. The very political processes noted by critics of the Sonderweg continued to develop during the Weimar Republic. Reassessments point to intensive politicization in the late nineteenth century to undermine accounts of late German political modernization, but the growth of political activity in late imperial Germany did not give way to mass democracy at all levels of government until the Weimar Republic. On the local level, Weimar Germany's democratic transition marked the further development of one important form of modern politics.

Recovery and Democratization in Düsseldorf, Frankfurt, and Hanover

Municipal history is often the province of case studies of individual cities, but a comparative study, in this particular case of Düsseldorf, Hanover, and Frankfurt am Main, provides an opportunity to detail overall patterns in the politics and policies of Weimar municipal recovery. Municipal politics in Frankfurt during the Weimar Republic showed both the new strength of Social Democracy and the lingering influence of Liberalism. The SPD became the largest single party in Frankfurt's city parliament during the Weimar Republic, but a long tradition of Left-Liberal administration, which stretched back to Mayor Franz Adickes in the late nineteenth century, continued as Ludwig Landmann, a member of the German Democratic Party (DDP), was elected mayor in 1924 by a majority of the city parliament consisting of the DDP, the Center Party, and the SPD.[64]

A study relying solely on Frankfurt might overstate the political roles of Liberals and Social Democrats. Although these did leave their stamp on programs of recovery, so, too, did municipal leaders with ties to parties of the bourgeois Right, which were extremely influential in numerous cities. For that reason, Düsseldorf and Hanover offer useful contrasts to Frankfurt.

Hanover, a long standing regional center, was one of the few large cities in which the revolution of 1918 brought a Socialist mayor, the decidedly moderate local party secretary Robert Leinert, to office. Leinert was elected mayor by a committee of members of the city parliament and Magistrat after the city's longtime Stadtdirektor, Heinrich Tramm, abruptly resigned rather than remaining to face the possible wrath of revolutionary soldiers in November 1919.[65] Vilified by the right for having served on the Prussian delegation to the Paris Peace Conference, prevented by inflation from undertaking plans to speed recovery, and politically crippled by the absence of a Social Democratic majority in Hanover's city parliament, Leinert confronted a movement of bourgeois reaction.[66] In 1924 a local bourgeois block known as the Ordnungsblock (Order Block) joined forces with the regionalist Deutsch Hannoveraner (German Hanoverians), heirs to anti-Prussian feeling dating from Hanover's incorporation into Prussia in 1867, and small bourgeois parties to forge a narrow but firm majority in the city parliament. The new majority of the Right voted to remove Leinert from office to save money (Leinert agreed to resign) and replaced him with Arthur Menge, the Director of Hanover's streetcar company and the former leader of the Deutsch Hannoveraner in the city parliament.[67]

Düsseldorf, a longtime center of trade and an important industrial city, was also dominated by parties on the Right during the Weimar period of stabilization, though, unlike Hanover, Düsseldorf had a large Catholic population. After a period of mutual enmity in the late nineteenth century, Düsseldorf's Liberals and Center Party had begun to cooperate in municipal affairs after 1900 when conservative Liberals took alarm at the growth of Düsseldorf's relatively radical SPD.[68] With the birth of the Weimar Republic, Düsseldorf's civic leaders faced renewed challenges from the Left, first from a brief Spartacist uprising in January 1919 and then from the emergence of a strong local KPD. By the period of stabilization, the Center Party and established bourgeois parties, in particular the German National People's Party (DNVP), dominated municipal politics, electing Robert Lehr, a former department head of police and city treasurer, mayor in 1925.[69] As Peter Hüttenberger, the leading historian of modern Düsseldorf concluded, Lehr's administration "supported itself ... politically on the Right camp."[70]

As a survey of communal politics in Düsseldorf, Frankfurt, and Hanover indicates, municipal recovery took place under a wide range of political conditions. Parties from the SPD on the Left to the DNVP on the Right all proved capable of gaining a strong voice in civic affairs. This variation created the potential for distinct approaches to recovery, but at the same time, municipal politicians from different parties faced common pressures. Indeed, the urgent tasks of recovery and competition to fulfill local demands for recovery created favorable conditions for greater convergence between the policies of the Weimar Republic's diverse parties on the local level.

State Expansion, Society, and Politics in Weimar Germany

Because they took part in the rapid expansion of state activity, municipalities provide useful sites for analyzing how the complex relationship between state and society shaped politics in Weimar Germany before the National Socialists' political breakthrough of 1930. The pursuit of recovery brought about the expansion of state activity at all levels of government, most notably in the area of social provision. "The most immediately striking economic consequence of the First World War," noted Harold James, "was the growth of the public sector." Public spending increased from 14.5 percent of national income in the period from 1910 to 1913 to 24 percent of national income between 1925 and 1929. Social spending, the fastest growing area of state expenditure, rose from 20.5 marks per resident in 1913 to 64.7 marks per resident in 1925 and reached 101.6 marks per resident by 1929.[71]

Evaluating the effects of this rapid expansion of state activity presents one of Weimar historiography's major problems. The growth of social provision might be termed one of the successes of the Weimar Republic as new initiatives in social policy marked efforts to meet the ambitious social goals articulated in the Weimar Constitution. High expenditures made in pursuit of these lofty aims, however, did not secure lasting stabilization. Why did Weimar recovery ultimately fail despite the many achievements of recovery programs? Investigating the shortcomings of stabilization, economic historians have argued that the Weimar State tried to do too much, in the process weakening the economy and provoking a backlash from a wide array of economic and social interest groups. Historians of social policy, while recognizing Weimar's social achievements, have also pointed to the difficulty of meeting expectations raised by the constitution.[72] As Elizabeth Harvey noted, "many expectations raised by pledges in the constitution were not fulfilled."[73] Combining the perspectives of economic and social historians therefore suggests that the Weimar State simultaneously did too little and too much.

Similar contradictions marked the expansion of state activity at the local level. Despite their considerable achievements, recovery programs in cities, as in the Weimar Republic as a whole, did not bring long-term stability. Indeed, municipal policy raised the ire of diverse critics ranging from financial authorities to local populists. A municipal history of Weimar stabilization must therefore explain how the same programs that were celebrated by civic leaders also provoked waves of reaction. Investigating the paradoxes of Weimar stabilization at the local level, this study explores the municipal politics of recovery through analysis of municipal records, files of the German Association of Cities, records of the Reich Economic Ministry, the contemporary press, and other sources. Administrative records and stenographic reports of city parliaments provide especially useful sources for following the municipal politics of recovery.

Analysis of municipal records and other primary and secondary sources supports several arguments about the contradictions of recovery. In the first place, comprehensive municipal recovery programs were at least partially successful in meeting the goals of civic leaders through the late 1920s. Even as late as 1928, and in some cases 1929, municipal leaders from parties of the Left and Right vied to take credit for the achievements of recovery. Secondly, municipal history shows that programs of recovery won support from established parties, from the SPD to parties of the bourgeois Right. Although deep cleavages between Germany's fragmented political milieus or camps continued to generate tension during the Weimar Republic, the politics of recovery cut across party, class, and confessional boundaries. Competition to represent civic needs after the introduction of universal equal suffrage encouraged the formation of a broad consensus in support of a wide array of recovery programs.

Reaction against policies and politics of municipal recovery cannot be attributed to a single cause.[74] The costs and the problematic means used to finance municipal programs of recovery provided, perhaps, the most obvious reasons for opposition to Weimar municipal authorities. However, excessive spending was only one of several major charges levelled against city governments by their critics well before the full scale financial crisis of 1931. Reaction against municipalities drew on political, economic, and, in some cases, cultural grievances.

The broad political consensus of recovery paradoxically created extraordinarily destructive political conflict. The powerful political backlash against programs and politics of recovery cannot be explained primarily as a reaction by parties of the Right against Social Democrats or progressive alliances. Rather, the consensus of recovery suffered immense damage from the emergence of contradictory evaluations of the state on the bourgeois Right. Responding to local pressure for recovery by taking part in the expansion of municipal activity, bourgeois civic leaders from established parties simultaneously confronted demands for curtailing state expansion from splinter parties and local populists. Municipal politicians from established parties of the Right found it increasingly difficult to reconcile participation in the expansion of state activity with demands for municipal thrift.

Political conflict within the bourgeois Right gained force from a collision between the politics of milieus and the politics of recovery. Advocates of a politics of milieus dominated by sharp boundaries between rival political groupings viewed the emergence of a consensus that cut across existing political boundaries with deep suspicion. For splinter parties and local populists of the bourgeois Right, participation by established parties of the Right in the politics of recovery was nothing less than a betrayal of bourgeois ideals.

Exploring recovery and reaction in Weimar cities, this book first sets out to explain the development of recovery programs. Chapter 1 introduces municipal recovery programs of economic promotion, social welfare, promotion of housing construction and leisure. Chapter 2 analyzes the politics of recovery, detailing the strong support for recovery programs across the political spectrum from Social Democrats to parties of the bourgeois Right.

Having outlined the emergence of a broad consensus in favor of ambitious recovery programs, the remainder of this study examines the development of reaction against municipal policy and politics. Chapter 3 outlines the financial pressures created by recovery programs in municipal budgets, which created widespread anxiety in municipal governments by the end of the period of stabilization. Municipal pursuit of credit, as chapter 4 explains, also fostered resentment against cities on the part of leading financial authorities and economic interest groups. Their case against municipalities, chapter 5 notes, attacked the utility as well as the costs of municipal recovery programs. Returning to the local level, chapter 6 explains how disputes over the organization of recovery programs fragmented the civic public and weakened the consensus in favor of municipal policy. Chapter 7 reveals how the political contradictions of recovery fragmented bourgeois politics by the end of the period of stabilization. The Conclusion, finally, analyzes the roots of the diverse waves of reaction against municipal policy and politics of recovery in a broad crisis of "classical modernity."

Notes

1. Gerald D. Feldman, *The Great Disorder: Politics, Economics and Society in the German Inflation, 1914-1924* (New York, 1993).

2. Fritz Rene Allemann, *Bonn ist nicht Weimar* (Cologne, 1956).

3. For an interpretation of revolutionary politics as a choice between social revolution allied with advocates of proletarian dictatorship or a parliamentary republic allied with conservative elites see Karl Dietrich Erdmann, "Die Geschichte der Weimarer Republik als Problem der Wissenschaft," *Vierteljahrshefte für Zeitgeschichte* 3 (1955): 1-19. For discussion of the workers' councils see Eberhard Kolb, *Die Arbeiterräte in der deutschen Innenpolitik 1918-1919* (Düsseldorf, 1962); and Reinhard Rürup, *Probleme der Revolution in Deutschland 1918/19* (Wiesbaden, 1968).

4. Wolfgang J. Mommsen, "Die deutsche Revolution 1918-1920: Politische Revolution und soziale Protestbewegung," *Geschichte und Gesellschaft* 4 (1978): 391; Ulrich Kluge, *Die deutsche Revolution 1918/1919: Staat, Politik und Gesellschaft zwischen Weltkrieg und Kapp Putsch* (Frankfurt am Main, 1985), p. 136; Rürup, *Probleme der Revolution*, p. 45; and Kolb, "Rätewirklichkeit and Räteideologie in der deutsche Revolution von 1918/19," in *Vom Kaiserreich zur Weimarer Republik*, ed. Eberhard Kolb (Cologne, 1972), pp. 165-84.

5. Richard Bessel, *Germany after the First World War* (Oxford, 1993), pp. 101, 123, 128, 212-13, 221-22, 273.

6. Feldman, *The Great Disorder*. See list of some of Gerald D. Feldman's other work on inflation in bibliography and also Carl-Ludwig Holtfrerich, *The German Infla-*

tion 1914-1923, trans. Theo Balderston (Berlin, 1986); Peter J. Lyth, *Inflation and the Merchant Economy: The Hamburg Mittelstand, 1914-1924* (New York, 1990); and Niall Ferguson, *Paper & Iron: Hamburg Business and German politics in the era of inflation, 1897-1927* (Cambridge: Cambridge University Press, 1995).

7. Feldman, *The Great Disorder*, pp. 555, 673-681, 805.

8. Knut Borchardt, "Zwangslagen und Handlungsspielräume in der großen Weltwirtschaftskrise der frühen dreißiger Jahre;" and "Wirtschaftliche Ursachen des Scheiterns der Weimar Republik," in Knut Borchardt, *Wachstum, Krisen, Handlungsspielräume der Wirtschaftspolitik: Studien zur Wirtschaftsgeschichte des 19. und 20. Jahrhunderts* (Göttingen, 1982), pp. 165-82, 183-205. For discussion of Borchardt's analysis see Carl-Ludwig Holtfrerich, "Zu hohe Löhne in der Weimarer Republik? Bemerkungen zur Borchardt-These," *Geschichte und Gesellschaft* 10 (1984): 122-41; Charles Maier, "Die Nicht-Determiniertheit ökonomischer Modelle: Überlegungen zu Knut Borchardt's These von der 'kranken Wirtschaft' der Weimarer Republik, *Geschichte und Gesellschaft* 11 (1985): 275-94; and Jürgen Baron von Kruedener, ed., *Economic Crisis and Political Collapse: The Weimar Republic 1924-1933* (New York, 1990). See also Harold James, *The German Slump: Politics and Economics 1924-1936* (Oxford, 1986); and Peter Stachura, ed., *Unemployment and the Great Depression in Weimar Germany* (New York, 1986).

9. The literature on the National Socialist acquisition of power is vast. For guides to historiography see Kolb, *The Weimar Republic*, trans. P.S. Falla (London, 1988); Stachura, *The Weimar Era and Hitler: A Critical Bibliography* (Oxford, 1977); and Ian Kershaw, *The Nazi Dictatorship: Problems and Perspectives of Interpretation*, 2nd edition (London, 1989). For the first classic account, see Karl Dietrich Bracher, *Die Auflösung der Weimarer Republik: Eine Studie zum Problem des Machtverfalls in der Demokratie* (Villingen, 1955; 6th edition, Düsseldorf, 1978). For analysis of elections see Jürgen Falter, *Hitlers Wähler* (Munich, 1991); and Thomas Childers, *The Nazi Voter: The Social Foundations of Fascism in Germany, 1919-1933* (Chapel Hill, 1983). For influential studies of National Socialist mobilization in a single town see William Sheridan Allen, *The Nazi Seizure of Power: The Experience of a Single German Town*, revised edition (New York, 1984); and Rudy Koshar, *Social Life, Local Politics, and Nazism: Marburg 1880-1935* (Chapel Hill, 1986). For analysis of political violence see Richard Bessel, *Political Violence and the Rise of Nazism: The Stormtroopers in Eastern Germany 1925-34* (New Haven, 1984); Eve Rosenhaft, *Beating the Fascists? The German Communists and Political Violence 1929-1933* (Cambridge, 1983); and Christian Striefler, *Kampf um die Macht: Kommunisten und Nationalsozialisten am Ende der Weimarer Republik* (Frankfurt am Main, 1993).

10. Gerhard Schulz, *Zwischen Demokratie und Diktatur Verfassungspolitik und Reichsreform in der Weimarer Republik*, 3 vols., (Berlin, 1963, 1987, 1992).

11. Michael Stürmer, *Koalition und Opposition in der Weimarer Republik 1924-1928* (Düsseldorf, 1967), 265-273. See also Ilse Maurer, *Reichsfinanzen und Große Koalition: Zur Geschichte des Reichskabinetts Müller (1928-1930)* (Frankfurt am Main, 1973); and Hans Mommsen, *Die verspielte Freiheit: Der Weg der Republik von Weimar in den Untergang 1918 bis 1933* (Berlin, 1989), pp. 200, 205, 225, 261.

12. M. Rainer Lepsius, "Parteien System und Sozialstruktur. Zum Problem der Demokratisierung der deutschen Gesellschaft," in *Wirtschaft, Geschichte und Wirtschaftsgeschichte: Festschrift zum 65. Geburtstag von Friedrich Lütge*, ed. W. Abel (Stuttgart, 1966), pp. 37-93; and Lepsius, "From Fragmented Party Democracy to Government by Emergency Decree and National Socialist Takeover:

Germany," in *The Breakdown of Democratic Regimes*, ed. Juan J. Linz and Alfred Stepan (Baltimore, 1978), pp. 41-42.

13. Larry Eugene Jones, *German Liberalism and the Dissolution of the Weimar Party System, 1918-1933* (Chapel Hill, 1988).

14. Barbara Miller Lane, *Architecture and Politics in Germany, 1918-1945* (Cambridge Massachusetts, 1968). See also Jost Hermand and Frank Trommler, *Die Kultur der Weimarer Republik*. (Munich, 1978); and John Willett, *The New Sobriety Art and Politics in the Weimar Period 1917-1933* (London, 1978).

15. Peter Gay, *Weimar Culture: The Outsider as Insider* (New York, 1968), pp. 128, 132-33, 140.

16. Walter Laqueur, *Weimar: A Cultural History 1918-1933* (New York, 1974), 36-37. See also Willett, *The New Sobriety*.

17. Alan E. Steinweis, "Weimar Culture and the Rise of National Socialism: *The Kampfbund für deutsche Kultur*," *Central European History* 24 (1991): 402-23; Steinweis, *Art, Ideology and Economics in Nazi Germany: The Reich Chambers of Music, Theater and the Visual Arts* (Chapel Hill, 1993).

18. Mommsen, Dietmar Petzina, and Bernd Weisbrod, eds. *Industrielles System und politische Entwicklung in der Weimarer Republik* (Düsseldorf, 1974), pp. 693-704, 762-835. See also Heinrich August Winkler, *Mittelstand, Demokratie und Nationalsozialismus: die politische Entwicklung von Handwerk und Kleinhandel in der Weimarer Republik* (Cologne, 1972). For early research on agrarian discontent see Gerhard Stoltenberg, *Politische Strömungen im schleswig- holsteinischen Landvolk 1918-1933: Ein Beitrag zur politischen Meinungsbildung in der Weimarer Republik* (Düsseldorf, 1962); and Rudolf Herberle, *Landbevölkerung und Nationalsozialismus: Eine soziologische Untersuchung zur politischen Willensbildung in Schleswig-Holstein 1918-1932* (Stuttgart, 1963).

19. Bernd Weisbrod, *Schwerindustrie in der Weimarer Republik: Interessenpolitik zwischen Stabilisierung und Krise* (Wuppertal, 1978); Michael Schneider, *Streit um Arbeitszeit: Geschichte des Kampfes um Arbeitsverkürzung in Deutschland* (Cologne, 1984); Henry Ashby Turner, *German Big Business and the Rise of Hitler* (New York, 1985), pp. 40-43; Feldman and Irmgard Steinisch, "Notwendigkeit und Grenzen sozialstaatlicher Intervention: Eine vergleichende Fallstudie des Ruhrenstreits in Deutschlands und der Generalstreiks in England," *Archiv für Sozialgeschichte* 20 (1988); Johannes Bähr, *Staatliche Schlichtung in der Weimarer Republik* (Berlin, 1989), pp. 267-68; and David Abraham, *The Collapse of the Weimar Republic: Political Economy and Crisis* (Princeton, 1981), pp. 254-57. Abraham argued that growing discontent among industrialists by 1928 and a return to leadership by heavy industry eroded previous readiness by exporters to compromise with Weimar policies.

20. Winkler, *Mittelstand, Demokratie und Nationalsozialismus*; Peter Wulf, *Die politische Haltung des schleswig- holsteinischen Handwerks 1928-1932* (Cologne, 1969); Klaus Schaap, *Die Endphase der Weimarer Republik im Freistaat Oldenburg 1928-1933* (Düsseldorf, 1978), p. 99; Peter Fritzsche, *Rehearsals for Fascism: Populism and Political Mobilization in Weimar Germany* (New York, 1990); and Jürgen Bergmann, "Politische Anschauungen und politische Kultur des Handwerks in der Weimarer Republik im Spannungsverhältnis von Tradition, Ideologie und materiellen Interessen," in *Pluralismus als Verfassungs- und Gesellschaftsmodell: Zur politischen Kultur in der Weimarer Republik*, ed. Detlef Lehnert and Klaus Megerle (Opladen, 1993), pp. 131-213; Detlef Lehnert, "Organisierter Hausbe-

sitz und Kommunalpolitik in Wien und Berlin 1890-1933," *Geschichte und Gesellschaft* 20 (1994): 29-56.

21. Dieter Gessner, *Agrarverbände in der Weimarer Republik: wirtschaftliche und soziale Voraussetzungen agrarkonservativer Politik vor 1933* (Düsseldorf, 1976); Arno Panzer, *Das Ringen um die deutsche Agrarpolitik von der Währungsstabilisierung bis zur Agrardebatte im Reichstag im Dezember 1928* (Kiel, 1970); and Jonathan Osmond, *Rural Protest in the Weimar Republic: The Free Peasantry in the Rhineland and Bavaria* (New York, 1993), p. 133.

22. Winkler, *Der Schein der Normalität: Arbeiter und Arbeiterbewegung in der Weimarer Republik 1924 bis 1930* (Berlin, 1985).

23. Borchardt, "Wirtschaftliche Ursachen des Scheiterns der Weimarer Republik," in Borchardt, *Wachstum, Krisen, Handlungsspielräume*, pp. 183-205; and James, "Economic Reasons for the Collapse of Weimar," in *Weimar: Why did German Democracy Fail?*, ed. Ian Kershaw (New York, 1990), pp. 38-40.

24. James, *The German Slump*; and William C. McNeil, *American Money and the Weimar Republic: Economics and Politics on the Eve of the Great Depression* (New York, 1986).

25. Michael Hughes, *Paying for the German Inflation* (Chapel Hill, 1988), p. 184; and Thomas Childers, "Interest and Ideology: Anti-System Politics in the Era of Stabilization 1924-1928," in *Die Nachwirkungen der Inflation*, ed. Feldman, pp. 1-20.

26. Feldman, *The Great Disorder*, pp. 837, 843-48, 854; and Jones, *German Liberalism*, p. 208.

27. Christoph Sachße and Florian Tennstedt, *Fürsorge und Wohlfahrtspflege 1871 bis 1929*, vol. 2 of *Geschichte der Armenfürsorge in Deutschland Band 2* (Stuttgart, 1988); Detlev Peukert, *Grenzen der Sozialdisziplinierung: Aufstieg und Krise der deutschen Jugendfürsorge von 1878 bis 1932* (Cologne, 1986); Peukert, *Die Weimarer Republik*, p. 134; Elizabeth Harvey *Youth and the Welfare State in Weimar Germany* (Oxford, 1993); and Peter Stachura, *The Weimar Republic and the Younger Proletariat: An Economic and Social Analysis* (London, 1989), p. 43.

28. Peukert, *Die Weimarer Republik*, pp. 9-11.

29. James on occasion notes the appeal of social stabilization, but his analysis ultimately concentrates far more on the economic consequences of stabilization than on the politics of recovery. See James, *The German Slump*, pp. 87, 108-9; and McNeil, *American Money and the Weimar Republic*, pp. 77-78.

30. Stürmer, *Koalition und Opposition*; and Dietrich Orlow, *Weimar Prussia, 1925-1933: The Illusion of Strength* (Pittsburgh, 1991).

31. See for example, Geoff Eley, *Reshaping the German Right: Radical Nationalism and Political Change After Bismarck* (New Haven, 1980).

32. Christian Engeli, *Gustav Böß Oberbürgermeister von Berlin 1921 bis 1930*, (Stuttgart, 1971); Detlef Lehnert, *Kommunale Politik, Parteiensystem und Interessenkonflikte in Berlin und Wien 1919-1932: Wohnungs-, Verkehrs- und Finanzpolitik im Spannungsfeld von städtischer Selbstverwaltung und Verbandseinflüssen* (Berlin, 1991); Wolfgang Hofmann, *Zwischen Rathaus und Reichskanzlei: Die Oberbürgermeister in der Kommunal- und Staatspolitik des Deutschen Reiches von 1919 bis 1933* (Stuttgart, 1974); Hermann Hanschel, *Oberbürgermeister Hermann Luppe: Nürnberger Kommunalpolitik in der Weimarer Republik* (Nuremberg, 1977); Dieter Rebentisch, *Ludwig Landmann: Frankfurter Oberbürgermeister der Weimarer Republik* (Wiesbaden, 1975); Hugo Stehkämper, ed., *Konrad Adenauer: Oberbürgermeister von Köln* (Cologne, 1976); Hans-Peter Schwarz, *Konrad Adenauer: A German Politician and Statesman in a Period of War, Revolution and Reconstruction*, vol. 1, trans.

Louise Willmot (Providence, 1995); and Peter Steinborn, *Grundlagen und Grundzüge Münchener Kommunalpolitik in den Jahren der Weimarer Republik: Zur Geschichte der bayerischen Landeshauptstadt im 20. Jahrhundert* (Munich, 1968).

33. Kolb, *Die Arbeiterräte in der deutschen Innenpolitik 1918 bis 1919* (Düsseldorf, 1962); Richard A. Comfort, *Revolutionary Hamburg: Labor Politics in the early Weimar Republic* (Stanford, 1966); Ulrich Kluge, *Soldatenräte und Revolution: Studien zur Militarpolitik in Deutschland* (Göttingen, 1975); Rürup, ed., *Arbeiter- und Soldatenräte im rheinisch- westfälischen Industriegebiet* (Wuppertal, 1975); Jurgen Tampke, *The Ruhr and Revolution: The Revolutionary Movement in the Rhenish-Westphalian Region, 1912-1919* (London, 1979); and Robert Scholz, "Die Auswirkungen der Inflation auf Das Sozial- und Wohlfahrtswesen der neuen Stadtgemeinde Berlin," in *Konsequenzen der Inflation*, ed. Feldman (Berlin, 1989), pp. 45-75.

34. Feldman, *The Great Disorder*, pp. 609-22, 766-67; Merith Niehuss, "Lebensweise und Familie in der Inflationszeit," in *Die Anpassung an die Inflation*, ed. Feldman, pp. 253, 256; Niehuss, *Arbeiterschaft In Krieg und Inflation: Soziale Schichtung und Lage der Arbeiter in Augsburg und Linz 1910 bis 1925* (Berlin, 1985); Norbert Ranft, "Erwerbslosenfürsorge, Ruhrkampf und Kommunen: Die Trendwende in der Sozialpolitik im Jahre 1923," in *Die Anpassung an die Inflation*, ed. Feldman, pp. 186, 190-91, 193; and Jürgen Freiherr von Kruedener, "Die Entstehung des Inflationstraumas: Zur Sozialpsychologie der deutschen Hyperinflation 1922/23," in *Konsequenzen der Inflation*, ed. Feldman, p. 237.

35. Feldman, *The Great Disorder*, pp. 557-563; Reulecke, "Die Auswirkungen der Inflation auf die städtischen Finanzen" in *Die Nachwirkungen der Inflation*, ed. Feldman," pp. 101, 111; and Scholz, "Die Auswirkungen der Inflation," pp. 69, 71.

36. Karl-Heinrich Hansmeyer, ed., *Kommunale Finanzpolitik in der Weimarer Republik* (Stuttgart, 1973), pp. 64-69.

37. Peter Hüttenberger, *Die Industrie- und Verwaltungsstadt (20. Jahrhundert)*, vol. 3 of *Düsseldorf Geschichte von den Ursprüngen bis ins 20. Jahrhundert*, ed. Hugo Weidenhaupt (Düsseldorf, 1989), p. 133.

38. David Blackbourn and Geoff Eley, *The Peculiarities of German History: Bourgeois Society and Politics in Nineteenth Century Germany* (Oxford, 1984), p. 199.

39. BVK Hannover 1919-1920, p. 3115; and StA Frankfurt S1723 IV, Verwaltungsrat der Palmengarten-Gesellschaft to Landmann, 14 September 1925.

40. BVK Hannover, 1923-1924, p. 506; Brauer, "Die Sozialdemokratie und der Kommunalgroßwahltag unter Berücksichtigung der Wahlen in Preussen," *Die Gemeinde* 6 (1929): 980; and Chr. Lill, "Wohlfahrtspflege in Frankfurt a.m.," *Kommunalpolitische Blätter* 20 (1929): 204.

41. Peter-Christian Witt, "Inflation, Wohnungszwangswirtschaft und Hauszinssteuer. Zur Regelung von Wohnungsbau und Wohnungsmarkt in der Weimarer Republik," in *Wohnen im Wandel: Beiträge zur Geschichte des Alltags in der bürgerlichen Gesellschaft*, ed. Lutz Niethammer (Wuppertal, 1979), pp. 390, 402.

42. StVV Frankfurt, 1926, p. 143.

43. StVV Düsseldorf, 1925, pp. 51-52.

44. BVK Hannover, 1921-1922, p. 567; StVV Düsseldorf, 1925, p. 88; and Arthur Schloßmann, ed., *GE-SO-LEI, Grosse Ausstellung Düsseldorf 1926 für Gesundheitspflege, soziale Fürsorge und Leibesübungen* (Düsseldorf, 1927), vol. 2, pp. 636-37.

45. BVK Hannover 1925-1926, p. 413.

46. Schloßmann, "Entstehung und Ziele der grossen Ausstellung für Gesundheitspflege, soziale Fürsorge und Leibesübungen Düsseldorf 1926," *Gesolei* 1 (1925): 3-4.

47. For a definition of social reproduction see David Byrne, "The Standard of Council Housing in Inter-War North Shields – A Case Study in the Politics of Reproduction," in *Housing, Social Policy and the State*, ed. Joseph Melling (London, 1980), p. 168. For a functionalist analysis of social reproduction see Cynthia Cockburn, *The Local State: Management of Cities and People* (London, 1977), pp. 52-53. For a critique of functionalism see R.W. Connell, *Which Way is Up? Essays on Sex, Class, and Culture* (Sydney, 1983), pp. 148, 159.

48. Juan Rodriguez-Lores, "Stadthygiene und Städtebau" in *Stadtbaureform 1865-1900, von Licht, Luft und Ordnung in der Stadt der Gründerzeit*, vol. 1, ed., Gerhard Fehl and Juan Rodriguez-Lores (Hamburg, 1985), pp. 29, 35-38; Andrew Lees, *Cities Perceived: Urban Society in European and American Thought, 1820-1940* (Manchester, 1985), pp. 142-43; Young-Sun Hong, "The Contradictions of Modernization in the German Welfare State: Gender and the Politics of Welfare Reform in First World War Germany," *Social History* 17 (1992): 253; and David Crew, "German Socialism, the State and Family Policy, 1918-1933," *Continuity and Change* 1 (1986): 237-38.

49. Schwarz, *Konrad Adenauer*, p. 195.

50. Regina Jeske, "Kommunale Amtsinhaber und Entscheidungsträger – die politische Elite," in *Stadt und Bürgertum im Übergang von der traditionalen zur modernen Gesellschaft*, ed. Lothar Gall (Munich, 1993); Heinrich Heffter, *Die deutsche Selbstverwaltung im 19. Jahrhundert: Geschichte der Ideen und Institutionen* (Stuttgart, 1950); and Hofmann, *Zwischen Rathaus und Reichskanzlei*, pp. 32-33.

51. Jürgen Reulecke, *Geschichte der Urbanisierung in Deutschland* (Frankfurt am Main, 1985); Horst Matzerath, *Urbanisierung in Preussen 1815-1914* (Stuttgart, 1985); Brian Ladd, *Urban Planning and Civic Order in Germany, 1860-1914* (Cambridge, Massachusetts, 1990), pp. 236-51; and Blackbourn and Eley, *The Peculiarities of German History*, p. 149. For a study of the constraints upon solutions to the problems of urbanization see Richard Evans, *Death in Hamburg: Society and Politics in the Cholera Years 1830-1910* (Oxford, 1987).

52. Frederic Howe, *European Cities at Work* (New York, 1914), p. 3; and Ladd, *Urban Planning*, p. 1.

53. Gustav Böß, *Die sozialen Aufgaben der Kommunalpolitik* (Berlin [1928]), p. 11.

54. H. Heimrich, "Städtische Kulturpflege," *Die Lebendige Stadt* 1 (1929): 71-72; Heimrich, "Von Jarres bis Reuter," *Die Lebendige Stadt* 1 (1929): 101-2; and Heimrich, "Kommunale Industriepolitik," *Die Lebendige Stadt* 2 (1930/31): 21-24.

55. Special magazines included *Das neue Berlin*, *Das neue Frankfurt* and Mannheim's *Die lebendige Stadt*. The book *Die rote Stadt im roten Land*, ed. Parteitagkomitee (Magdeburg, 1929) depicted socialist policy in Magdeburg, and Paul Th. Hoffmann, ed., *Neues Altona 1919-1929: Zehn Jahre Aufbau einer Groszstadt*, 2 vols. (Jena, 1929) publicized Altona's policies. See also Lees, *Cities Perceived*, p. 271.

56. Fritzsche, *Rehearsals for Fascism*; and Koshar, *Social Life, Local Politics, and Nazism*.

57. Roger Wells, *German Cities: A Study of Contemporary Municipal Politics and Administration* (Princeton, 1932), pp. 33-35. Note that a third type of city government, the Stadtratverfassung, which combined the city parliament with the executive, was common in Bavaria.

58. Richard Robert Rive, *Lebenserinnerungen eines deutschen Oberbürgermeisters* (Stuttgart, 1960), pp. 94-97, 171; *Die rote Stadt im roten Land*, pp. 16-18; Dieter Rebentisch, "Die Selbstverwaltung in der Weimarer Zeit," in *Handbuch der kommunalen Wissenschaft und Praxis* vol. 1, ed. Günter Püttner (Berlin, 1981), p. 88; and Evans, *Death in Hamburg*, pp. 519-21, 546-51.

59. James Sheehan, "Liberalism and the City in Nineteenth-Century Germany," *Past and Present* 51 (1971): 116-37; and Dieter Langewiesche, *Liberalismus in Deutschland* (Frankfurt am Main, 1988), pp. 206-7.

60. Eley, *Reshaping the German Right*, p. 155.

61. Ralf Dahrendorf, *Society and Democracy in Germany* (London, 1968); and Barrington Moore, *Social Origins of Dictatorship and Democracy* (London, 1967). See also Hans-Ulrich Wehler, *The German Empire 1871-1918*, trans. Kim Traynor (Leamington Spa, 1985).

62. Blackbourn and Eley, *The Peculiarities of German History*; and Stanley Suval, *Electoral Politics in Wilhelmine Germany* (Chapel Hill, 1985).

63. Peukert, *Die Weimarer Republik*, pp. 10-11, 87-91; David Crew, "The Pathologies of Modernity: Detlev Peukert on Germany's Twentieth Century," *Social History* 17 (1992): 319-28; and Ben Lieberman, "Testing Peukert's Paradigm: The 'Crisis of Classical Modernity' in the 'New Frankfurt,' 1925-1930," *German Studies Review* 17 (1994): 287-88.

64. Hans Kilian Weitensteiner, *Karl Flesch: Kommunale Sozialpolitik in Frankfurt am Main* (Frankfurt am Main, 1976), pp. 17-22.

65. Friedhelm Boll, *Massenbewegungen in Niedersachsen 1906-1920: Eine sozialgeschichtliche Untersuchung zu den unterschiedlichen Entwicklungstypen Braunschweig und Hannover* (Bonn, 1981), pp. 254-56.

66. BVK Hannover, 1919-1920, p. 21; 1920-1921, pp. 2273, 2385-88; 1921-1922, pp. 593, 741; and 1922-1923, p. 500.

67. Waldemar Röhrbein and Franz R. Zankl, eds., *Hannover im 20. Jahrhundert: Aspekte der neueren Stadtgeschichte*, (Hanover, 1978), p. 118.

68. Hüttenberger, *Die Industrie- und Verwaltungsstadt*, pp. 150- 69.

69. Ibid., pp. 287-88, 291, 294, 318-19, 328, 362-63.

70. Ibid., pp. 318-19.

71. James, *The German Slump*, pp. 39, 48-49, 85; and Schulze, *Weimar Deutschland*, p. 66.

72. Borchardt, "Wirtschaftliche Ursachen," pp. 191, 195-96.

73. Harvey, *Youth and the Welfare State*, pp. 5-6; Peukert, *Die Weimarer Republik*, p. 137; and Bessel, "Die Krise der Weimarer Republik als Erblast des verlorenen Krieges," in *Zivilisation und Barbarei: Die widersprüchlichen Potentiale der Moderne; Detlev Peukert zum Gedenken*, ed. Frank Bajohr (Hamburg, 1991), pp. 99, 106.

74. Kolb, *The Weimar Republic*, p. 193.

Chapter 1

STABILIZATION AND STATE EXPANSION

Comprehensive City Planning

The common historical practice of identifying Weimar stabilization as illusory or false, though useful for building a linear narrative from hyperinflation to depression, does not help to explain how Germany actually continued the process of stabilization after the end of hyperinflation in 1923/24. On the municipal level, the period of stabilization brought intensive pursuit of recovery until at least 1929. Evident at all levels of government, the rapid expansion of state activity of the Weimar Republic took striking form in Germany's large cities during the era of recovery. Few, if any, areas of civic life, whether economic, social or cultural, were left untouched by municipal intervention.

Municipal leaders wished to begin work on programs of recovery before 1924, but inflation obstructed stabilization even as the collapse of currency added to the list of social and economic problems demanding state attention. Inflation rapidly shrank even large appropriations to negligible proportions, leaving Germany's mayors and municipal politicians frustrated and pessimistic. During the discussion of Hanover's budget for 1923, the city's chief financial official lamented that the budget plan gave a "clear picture of how far … we have become impoverished."[1]

With the onset of monetary stabilization, the mood of Germany's civic leaders rapidly shifted. German mayors proclaimed that the time had come to begin work on programs of recovery as soon as it became evident that hyperinflation had actually come to a final end. Ludwig Landmann, in his first speech as mayor to Frankfurt's city parliament, told city councilors in 1924 that "we stand at a turning point. The time of chaotic disruptions is over, the time of reconstruction begins." There was little doubt that reconstruction would entail large projects. Düsseldorf's Mayor Robert Lehr informed city councilors in January 1925 that "we have taken up big plans… If a place in the sun is to be reconquered, such plans must be carried out."[2]

The broad commitment by civic leaders to pursuit of recovery encompassed varied ultimate goals. Recovery often meant, as it did for Düsseldorf's Mayor Lehr, recapturing the qualities that had distinguished German cities before 1914. Lehr declared that "our path is clearly marked for us through the past."[3] Defining recovery as a clear-cut process of reconstruction appealed to many municipal leaders, for German cities had enjoyed an international reputation as pinnacles of urban progress before the First World War.[4]

While many municipal leaders, including Lehr, looked to past achievements to find a guide for reconstruction, recovery also provided occasion to re-evaluate civic goals and achievements of the prewar era. Pursuit of recovery spurred renewed debate about the appropriate form of urban living. For all the accolades showered on prewar German city planning for improvements to hygiene and infrastructure, prominent city planners and municipal leaders of the Weimar Republic stressed the failure of their predecessors to confront some of the major drawbacks of urban living, particularly the lack of good housing and space for leisure. Redressing urban shortcomings often took the form of improving upon past urban policy by striving to provide a broader array of services for all urban residents.

Moving beyond this goal of expanding social provision, the most ambitious mayors and municipal planners saw recovery as an opportunity, not simply to repair damage of the last decade or even to take up previously neglected tasks, but also to remake their cities into "new" cities. Frankfurt's Mayor Landmann, for example, wished to transform Frankfurt into a "new Frankfurt." Landmann and other advocates of "new" cities sought to apply modern techniques to the task of improving the living conditions for urban residents.

Economic Promotion

Whatever the ultimate goal of recovery, municipal governments began work on a wide array of projects during the period of stabilization. Municipal policy was not easy to categorize, for many projects had dual purposes, but in nearly all cases city governments expanded their attention to the promotion of housing construction, social welfare, the provision of leisure and economic promotion.

City governments of Weimar Germany paradoxically devoted increased resources to economic promotion even while reducing involvement in some economic activities. At first glance, the Weimar Republic actually appeared to bring the curtailment of economic activity by city governments: municipalities dismantled offices established during the First World War for procuring and distributing food, fuel, and clothing.[5] Yet even as city governments discarded economic duties assumed to meet emergencies created by war, civic leaders took up a wide array of projects to boost local economic activity. As Wolfgang Hofmann notes, economic and industrial promotion received unprecedented attention from municipal leaders during the Weimar Republic.[6]

In the simplest conception of municipal economic promotion, civic leaders presumed that spending for construction projects of all sorts increased employment. Even a mayor such as Hanover's Arthur Menge who took a relatively cautious approach to economic promotion argued that municipal promotion of housing construction, along with other projects, provided workers with employment and local companies with business opportunities. He boasted in 1927 that the execution of municipal projects "serves to help trade and industry over the difficulties of the present time."[7]

Advocating more elaborate plans of economic development, most mayors saw economic promotion as more than simply a fortunate secondary effect of municipal spending on construction projects. Frankfurt's Ludwig Landmann, the architect of a particularly ambitious program of municipal economic promotion, had actually begun to outline a plan for future economic development in 1917 when he was still a *Stadtrat*. In 1917 Landmann suggested building a base for economic growth by improving transportation and securing low prices for power, goals which remained central to his economic plans as Frankfurt's mayor after 1924. As mayor, Landmann actively sought to encourage the settlement of industry in Frankfurt.[8]

More so than for any other major branch of municipal activity, economic promotion was closely built according to the practices of the prewar era. In the Weimar Republic it usually began with renovation of the core firms of the communal economy established before 1914. Investing in communal utilities, municipal authorities held in mind the profits that city governments could earn by selling gas, water, and electricity, but municipal officials did not see city governments as the sole beneficiaries of plans to renovate utilities.

Though leading economic interest groups and the Reichsbank came to question the need for maintaining public utilities, municipal officials asserted that private industry stood to gain from improvements to public water works and power plants. Arguing along these lines, Frankfurt's City Treasurer Bruno Asch suggested that investment in municipal utilities reduced production costs, aiding the entire economy.[9]

To preserve the gas, water, and electrical utilities at the core of the existing communal economy, Weimar municipal authorities modernized gas and water distribution systems and electrical power plants. Pressure for upgrading utilities was especially strong in the case of electrical power plants because demand for electricity soared after 1923. Most large cities, including Düsseldorf and Frankfurt, took up work on improvements to power plants as soon as they could, though Hanover, in contrast, first negotiated a contract in 1925 to purchase electricity from Prussia before undertaking the modernization of its electrical utility in 1927 and 1928.[10]

Frankfurt branched out very far in the area of communal supply. Seeking to ensure continued possession of an independent supply of gas in the face of competition from the Ruhr coal syndicate, which he suspected of designing a gas monopoly, Landmann persuaded the Frankfurt Gas Company to purchase a coal field in 1927 from *Rheinisches Stahlwerk* for RM 16 million. Frankfurt's city parliament subsequently provided funds and loan guarantees to create a regional gas system.[11]

Along with modernization of communal utilities, city governments also engaged in economic promotion by carrying out an eclectic array of projects to stimulate commercial activity. Continuing to implement a far-ranging approach to economic promotion, Frankfurt's city government purchased a spa in the nearby town of Bad Homburg. Mayor Landmann believed that ownership of the spa would permit Frankfurt to prepare for possible future incorporation of Bad Homburg, and he argued that such ownership would draw travel and commerce to Frankfurt.[12] A number of other cities sought to attract more travel by building or supporting the construction of hotels. Mannheim's administration created a corporation to build a hotel and advanced loans to enable construction, and Nuremberg's city government, after deciding against municipal construction of a hotel, guaranteed a low-interest mortgage for the private builder of a hotel.[13]

Among a wide variety of measures, municipal governments most often worked to boost commercial activity by making improvements to transportation and by holding trade fairs and exhibitions. Ludwig Landmann, one of many mayors to attribute enormous economic benefits to trade fairs, argued that Frankfurt's trade fair brought business for local firms and provided the entire city with publicity.[14] Similar logic appealed to Landmann's counterparts in cities across Germany. Trade fairs in fact proliferated after the First World War at a rate that alarmed some observers. They "shot up out of the ground like mushrooms," remarked the secretary of Düsseldorf's Chamber of Industry and Commerce.[15] Many of the new fairs soon struggled to survive alongside Leipzig's preeminent trade fair.[16] Thus, Frankfurt's entry in the trade fair sweepstakes faced stiff competition from trade fairs in cities including Leipzig, Munich, Königsberg, and Breslau.[17]

For municipal officials looking to boost economic activity, the allure of exhibitions rivalled that of trade fairs. Major municipal exhibitions of the Weimar period of stabilization included Essen's Gruga, a gardening exhibition, Cologne's Pressa, a press exhibition, the Magdeburg theater exhibition, an electrical exhibition in Darmstadt, and Frankfurt's Summer of Music of 1927. The Summer of Music, a series of concerts held in conjunction with an exhibition on international music, initially won praise as a great success: city councilors from the SPD and the DVP respectively termed the exhibition a "complete success" and "a cultural feat for Frankfurt."[18]

Like many of his counterparts, Düsseldorf's Mayor Robert Lehr placed highest priority on making his city a center for exhibitions. After holding a Thousand Year Fair in 1925, Düsseldorf hosted the Gesolei in 1926, an exhibition which publicized hygiene, social welfare, and physical exercise as methods for treating social damage caused by war and inflation. Looking to the past as a guide for future economic promotion, Lehr believed that the Gesolei would renew Düsseldorf's reputation as a good host for exhibitions and meetings. Permanent exhibition buildings constructed for the Gesolei would aid Düsseldorf in competition with neighboring cities to host future exhibitions.[19]

The mayor of a city in a region of many cities, Lehr took economic competition with other cities very seriously. He warned a city councilor who objected to the design of the permanent exhibition buildings that internal disunity could prevent Düsseldorf from gaining a "place in the sun in the hot competition with the neighboring cities."[20] Lehr expected the Gesolei to permit Düsseldorf to gain a step on its competitors, the other large cities in the Rhineland and the Ruhr, though he later modified his combative tone, suggesting that economic competition between cities did not have to produce winners and losers; the cities of western Germany could all develop their separate individual areas of strength.[21]

Beyond advocating general efforts to stimulate economic activity, both Lehr and Landmann favored measures to cultivate particular trades, industries, and companies. Düsseldorf's administration developed a close relationship during the period of stabilization with the steel conglomerate Vestag (*Vereinigten Stahlwerke*), which established its headquarters in Düsseldorf. Lehr, possibly exaggerating his influence, ascribed Vestag's decision to his own lobbying. In any case Lehr subsequently cooperated with Vestag on a plan to build a second bridge across the Rhine at Düsseldorf. Vestag agreed to guarantee a loan for RM 8 million of the total RM 14 million cost of bridge construction.[22]

Ludwig Landmann was another mayor who worked to draw individual companies and specific branches of trade and industry to his city. Guided by the intention of making Frankfurt the chief hub for the distribution of food and fruit in southern Germany, Landmann took up long-delayed plans to build a new market hall. Landmann maintained that the new market hall would both safeguard public health and win a higher proportion of the distribution of food for Frankfurt.[23]

In his chief feat of industrial policy, Landmann helped to locate the chemical conglomerate I.G. Farben in Frankfurt by incorporating the town of Höchst, the site of many of I.G. Farben's factories. Landmann argued that incorporating Höchst would enable Frankfurt to counter the trend towards economic concentration in Berlin, and I.G. Farben, which owned plans in both Frankfurt and Höchst favored Landmann's plan. With I.G. Farben's decision to place its headquarters in Frankfurt, the city became the chief center for the German chemical industry.[24]

Extending from patronage of trade fairs and exhibitions to policies designed to foster particular industries, municipal economic promotion of the Weimar period of stabilization nearly always included efforts to improve transportation. City governments drew on the prewar record of municipal activity to take up projects such as harbors and waterways – Frankfurt undertook an ambitious project to become a major inland port – but the growth of aviation created a new focus for municipal promotion of transportation. Commercial aviation, though still in its fledgling phase, fascinated municipal officials who predicted that air travel would continue to gain in importance. Frankfurt's Mayor Landmann compared contemporary air travel to railways in the 1840s.[25] Timely action could make Frankfurt a future center of international air travel.

Competition between cities helped to propel municipal promotion of aviation. Civic leaders spoke of a contest between cities to gain air traffic. Reporting on airports in other German cities, a committee of Frankfurt's city parliament advised that "Frankfurt can not and may not stand behind."[26] Even Hanover's Mayor Menge dropped his customary caution in matters of economic promotion and claimed that the acquisition of an airport would prevent Hanover from falling behind other cities in competition for aviation.[27]

By the late 1920s, numerous cities including Düsseldorf, Frankfurt, and Hanover possessed airports. Frankfurt held a controlling interest in a company that operated the city's new airport, while Hanover's municipal government operated its airport directly.[28] Düsseldorf faced greater obstacles than either Frankfurt or Hanover to entering competition for aviation: the occupation of the Rhineland hindered the development of aviation in Düsseldorf, and both the national and Prussian governments wished to concentrate regional aviation at Cologne and Essen. Düsseldorf's air field only managed to obtain the status of landing field, a level below that of airport, but Düsseldorf's municipal government persevered, and Düsseldorf began to obtain more scheduled flights in 1929.[29]

Social Welfare

Support for trade fairs, exhibitions, transportation projects and the modernization of power plants and gas works made economic development a major municipal endeavor of the Weimar Republic, but the most rapid proliferation of municipal tasks after the First World War occurred, not in economic promotion, but in social provision. The authors of the chief survey of modern Germany social policy note that "the extension of the welfare state was the centerpiece of the political compromise which sought to anchor the Weimar Republic." Social spending rose from 20.5 marks per resident in 1913 to 64.7 marks per resident in 1925 and reached 101.6 marks per resident by 1929, and all levels of the German social state acquired new responsibilities.[30]

As a component of a complex and decentralized social state, German municipal governments helped to fund and oversee an ever-growing list of social welfare programs. Under the terms of national welfare legislation of 1924, the individual federal states established district welfare authorities in every city with the status of county (*Bezirk*) and in rural counties. Besides supporting people formerly tended to by poor relief, each welfare district assisted recipients of invalidity and employees' insurance who were not fully cared for by the insurance offices.[31]

The complex social state of the Weimar Republic incorporated both public institutions and private organizations at the local level. District welfare authorities relied heavily on volunteers from private organizations. In 1925 Frankfurt's district welfare authority had 2,375 active volunteers and Düsseldorf's had 1,133 active volunteers.[32] The actual recipients of social welfare during the Weimar Republic included new categories of the needy, the legally-recognized victims of war and inflation. Wounded veterans and surviving dependents were eligible for welfare. So too were pensioners who had lost their savings to inflation. In 1928, victims of inflation, the *Sozialrentner* and *Kleinrentner* made up 33.1 percent of all recipients of open welfare in cities with a population of over 50,000 people.[33]

Youth also received special attention in welfare legislation of the Weimar Republic. The national law for youth welfare of 1922 recognized the right of children to receive education for "physical, mental, and social capability" and mandated the creation of youth welfare offices; although, a final national law for youth welfare of 1924 permitted other communal authorities to provide youth welfare.[34] Methods of complying with the youth welfare law varied in practice as some cities set up youth welfare offices within existing welfare offices, while others created separate youth welfare offices. Hamburg's substantial Youth Welfare Department, which actually predated the national youth welfare law, had a staff of 665 civil servants and white-collar employees by 1926.[35]

Youth welfare included rehabilitation of juvenile offenders, subsidized holidays, and special education. Cities sent thousands of children to special schools and hostels for rest care. Düsseldorf, Frankfurt, and Hanover all operated rest homes for children, and children also received medical care at homes specializing in the treatment of tuberculosis and at a variety of clinics operated by private welfare associations with municipal financial support.[36]

At least in Prussia, families as well as children received special attention under welfare legislation of the Weimar Republic. The Prussian Housing Law of 1918 instituted a system of family welfare. In most cases, municipal governments assigned family welfare to existing welfare authorities. Only a few cities, including Düsseldorf, set up separate family care offices. Providers of family care delivered advice on legal problems, health questions, including the care of infants and children, and gave material aid in the form of rent supplements, shoes, and clothing.[37]

District welfare authorities provided considerable discretion to case workers in determining and adjusting the benefits of applicants within the various branches of welfare. Professional and volunteer case workers alike investigated the personal problems, living conditions, and habits of applicants for welfare, evaluating the circumstances of individual applicants in order to determine how much support the applicant merited. Case workers could recommend higher levels of support for those judged to be needy. In Frankfurt, the District Welfare Authority could raise rates of support by 30 percent. Increases of 50 percent in rates required the approval of the next level of Prussian welfare authorities, the *Kreisverband*, and increases of more than 50 percent in welfare rates required the approval of still higher levels of the Prussian welfare administration.[38] Investigations carried out by welfare case workers could, on the other hand, also bring penalties for welfare applicants.[39] Case workers judged applicants according to moral standards: those determined to be "asocial" merited lower levels of support than other applicants. The ranks of the asocial included "the work-shy," drinkers and the "spendthrift" (*Unwirtschaftlich*).

There were municipal politicians, especially on the bourgeois Right, who applauded efforts to weed the asocial from the ranks of welfare recipients. Councilor Schwietzke of the German National People's Party (DNVP) in Düsseldorf believed that welfare encouraged the unemployed to remain idle. Advising the unemployed to resort to self help, Schwietzke argued that self-help would lie dormant so long as "the law of public welfare stipulates care for subsistence." In 1928 he declared that the welfare system was unsuitable for those of "weak will."[40] Even officials who presumed that the unemployed desired work often defended the practice of examining individual welfare recipients. Mayor Gustav Böß of Berlin asserted that the "individual treatment of the separate needy" was the "chief principle of modern welfare."[41]

Social Democrats were far more critical than their bourgeois counterparts of the practice of adjusting levels of welfare support according to moral criteria. The SPD in Frankfurt became increasingly dissatisfied with a policy that made the level of benefits received by welfare recipients dependent upon the moral examinations conducted by volunteer case workers. In 1928 councilor von Bauer, the SPD's specialist on welfare in Frankfurt's city parliament, called for a shift to schematic rates in order to "free the individual from being dependent on the good will of others."[42] With schematic rates, a welfare recipient's support would not be adjusted by a case worker.

Noting the practice of classifying welfare applicants according to moral criteria, some historians have argued that the welfare system of the Weimar Republic did not break with the practices of prewar poor relief. Welfare was still not entirely treated as a civic right for those in reduced circumstances. Investigations of alcoholism and sloth suggested that poverty resulted from moral faults.[43] Though volunteer case workers continued to apply principles used in administering poor relief, Weimar welfare programs however did not make up a slightly updated copy of poor relief. The new welfare system bestowed benefits on a more democratic basis. Unlike prewar recipients of poor relief, welfare recipients suffered no reduction of their rights as citizens including the right to vote.[44]

Despite some continuities between prewar poor relief and postwar welfare, the very magnitude of welfare programs during the Weimar Republic undermined practices formerly used in poor relief. The total package of welfare legislation of the Weimar Republic left cities to provide support for unprecedented numbers of needy residents. Frankfurt, for example, had assisted 3,800 people with forms of welfare in 1913, but in 1925 Frankfurt's municipal government helped to support 8,726 wounded veterans and surviving dependents, 6,725 pensioners and 14,814 others in a city with a population of over 400,000 people. Düsseldorf, a city of similar size, assisted 4,630 wounded veterans and surviving dependents, 5,317 pensioners and 18,059 other recipients of welfare in 1925.[45]

The swollen numbers of welfare recipients slowly altered welfare practices, eroding efforts by welfare professionals to uphold the practice of tailoring welfare support to individual circumstances. The enormous numbers of welfare recipients placed tremendous strain on the local welfare authorities. Volunteer and professional welfare workers struggled with limited success to preserve the investigation of individual applicants as a component of the welfare system.[46] In 1928 councilor von Bauer, the SPD's welfare expert in Frankfurt's city parliament, pointed out the difficulty of following the principle of individual examination. The number of applicants for welfare had swamped the welfare system. As the Association of Cities noted, "battle against mass deprivation took the place of the formerly-practiced individual welfare."[47]

The lack of clear separation, in the social legislation of the Weimar Republic, between welfare and support for the unemployed made the numbers of recipients of welfare subject to large fluctuations. Between 1924 and 1927, cities paid one-sixth of the benefits for support for the unemployed for up to twenty-six to thirty-nine weeks under a system that restricted unemployment assistance to those who had contributed to state health insurance for at least three months during the previous year.[48] The establishment of unemployment insurance in 1927, in which contributions from employers and employees provided benefits for twenty-six to thirty-nine weeks for those who had worked at least fifty-two weeks in the preceding two years, did not end municipal assistance for the unemployed. Responsible for paying one-fourth of the benefits for an intermediate system of "crisis support" (*Krisenunterstützung*) established in 1926 for those whose unemployment benefits had expired, municipal governments still extended welfare benefits to large numbers of the unemployed during any economic downturn.[49]

Though annoyed by the readiness of the national and state governments to leave cities with the task of providing welfare for the unemployed who had either exhausted or failed to qualify for unemployment support, a considerable number of municipal officials and politicians argued that providing social welfare for the unemployed at least had the virtue of complementing economic rationalization. A report issued by Frankfurt's Magistrat in 1927 underscored the close relationship between welfare and rationalization, declaring: "Without the welfare work of the municipalities, the rationalization efforts of the economy could never have been realized." Frankfurt's Mayor Landmann told an assembly of the Association of German Industry in 1927 that cities played a vital part in rationalization by aiding unemployed workers and white collar employees.[50] Social welfare, maintained Gustav Reuter, Düsseldorf's *Beigeordneter* for welfare, was especially useful during the first phase of rationalization when workers tended to be laid off. Social welfare preserved the capacity for work of the unemployed until they could be reintegrated into production at a later stage of rationalization.[51] By this calculation, social welfare prevented the deterioration of human capital.

The most direct method of ensuring that the unemployed retained the ability to work was to put them to work. City governments provided emergency work (*Notstandsarbeit*), most often through projects that required moving large amounts of earth such as flood regulation, cemetery expansion, and the construction of sports stadiums. Although civic leaders favored work creation projects, the recipients of employment were not necessarily thankful for their fortune in obtaining emergency work instead of welfare support. Working with inadequate equipment on flood control projects was not the most popular of occupations.[52]

Promotion of Housing Construction

The growth of municipal activity evident in social welfare during the Weimar Republic was, if anything, even more remarkable in housing policy. Of all types of social policy, the promotion of housing construction was most closely identified with municipal governments. Civic leaders often decried the burdens placed by other levels of government on local authorities when they discussed welfare, but many boasted of municipal achievements in organizing housing construction. "It will always remain a glorious chapter of the German cities," wrote Oberbaurat Peters of Hamburg, "how they practically took up the supply of housing after the unfortunate end of the World War."[53]

For municipal leaders, creating housing promised not only to satisfy public demand for apartments, but also to revitalize and invigorate a population held to have suffered grave injuries from war and inflation. Stressing the benefits of suitable housing for health and fitness, Oskar Mulert, President of the Association of Cities, wrote that the "preservation of public health and national strength … depends inseparably on the satisfaction of the need for housing suitable for human beings."[54] Such faith in the capacity of new housing to boost health and vigor was widespread. At one political extreme, Communists such as councilor Cremer of Düsseldorf's KPD claimed that only good housing could preserve the health of workers, and many bourgeois politicians, for their part, also thought that new housing fostered public health and capacity to work.[55] Describing the "preservation … of capacity for work" as a duty for all levels of government, councilor Boehmecke of Hanover's Deutsch-Hannoveraner spoke of "our task to create better apartments.[56] For bourgeois parties, concludes the historian Adelheid von Saldern, a solution to the housing problem "corresponded … to the ideas about social hygiene, morality, preservation of 'national strength,' 'productive welfare' as well as the raised demand of the economy for the reproduction of working men."[57]

Reflecting the lofty and, perhaps, elusive goals of Weimar planners, state action to improve housing conditions during the Weimar Republic went far beyond any measures taken before 1914. State intervention into housing policy during the imperial era was restricted to the introduction of zoning regulations and to modest efforts in cities including Frankfurt to encourage housing production by leasing land at low cost to non-profit housing companies, but such programs had limited effect. In 1913, only 16 of 123 cities responding to a poll from the Prussian Association of Cities reported having built housing for those of modest means at a total cost of only 7.5 million marks.[58] The previously slow pace of state intervention into the housing market accelerated during the Weimar Republic as public authorities controlled rents and helped to organize housing construction. The *Wohnungszwangswirtschaft* (state housing control), introduced to check soaring housing prices, set rents for apartments in buildings constructed before 1 July 1918 *(Altbauwohnungen)* in relation to pre-war rents and obligated landlords to make apartments available to tenants listed by communal housing offices.[59] Municipal officials and politicians saw rent control as a necessary stop-gap measure until the supply of apartments more closely balanced demand.

To spur housing production, the Weimar State increased spending for the promotion of housing construction at a faster rate than for any other type of social spending. "State housing construction policy," notes Werner Abelshauser, "developed the greatest financial dynamism and social relevance."[60] Rising even more sharply than total social spending, which multiplied almost five-fold between 1913 and 1929, state spending for housing construction stood at thirty-three times the level of 1913 by 1929. Much of this funding came from the rent tax of 1924 *(Hauszinssteuer* or HZS in Prussia), a tax levied on housing built before monetary stabilization in order to balance rents for old housing and housing built after hyperinflation.[61] Excluding loans, public spending for housing construction accounted for 13 percent of social expenditures in 1929.[62]

With increased public spending for housing construction, the number of apartments built with assistance from cities rose throughout the Weimar period of stabilization. The total number of housing units constructed in municipal housing programs in cities with a population of more than 50,000 increased from 81,578 in 1926 to 114,583 in 1927, 117,163 in 1928, and 158,637 in 1929.[63]

However, this general trend towards larger housing construction programs obscured fluctuations in individual cities. Düsseldorf, for example, increased promotion of housing construction sharply from approximately 1,500 or 1,600 apartments in 1926 to between 3,600 units and 3,800 units in 1927, but lack of capital forced the administration to cut back Düsseldorf's promotion of housing construction to fewer than 2,000 dwellings in 1928. To give housing construction new impetus, the administration then drafted a four-year plan to aid construction of 11,200 apartments between 1929 and 1932.[64]

The size of Frankfurt's housing programs increased more steadily from approximately 1,500 dwellings in 1925 to well over 3,000 units annually by the end of the period of stabilization. Frankfurt, like Düsseldorf, began a four-year program in 1929. Under the terms of this plan, Frankfurt intended to support the construction of 4,000 dwellings a year. Frankfurt helped to finance the construction of a total of nearly 20,000 housing units between 1924 and 1931.[65]

Hanover also avoided any major downturns in housing construction. Hanover's housing program for 1926 provided for the construction of 2,438 dwellings, a total more than double the 907 dwellings in the city's housing program of 1925. Hanover's Stadtbaurat Elkart outlined still-larger programs in the next two years as Hanover promoted the construction of more than 3,600 dwellings in both 1927 and 1928.[66]

While city governments clearly sought to increase housing production, the exact role of municipal governments in housing construction during the Weimar Republic has caused considerable confusion. It is far more accurate to refer to municipal promotion of housing construction, rather than to municipal housing production, for mayors and city councilors of the Weimar Republic generally preferred to avoid direct sponsorship of construction, the most dramatic form of municipal intervention into housing construction. Cologne's Konrad Adenauer, reflecting the views of most mayors, supported construction, not by city governments, but by non profit-building societies.[67] The standard arguments against municipal sponsorship of housing construction, as outlined by Hanover's Stadtbaurat Elkart, stressed the difficulty of obtaining funds and the burden of administering apartments. Even Social Democrats, though more inclined than their bourgeois colleagues to back direct sponsorship of construction, favored reliance on non-profit building societies in cities including Berlin.[68] Most German cities sponsored little construction directly, and direct municipal sponsorship of housing construction declined during the period of stabilization. In 1926 only three of the twenty-three cities with a population of more than 200,000 sponsored construction of at least 40 percent of all new dwellings, and another two cities, including Frankfurt, sponsored construction of at least 20 percent of all new dwellings. By 1929 only one of Germany's twenty-seven cities with a population more than 200,000 sponsored construction of more than 40 percent of all new dwellings, and another three sponsored at least 20 percent of all new dwellings.[69]

Statistics of municipal sponsorship did not reveal the full extent of Frankfurt's oversight of local housing construction. Frankfurt's municipal government directly sponsored the construction of the

TABLE 1.1 New apartments paid for in part with subisidies in Düsseldorf, Frankfurt and Hanover between 1925 and 1929

The Association of Cities' Count of New Apartments

	1926	1927	1928	1929
Düsseldorf	1,474	3,591	739	2,341
Frankfurt	2,212	2,193	2,902	3,349
Hanover	1,534	2,511	3,319	4,208

Municipal Counts of New Apartments in Frankfurt and Hanover

	1925	1926	1927	1928	1929
Frankfurt	1,432	2,212	2,866	3,319	3,640
Hanover	907	2,438	3,666	3,659	3,039

Düsseldorf's Statistical Yearbook's Count of New Apartments

	1925	1926	1927	1928	1929	1930
Düsseldorf	562	1,638	1,629	3,747	1,819	2,817

Sources: Statistisches Jahrbuch deutscher Städte 23 (1928), p. 60; 24 (1929), p. 45; 25 (1930), p. 211; 26 (1931), p. 72. Dietrich Andernacht and Gerd Kuhn, "Frankfurter Fordismus," in *Ernst May und Das neue Frankfurt*, ed. Deutsches Architekturmuseum (Berlin, 1986), p. 45. BVK Hanover 1929-1930, 24 March 1930, Wohnungsbauprogramm 1930. *Jahresbericht des Statistischen Amts Düsseldorf* (1925), p. 53; (1926), p. 68; (1927), p. 130; (1928), p. 92; (1929), p. 120; and (1930), p. 54.

Praunheim housing settlement of 1,441 apartments as well as some smaller settlements, and when Frankfurt reduced municipal sponsorship of housing construction in the late 1920s, companies owned by the city, most notably the Corporation for Small Apartments (AG für kleine Wohnungen) and the Rental Home Corporation (Mietheim AG) – later the Garden City Corporation – sponsored construction of large housing settlements including the Römerstadt settlement of 1,220 apartments, the Bornheimer Hang settlement of 1,234 apartments and the Bruchfeldstrasse settlement of 643 apartments.[70] Frankfurt's highest-ranking municipal officials held the chief posts on the boards of directors of these companies. Mayor Ludwig Landmann chaired the Board of Directors of the Corporation for Small Apartments until 1927 when Ernest May replaced him in that position, and Frankfurt's City Treasurer Asch chaired the board of directors of the Garden City Corporation.[71]

Municipal authorities in most cities including Düsseldorf and Hanover were more wary of relying on municipal companies to sponsor housing construction. In 1925 Düsseldorf's administration solicited opinions from local economic interest groups, including the Chamber of Industry and Commerce, the Organization of Düsseldorf's Banks and Bankers, and the Association of Industrialists of Düsseldorf and Environs, to undercut recommendations by the Center Party and the DVP to create a municipal housing construction company.[72] But despite resisting moves to found a municipal housing construction company, Düsseldorf's administration displayed flexibility, making increasing use of the city's existing Office Building Company (Bürohausgesellschaft) to sponsor construction of small apartments for those of modest means.

In most cities, it was not direct sponsorship of construction, but control of distribution of public funding that provided municipal authorities with a powerful tool for organizing local housing construction. Municipal housing programs typically set targets for the number and type of apartments to be constructed with public financial assistance. Attaching conditions for the use of low-interest mortgages and other loans, municipal authorities steered public funds towards the construction of particular categories of housing such as small apartments or housing earmarked for those of modest means. In Düsseldorf, for example, the administration's housing program of 1928 set the size and number of rent-tax mortgages available for the construction of apartments of two, three, and four rooms by private contractors and cooperatives, and also set aside separate rent-tax mortgages for the construction of 275 apartments for residents defined as asocial.[73]

Covering the selection of targets for the number, size, and cost of new apartments, municipal promotion of housing construction only extended to the choice of housing design in a minority of large cities. Hamburg was one city that obliged recipients of public funds to follow technical and planning guidelines set by city planners, and Berlin's city planner Martin Wagner also sought to influence construction techniques, but no large city shaped construction methods and design more closely than Frankfurt am Main during Ernst May's tenure as the city's chief housing official.[74] Invited to join Frankfurt's administration in 1925 by Mayor Ludwig Landmann, May held the titles of Department Head for the Hochbauamt (Office for Above-Ground Construction), the Siedlungsamt (Housing Development Office), and the building police, an unusual combination of posts that allowed him to shape all aspects of housing construction.[75]

Analyzing the influence of government intervention on housing design of the Weimar Republic, it is tempting for historians to emphasize the adoption of a new architectural style and of new construction techniques in Weimar housing settlements, but as Anthony McElligott notes, the majority of new housing units did not incorporate a new building style.[76] City planners who wished to introduce a new housing style could not count on gaining approval from local politicians. The Weissenhof housing exhibition of 1927, one of the best known Weimar displays of modern architecture, left the impression that Stuttgart was a center of architectural innovation, but Stuttgart's Deputy Mayor and city planner Daniel Sigloch actually failed to persuade Stuttgart's city parliament to approve of new methods of construction in the city's new housing settlements.[77]

If McElligott is correct in pointing out that most new housing settlements were not sites for architectural experiments, it remains true that municipal innovation in housing design and building techniques gained public attention during the Weimar Republic. Frankfurt, in particular, won an international reputation as a center for new building methods and new housing. Convinced that prewar housing did not provide a suitable model for postwar planning, Ernst May claimed that the First World War had revealed the defects of urban living conditions. "When the world war unmasked human culture," it became apparent that "things went on daily ... scarcely less brutally at home than on the battle field."[78] May condemned prewar urban housing, especially the "five-story rent barracks with cement courtyards."[79] While he perhaps exaggerated the prevalence of rent barracks, the vehemence of his criticism of these housing blocks reflected widespread desire among city planners to make recovery the occasion for urban transformation.

To create a "new Frankfurt," May and his associates combined lessons of the Garden City movement with the rationalization of construction and a new building style. Drawing on his experience between 1910 and 1912 working for Raymond Unwin of the Garden City movement, May placed new housing settlements on Frankfurt's outskirts where residents could live near green space. He worked to lower the costs of these housing settlements through rationalization, the technical solution of choice for so many professional groups during the Weimar Republic. Rationalization in Frankfurt encompassed all aspects of building: Frankfurt's planners and architects drew up blueprints for large groups of apartments; designed apartments with standardized elements such as windows, ovens, and doors; and experimented with new construction materials, chiefly precast concrete panels, which Frankfurt purchased from private companies and also manufactured itself in the trade fair's House of Technology. An advocate of new building techniques,

May also championed a new building style. It was this new style of flat roofs, flat surfaces, and horizontal bands that truly made the satellite housing settlements rising on the city's periphery look like a "new Frankfurt."[80]

Approaches to housing policy varied greatly from Ernst May's ambitious effort to create a "new Frankfurt" to the more cautious approach to planning of municipal politicians and officials in cities like Düsseldorf and Hanover, but promotion of housing construction became a major municipal task in all cities during the Weimar period of stabilization. Once the rent tax was in place, the Reichstag and Reich Ministry of Labor had little control over the actual organization of the promotion of housing construction. From 1924 to 1929, the work of ending the much-lamented housing shortage proceeded in Germany's local administrations.

Promotion of Leisure

Assistance for housing construction, whether restricted to the distribution of public funding or encompassing the selection of building techniques and housing styles, was part of a pattern of expansion of state responsibility for satisfying public needs. The growth of municipal duties began in the nineteenth century with the protection of basic sanitation and was extended during the Weimar Republic to cover both support for housing construction and promotion of leisure.

As in the case of housing construction, the growth of municipal support for leisure often encouraged harsh reassessment of the prewar civic legacy. Municipal leaders of the 1920s rebuked their predecessors for having failed to consider the need of urban residents for contact with nature. Discussing the "large-city problem," Mayor Konrad Adenauer of Cologne feared that modern urban living had torn people away from their "necessary connections with nature." In one especially excited diatribe against the faults of nineteenth-century city planning, Düsseldorf's councilor Ellenbeck referred to areas of Düsseldorf where one found, not nature, but only "stones and more stones, miserable documents of the time when ... we did not master the problem of the city." Ellenbeck concluded that the nineteenth century had left a "facade-culture," a superficial front, which covered the misery of proletarian living conditions.[81]

The housing law of 1918 formalized the division of urban space into separate areas for housing and for business and industry, creating new zoning regulation heralded by city planners such as Düsseldorf's Beigeordneter Schilling, though Schilling did not halt at separating space for work and housing. His own general development plan for Düsseldorf divided space by its function for work, housing, and leisure.[82]

To provide urban residents with opportunities for leisure, Weimar municipal leaders favored plans to create green space. The provision of green space was, Dresden's Stadtbaurat Paul Wolf declared, a "vital question" in large cities.[83] German cities had built parks in the nineteenth century, but it was only towards the turn of the century and the immediate prewar years that planners began to treat space for leisure as a requirement for recuperation in an urban setting, rather than as an ornament. By the 1920s, space for leisure was firmly enshrined as one of the three functional components of city planning along with space for work and housing.[84]

Municipal provision of green space for urban residents took most striking form in the construction of green belts. The Essen planner Ehlgötz described green belts as "the essential part of general settlement planning." Cologne received the most renown for its new green belt, a band of parks, gardens, and sports fields approximately 40 kilometers in length, which stretched around much of the city; Kiel, and Altona, among other large cities, also built green belts.[85]

The expansion of municipal promotion of leisure coincided with the rapid emergence of new trends in leisure, most notably a postwar sports boom. After a period of steady growth in the late imperial era, sports became a mass phenomenon during the Weimar Republic as Germans joined sports clubs and took to sports fields and stadiums in record numbers.[86] Membership in the German Soccer Federation, for example, rose from 9,317 in 1904 and 189,204 in 1913 to over 1,000,000 in 1921.[87] Even observers with experience of prewar sports found it difficult to fathom the level of postwar interest in sports. Heinrich Tramm, Hanover's prewar Stadtdirektor, noted in 1920 that he had never seen more than two or three thousand spectators at a sports event, but this figure was subsequently dwarfed by the tens of thousands of spectators at major sporting events of the Weimar era.[88]

How was this public enthusiasm for sport to be explained? The sports craze was often described as the result of a spontaneous and instinctive popular decision. Many credited troops with leading the sports movement. The *Hannoverscher Kurier*, a nationalist newspaper in Hanover, recounted in March 1919 that "front-line soldiers" hurried out of the trenches on to sports fields and playgrounds."[89]

Observers of the sports boom alternately suggested that German youths took up sports to preserve their physical strength against the debilitating effects of industrial labor. Perceiving a conjunction between industrialization and sport in England and Germany, the Stadtschulrat of Gelsenkirchen, a mining city in the Ruhr, concluded that German youth "took over the enthusiasm for physical exercise, which the oldest industrial people of the earth, the English, had proved as an excellent means to preserve national strength."[90]

Minimizing motives that historians might describe as social control, contemporary observers usually saw the Weimar sports boom as the product of popular choice, not as the result of any conscious program to achieve social harmony, but praise for the instincts of sports enthusiasts revealed the enormous benefits commonly attributed to sports during the Weimar Republic.[91] Sports promised both to replace military training and to raise public health and vitality. "Sport," explained Stadtrat Schmude, the municipal official who oversaw Frankfurt's promotion of physical exercise, was the "… best helper for the reconstruction of our fatherland."[92] Expressing similar confidence in the power of sport to revitalize Germans, the inscription on a pillar at the entrance of Hanover's new stadium read in part: "Help us create a new and strong generation after the wounds of the war."[93]

The postwar sports boom clearly fascinated officials and politicians. Mayor Rive of Halle, looking back on a long career in municipal administration, contrasted postwar enthusiasm for promoting sports with the opposition that his own proposals to aid sports had encountered from city councilors before 1914. Fritz Wildung, the General Secretary of the Workers' Gymnastics and Sports Association (Arbeiter Turn und Sport Bund), the umbrella organization for the workers' sport movement associated with the SPD, recalled that it was only a few years since professional politicians had held sports to be "at most a matter for people who did not know of anything better to do with their free time." Times had changed. Wildung remarked that "sports has attained such a great importance in public life, that no one can any longer leave it unnoted, least of all the statesman and politician."[94]

Among political institutions, municipal governments took the lead in promoting sports during the Weimar Republic. Dr. Wilms, a city councilor of the DVP in Düsseldorf, noted that "Gymnastics and sports have come to the forefront of interest; Reich, state, and cities compete in this area." Cities won any such competition.[95] In 1929 cities accounted for over two-thirds of public spending on sports.[96]

The largest part of municipal spending for sports went to pay for new stadiums. Constructing stadiums served to create both employment and opportunities for sporting activity, and many city governments first approved stadium projects in the early 1920s.[97] Hyperinflation slowed work on sports facilities, but Hamburg, Cologne, Munich, Breslau, Frankfurt, Essen, Dortmund, Düsseldorf, Hanover, Nuremberg, Gelsenkirchen, Duisburg, Mannheim, Altona, and Halle, among other cities, possessed new stadiums by the Weimar period of stabilization.[98] Frankfurt's stadium, a facility with an adjacent bicycle track, swimming pool, seats for 13,167 spectators and room for 67,400 standing spectators, was one of the more impressive of the new stadiums. Nuremberg also achieved renown as a center for sport, building a new sports complex with a stadium of more than 50,000 seats, practice fields, tennis courts, hockey and handball facilities, and a swimming pool.[99] As a group, the new municipal stadiums received enormous publicity. Reporting on his visit to the Thousand Year Exhibition of the Rhineland at Cologne in 1925, Carl Diem, the head of the National Committee for Physical Exercise (Reichsausschuß fur Leibesübungen), the umbrella group for sports clubs under bourgeois leadership, remarked that the title of the exhibition could have been "the stadium of our city!"[100]

Municipal governments supplemented construction of stadiums by building other sports facilities and by granting subsidies to encourage sports. Frankfurt guaranteed loans of RM 300,000 to pay for the construction of a sports hall next to its stadium.[101] At more modest cost, cities also extended subsidies and loan guarantees to sports clubs. Specific sporting events also received subsidies on occasion; Frankfurt gave funds to the International Workers Olympics in 1925.[102]

Eager to encourage the postwar sports boom, civic leaders simultaneously increased municipal assistance to an extremely wide array of other forms of leisure. Municipal promotion of leisure encompassed both support for rapidly-emerging popular pursuits and attempts to rescue sometimes-faltering cultural institutions that had been firmly established before the First World War. City governments of the Weimar Republic helped to preserve institutions of bourgeois culture, the theaters, museums, and botanical gardens dating from the late nineteenth century. Municipal authorities sympathetic to the plight of cultural institutions identified a duty to maintain a civic cultural legacy. Nuremberg's Mayor Hermann Luppe, noting the end of royal houses, the limited resources of the church, and the impoverishment of a large part of the class of cultural patrons, asked who was to replace the patrons of the prewar era. "It is our tasks as cities," he answered, "to replace in part these previous patrons, in which we maintain art collections, operate theaters, make musical performances possible, in which we give commissions for art work of all types."[103] Halle's Mayor Rive similarly termed city governments the heirs to princes as cultural patrons.[104]

The trend towards increased municipal support for culture began shortly before the First World War in cities such as Mannheim and Cologne and gathered speed during the Weimar Republic when most large cities took over operation of theaters and, in many cases, orchestras.[105] A sudden end to royal patronage forced the hand of municipal governments in cities such as Hanover, which acquired a state theater formerly subsidized by the Prussian monarchy. Other municipalities took over private theaters and operas that went bankrupt during the period of hyperinflation.[106] Even Berlin, which continued to benefit from cultural spending by the Prussian State, began to operate the bankrupt Charlottenburg opera. By the onset of stabilization, Frankfurt was actually one of the few cities that did not directly own a theater; however, Frankfurt's city government held 95 percent of the shares of a theater company that rented Frankfurt's playhouse until 1928 under a contract entitling it to apply to the city parliament for subsidies.[107]

Even private cultural institutions that retained a precarious independence asked municipal authorities for assistance. The directors of Frankfurt's Palm Garden, a private botanical garden, requested and received financial support from Frankfurt's administration. Reporting on the Palm Garden's postwar condition, Baudirektor Professor Elsaesser, one of Ernest May's colleagues, concluded that physical deterioration depressed attendance, magnified financial difficulties and prevented "a stirring visit and a profitable management."[108] To bolster the Palm Garden, the Magistrat introduced a motion in 1926 to help finance reconstruction of the garden by purchasing RM 160,000 of shares in the Palm Garden and loaning it RM 340,000.[109]

Comprehensive Functional Planning and the Promise of Weimar Recovery

On the municipal, as on the national level, the Weimar Republic brought a major new phase of state expansion in Germany. In the nineteenth century, municipal construction of urban infrastructure complemented state and national development of social insurance.

Following years of war and inflation, the Weimar period of stabilization marked a further era of intensive municipal activity in which German city governments took up new tasks. City governments of the Weimar Republic certainly built on prewar municipal duties, but they also extended their array of activity in economic promotion and social provision.

Municipal activism was a strong force for the growth of state intervention during the Weimar period of stabilization. If state activity grew from the top down as the national government delegated tasks, it also increased from the bottom up as local authorities expanded their own activities. Municipal authorities moved far beyond any prescribed duties in encouraging economic development and promoting housing construction and leisure.

Ambitious municipal programs of recovery carried the promise of democratizing access to improved living conditions. Despite widespread pride in the achievements of prewar municipal policy, many civic leaders concluded that city governments had not taken sufficient steps to improving living conditions for all urban residents during the imperial era. Taking particularly striking form in Frankfurt, strong criticism of the limits of past municipal achievements also surfaced elsewhere including Düsseldorf where councilor Ellenbeck charged that nineteenth-century urban planning had failed to address many problems of urban living. Criticism of prewar housing conditions combined with calls for ending the housing shortage to reinforce the goal of democratizing access to suitable housing. Efforts to ensure broad access to social provision were also more evident than ever before in municipal promotion of leisure.

Incorporating plans for improved social provision and economic development, Weimar municipal policy was comprehensive. *Das neue Frankfurt* and other magazines and books devoted to the deeds of city governments publicized the breadth of municipal endeavors.[110] Comprehensive policy was common both to cities such as Frankfurt where municipal leaders sought to create a "new" city, and to cities like Düsseldorf and Hanover where mayors and planners initially looked more to the past as a guide to recovery. Whether placed in the service of creating "new" cities or applied more narrowly to the goal of recovery, Weimar municipal policy was both comprehensive and functional. Civic leaders stressed that municipal policy, though far-ranging, was not a compendium of scattered and unconnected initiatives, but a functionally unified coherent set of policies of recovery. Altona's city planner Gustav Oelsner, one of the adherents of functional city planning, termed a city "an organic construction." Functional planning promised to secure the "'balance of interests' in a 'living organism.'"[111]

Advocates of comprehensive functional planning identified an economic imperative for social policy and, in some cases, for cultural policy that bound together social provision and economic promotion. Making the economic case for social policy, Oskar Mulert, President of the German Association of Cities, asserted that "social policy must be carried out... Intensive economic production of goods has a farseeing human economy *(Menschenökonomie)* as a prerequisite."[112] Dresden's Mayor Blüher termed man "the most valuable means of production" and explained in 1928 that municipal authorities sought to preserve and raise human "efficiency" through housing construction, education, "economic welfare," and public health care.[113]

The assertion of the economic utility of social provision transformed numerous desirable municipal activities into necessary preconditions for economic development. When the Oberbaurat of Mannheim announced that the future city of Mannheim was to be a city of work, it was only logical for him to argue that the "aim of planning must therefore be to prepare a city in which the economic, social, hygienic, and cultural requirements of the population find their satisfaction."[114] Municipal leaders regularly referred to the economic benefits of their endeavors to promote housing construction. Sports, too, figured as an instrument of economic development in civic explanations of municipal policy. Calling man "the best economic good," Mayor Gustav Böß of Berlin described his city's sports facilities as a component of economic planning.[115]

Even assistance for cultural institutions was a component of economic policy in the view of Frankfurt's Mayor Landmann. Underscoring the connection between cultural and economic promotion as explicitly as possible, Landmann told Frankfurt's city councilors that "this culture policy, which we are inaugurating and want to still further promote, is to be considered from this point of view as a significant part of economic policy." An active cultural policy raised the intellectual capabilities of the entire populace, "impregnating the people culturally ... in order to obtain a humanly intellectual and culturally higher achievement."[116]

Düsseldorf was host to an exhibition that provided one of the most striking displays of confidence in comprehensive functional planning. Outlining the economic rationale for comprehensive functional planning, Ernst Poensgen, the chief operating officer of the Vestag steel conglomerate and a member of the organizing committee for the Gesolei exhibition of 1926, argued that the economic challenge of making sufficient reparation payments to satisfy those states willing to reduce reparations required cultivating the capacity for work of the German labor force. Germany's economic "obligations," he stated, "cannot be paid off with the previously customary methods…," but demanded "a persistent maximum amount of full work and can only be accomplished if the men, from whom it is demanded, are completely healthy."

Recovery and reparations demanded that German industry operate at peak efficiency, yet the social damage of war and inflation jeopardized the ability of the work force to provide industry with efficient labor. The Gesolei illustrated how to overcome this apparent predicament by developing capacity for work "so that we can achieve lasting maximum performances." Concentrating on human recovery, the Gesolei correctly set "man in its center as the embodiment of all economic events." The Gesolei taught how to protect and improve human capacity for work through comprehensive functional planning. The exhibition, concluded Poensgen, spread knowledge of "rational human economy *(Menschenwirtschaft)*, suitable division of work and leisure, preservation and raising of the ability to work."[117]

Crafted to raise human efficiency, comprehensive functional planning also promised to emancipate urban residents from the constraints of urban life. Confidence in the power of planning to liberate urban residents emerged most distinctly in cities such as Frankfurt where municipal leaders proclaimed their intention of creating a "new" city. Defending Frankfurt's policies of investment in housing, sports, and culture, Landmann told his critics in 1930 that his aim was not merely to create an "external new Frankfurt." The city government's goal was nothing less than to "lay the foundations for the growth of a new generation, which pulled out of the crowded large apartment buildings of an over-settled old-city core …, understands how to maintain its physical and intellectual health and how to increase its attention for cultural wealth."[118]

Comprehensive functional planning, whether in its most ambitious form in cities of the "new city" movement or in cities with more cautious administrations, complied with many of the goals of the Weimar Republic. Municipal attention to housing construction and to the protection of capacity for work corresponded to aims listed in the Weimar constitution's extensive series of social clauses. Article 155 of the Weimar Constitution declared the state's intention "to secure a healthy dwelling for every German and a home … meeting their requirements for every German family especially for those with several children." Protection of the work force and its capacity for work emerged as official goals in article 157, which noted that "capacity for work (*Arbeitskraft*) stands under the special protection of the Reich," and in article 161, which referred to the creation of social insurance for "the preservation of health and ability to work" (*Arbeitsfähigkeit*). As we have seen, municipalities carried out much of the work of trying to meet these goals. In so doing, city governments ultimately acquired a considerable share of the responsibility for establishing the legitimacy of the Weimar Republic, for as Detlev Peukert notes, "the prestige of the new Republic was tied in particular with the promise to build up social policy."

Notes

1. BVK Hanover 1923-1924, p. 428.
2. StVV Frankfurt, 1924, p. 779; and StVV Düsseldorf, 1925, p. 4.
3. Schloßmann, *GE-SO-LEI*, vol. 1, p. 22.
4. Howe, *European Cities*, p. 3.
5. Fritz Elsas and Erwin Stein, eds., *Die deutschen Städte, ihre Arbeit von 1918 bis 1928* (Berlin, 1928), p. 18.
6. Hofmann, *Zwischen Rathaus und Reichskanzlei*, p. 99.
7. BVK Hanover, 1926-1927, p. 689.
8. Rebentisch, *Ludwig Landmann*, pp. 71, 116-17.
9. StVV Frankfurt, 1925, p. 1071.
10. BVK Hanover 1925-1926, pp. 616-23; and 1928-1929, p. 35.
11. Rebentisch, *Ludwig Landmann*, pp. 206-14; and StVV Frankfurt, 1927, pp. 349. 647-41, 750.
12. Rebentisch, *Ludwig Landmann*, pp. 149-50; and StVV Frankfurt, 1925, pp. 310-15.
13. Friedrich Walter, *Schicksal einer deutschen Stadt: Geschichte Mannheims, 1907-1945*, vol. 2 (Frankfurt am Main, 1950), p. 36; and Hermann Luppe, *Mein Leben* (Nuremberg, 1977), pp. 195-96.
14. StVV Frankfurt, 1925, p. 768.
15. Dr. Joseph Wilden, "Ausstellung oder Lehrschau," *Gesolei* 1 (1925): 47.
16. Rebentisch, *Ludwig Landmann*, pp. 235-38; and Elsas and Stein, eds., *Die deutschen Städte*, p. 48.
17. "Breslau 1918-1928: Ein kurzer Rückblick," in *Die deutschen Städte*, ed. Elsas and Stein, p. 108.
18. StVV Frankfurt, 1927, pp. 783, 788; and Schwarz, *Adenauer*, pp. 196-98.
19. StVV Düsseldorf, 1925, pp. 3, 214.
20. StA Düsseldorf III 683, Lehr to Wehner, 6 June 1925.

21. Ibid. III 685, Vortrag, 16 October 1926.
22. Hüttenberger, *Die Industrie- und Verwaltungsstadt*, pp. 371- 72; and StVV Düsseldorf, 1926, pp. 186-93.
23. StVV Frankfurt, 1926, pp. 576-79, 859-60; and Rebentisch, *Ludwig Landmann*, pp. 188-90.
24. Rebentisch, *Ludwig Landmann*, p. 181; and StVV Frankfurt, 1927, pp. 1213-16.
25. StVV Frankfurt, 1925, p. 10.
26. Ibid., 1927, p. 918.
27. *Hannoverscher Anzeiger*, 7 March 1928.
28. *Statistisches Jahrbuch deutscher Städte* (Jena, 1930), p. 316.
29. Hüttenberger, *Die Industrie- und Verwaltungsstadt*, pp. 383- 84.
30. Saachße and Tennstedt, *Fürsorge und Wohlfahrtspflege*, p. 77; Schulze, *Weimar Deutschland*, p. 66; and James, *The German Slump*, p. 48.
31. Wells, *German Cities*, pp. 162-64.
32. *Statistisches Jahrbuch deutscher Städte* 22 (1927), p. 436.
33. Ibid. 25 (1930), p. 476.
34. Stachura, *The Weimar Republic and the Younger Proletariat*, pp. 76-90; Peukert, *Grenzen der Sozialdisziplinierung*, pp. 196-97, 207-52; Sachße and Tennstedt, *Fürsorge und Wohlfahrtspflege*, p. 104; and Harvey, *Youth and the Welfare State*, pp. 168-72.
35. Harvey, *Youth and the Welfare State*, p. 174; and Frank Zadach-Buchmeier, "Staatliche Jugendpflege in der kommunalen Praxis: Das Beispiel Hannover," in *Stadt und Moderne*, ed. von Saldern, pp. 166-69.
36. *Kommunales Jahrbuch*, vol. 11, pp. 197, 245, 356; and *Statistisches Jahrbuch deutscher Städte* 25 (1930), p. 492.
37. Crew, "German Socialism, the State and Family Policy," pp. 243, 248-49.
38. StVV Frankfurt, 1926, p. 511.
39. Crew, "German Socialist and Family Policy," p. 249.
40. StVV Düsseldorf, 1927, p. 75; and 1928, p. 80.
41. Böß, *Die sozialen Aufgaben der Kommunalpolitik*, p. 16.
42. StVV Frankfurt, 1928, p. 1141.
43. Angela Dinghaus and Bettina Korff, "Wohlfahrtspflege im Hannover der 20er Jahre – Kontinuitätslinien repressiver Armenpflege und sozialer Disziplinierung," in *Stadt und Moderne*, ed. von Saldern, pp. 199-203.
44. Richard J. Evans, "Introduction," in *The German Unemployed: Experiences and Consequences of Mass Unemployment from the Weimar Republic to the Third Reich*, ed. Richard Evans and Dick Geary (New York, 1987), p. 2.
45. *Statistisches Jahrbuch deutscher Städte* 22 (1927), p. 441; and StVV Frankfurt 1926, p. 145.
46. Crew, "German Socialism, the State and Family Policy," pp. 256-57.
47. StVV Frankfurt, 1928, p. 1141; and LA Berlin STB 1533/I Städte Staat Wirtschaft, p. 39.
48. Elsas and Stein, eds., *Die deutschen Städte*, p. 66.
49. Evans, "Introduction," pp. 4-6; and Heidrun Homburg, "From Unemployment Insurance to Compulsory Labor," in *The German Unemployed*, ed. Evans and Geary, pp. 78-79.
50. StVV Frankfurt, 1927, p. 163; and *Mitglieder-Versammlung des Reichsverbandes der deutschen Industrie*, Veröffentlichungen des Reichsverbandes der deutschen Industrie, Heft 37 (Berlin, 1927), p. 14.
51. Schloßmann ed., *GE-SO-LEI*, vol. 2, p. 667.

52. Merith Niehuss, "From Welfare Provision to Social Insurance: The Unemployed in Augsburg 1918-27," in *The German Unemployed*, ed. Evans and Geary, pp. 60-65.

53. Albert Gut, ed., *Der Wohnungsbau in Deutschland nach dem Weltkriege: Seine Entwicklung unter der unmittelbaren und mittelbaren Förderung durch die deutschen Gemeindeverwaltung*, (Munich, 1928), p. 119.

54. Ibid., p. 9.

55. StVV Düsseldorf, 1925, p. 93.

56. BVK Hannover, 1925-1926, pp. 412-13.

57. Adelheid von Saldern, "Sozialdemokratie und Kommunale Wohnungsbaupolitik in den 20er Jahren – am Beispiel von Hamburg und Wien," *Archiv für Sozialgeschichte* 25 (1985): 185.

58. Ladd, *Urban Planning*, pp. 189-92, 196-97; and Henriette Kramer, "Die Anfänge des sozialen Wohnungsbaus in Frankfurt am Main 1860-1914," *Archiv für Frankfurt's Geschichte und Kunst* 56 (1978): 143.

59. Michael Ruck, "Wohnungsbaufinanzierung in der Weimarer Republik: Zielsetzungen, Ergebnisse, Probleme," in *Massenwohnung und Eigenheim: Wohnungsbau und Wohnen in der Großstadt seit dem Ersten Weltkrieg*, ed. Axel Schildt and Arnold Sywottek (Frankfurt am Main, 1988), p. 151.

60. Werner Abelshauser, "Die Weimarer Republik – ein Wohlfahrtsstaat?" in *Die Weimarer Republik als Wohlfahrtsstaat: Zum Verhältnis von Wirtschafts- und Sozialpolitik in der Industriegesellschaft*, ed. Werner Abelshauser (Stuttgart, 1987), p. 17.

61. Witt, "Inflation, Wohnungszwangswirtschaft, und Hauszinssteuer," p. 396.

62. Schulze, *Weimar Deutschland*, p. 66.

63. *Statistisches Jahrbuch deutscher Städte* 26 (1931), p. 69.

64. StA Düsseldorf XXIV 1113, Wohnungsbauprogramm der Stadt Düsseldorf für die Jahre 1929/1932. Note that the Association of Cities' statistics for construction in Düsseldorf in 1928 are wrong and that Düsseldorf's statistical office post-dated figures for annual housing construction by one year. See Table 1.1.

65. Dietrich Andernacht and Gerd Kuhn, "Frankfurter Fordismus," in *Ernst May und Das neue Frankfurt 1925-1930*, ed. Deutsches Architekturmuseum (Berlin, 1986), pp. 42, 45.

66. BVK Hannover, 1925-1926, p. 1003, Wohnungsbauprogramm 1926; 1927-1928, pp. 1-12; *Hannoverscher Anzeiger*, 11 March 1928; and BVK Hannover 1929-1930, 24 March 1930, Wohnungsbauprogramm 1930. Note that even Hanover's administration did not claim to promote housing construction at the levels reported in the Association of Cities' statistics. See Table 1.1.

67. Stehkämper, ed., *Konrad Adenauer*, p. 160.

68. Senator Stadtbaurat Elkart, "Städtische Wohnungsbaupolitik," *Bauamt und Gemeindebau* 8 (1926): 163-64; and Gough, *Die SPD in der Berliner Kommunalpolitik 1925-1933* (Berlin, 1984), p. 80.

69. *Statistisches Jahrbuch deutscher Städte* 23 (1928), p. 63; and (1931), pp. 74-75.

70. *Ernst May und das Neue Frankfurt*, pp. 111, 127, 139.

71. Andernacht and Kuhn, "Frankfurter Fordismus," pp. 43-45.

72. StVV Düsseldorf, 1925, pp. 88, 165; and StA Düsseldorf III 18223, 5 May 1925, 28 May 1925, 29 May 1925, 3 June 1925.

73. StA Düsseldorf XXIV 1113, Wohnungsbauprogramm 1928.

74. Ursula Büttner, *Politische Gerechtigkeit und sozialer Geist: Hamburg zur Zeit der Weimarer Republik* (Hamburg, 1985), p. 192.

75. Rebentisch, *Ludwig Landmann*, p. 133.

76. Anthony McElligott, "Workers' Culture and Workers' Politics on Weimar's New Housing Estates: A Response to Adelheid von Saldern," *Social History* 17 (1992): 104-5.

77. Richard Pommer and Christian F. Otto, *Weissenhof 1927 and the Modern Movement in Architecture* (Chicago, 1991), pp. 17-19.

78. Ernst May, "Das soziale Moment in der neuen Baukunst," *Das Neue Frankfurt* 2 (1928): 78.

79. May, "Wohnungspolitik der Stadt Frankfurt am Main," *Das Neue Frankfurt* 1 (1927): 93.

80. StVV Frankfurt, 1925, p.54; and 1927, p. 909; Nicholas Bullock, "Housing in Frankfurt 1925 to 1931 and the New Wohnkultur," *Architectural Review* 163 (1978): 338-49; and Lane, *Architecture and Politics*, p. 99.

81. Adenauer, "Das Großstadt-Problem," *Kommunalpolitische Blätter*, 18 (1927): 394; and *Düsseldorfer Nachrichten*, 29 August 1926.

82. Christoph Timm, *Gustav Oelsner und das Neue Altona: Kommunale Architektur und Stadtplanung in der Weimarer Republik* (Hamburg, 1984), p. 119; and StA Düsseldorf XXIV 1014, Generalbebauungsplan der Stadt Düsseldorf, pp. 2-3, 21, 24, 30.

83. Paul Wolf, "Die Siedlung als Form," *Bauamt und Gemeindebau* (1927): 240-41.

84. Heinz Wiegand, *Entwicklung des Stadtgrüns in Deutschland zwischen 1890 und 1925 am Beispiel der Arbeiten Fritz Enckes* (Berlin, 1982), pp. 16, 46, 81, 87; and Ladd, *Urban Planning*, pp. 67-70.

85. Adenauer, "Die Grünflächenpolitik der Stadt Köln," *Kommunalpolitische Blätter* 27(1930): 8-11; Gut, ed., *Der Wohnungsbau in Deutschland*, pp. 72-4; and Stehkämper, ed., *Konrad Adenauer*, pp. 157-59.

86. Jost Hermand and Frank Trommler, *Die Kultur der Weimarer Republik* (Munich, 1978), p. 75.

87. J. Brix, ed., *Handwörterbuch der Kommunalwissenschaften*, Ergänzungsband H-Z (Jena, 1927), p. 1323.

88. BVK Hannover, 1920-1921, pp. 1402-3.

89. StA Hannover XX B51, *Hannoverscher Kurier*, 2 March 1919.

90. StA Gelsenkirchen XI/5, "Festschrift zur Einweihung des Friedrich Ludwig Jahn Platz in Gelsenkirchen," p. 14; and StA Hannover XX B51, Festschrift zur Einweihung des Stadion der Stadt Hannover, pp. 7-8.

91. For an account of leisure during the Weimar Republic which points to the importance of social control see Jürgen von Reuss, "Freiflächenpolitik als Sozialpolitik," in *Martin Wagner, 1885-1957: Wohnungsbau und Weltstadtplanung: Die Rationalisierung des Glücks*, ed. Akademie der Künste (Berlin, 1985), p. 51.

92. StA Frankfurt U748 II, *Frankfurter Nachrichten*, 14 September 1925.

93. StA Hannover XX B51, "Festschrift zur Einweihung des Stadions," p. 5.

94. Rive, *Lebenserinnerungen*, pp. 171-72; and Fritz Wildung, "Der Sport im Haushalt von Staat und Gemeinde, *Die Gemeinde* 2 (1925): 595.

95. Schloßmann, ed., *GE-SO-LEI*, vol. 2, p. 939.

96. Hans Simons, Fritz Jahn, Helga Kluge et al., *Die Körperkultur in Deutschland von 1917 bis 1945*, vol. 3 of *Geschichte der Körperkultur in Deutschland*, ed. Wolfgang Eichel (Berlin, 1964), p. 90.

97. BVK Hannover, 1920-1921, p. 1402.

98. *Statistisches Jahrbuch deutscher Städte* 24 (1929), pp. 309, 699-702.

99. Ibid., 24 (1929), p. 700; and Hanschel, *Oberbürgermeister Hermann Luppe*, pp. 302-3.

100. Carl Diem, *Die Anlage von Spiel- und Sportplätzen* (Berlin, 1926), p. 7.
101. StVV Frankfurt, 1926, pp. 392, 637-43; and 1927, p. 1169.
102. StVV Frankfurt, 1925, p. 502.
103. Oberbürgermeister Luppe, "Kunstförderung durch die Städte," *Der Städtetag* 23 (1929): 325-26.
104. Rive, *Lebenserinnerungen*, p. 182.
105. Helmut Croon, "Aufgaben deutscher Städte in Ersten Drittel des 20. Jahrhunderts," in Wilhelm Rausch, ed., *Die Städte Mitteleuropas im 20. Jahrhunderts* (Linz, 1984), pp. 49-52.
106. John Willett, *The Theater of the Weimar Republic* (New York and London, 1988), p. 78.
107. Engeli, *Gustav Böß*, p. 146; and Rebentisch, *Ludwig Landmann*, p. 92.
108. StA Frankfurt S1723 IV, 1 September 1926.
109. StVV Frankfurt, 1926, p. 932.
110. Lees, *Cities Perceived*, p. 271.
111. Timm, *Gustav Oelsner*, p. 108.
112. Oskar Mulert, "Die Entwicklung der Selbstverwaltung" in *Zehn Jahre Deutsche Geschichte 1918-1928* (Berlin, 1928), pp. 387, 390.
113. Elsas and Stein, eds., *Die deutschen Städte*, p. 48.
114. Walter, *Schicksal einer deutschen Stadt*, vol. 2, pp. 28-9.
115. Elsas and Stein, *Die deutschen Städte*, p. 8.
116. StVV Frankfurt, 1926, p. 1179.
117. Schloßmann, ed., *GE-SO-LEI*, p. 16.
118. StVV Frankfurt, 1930, p. 189.

Chapter 2

STATE EXPANSION AND DEMOCRATIZATION

Surveying Weimar municipal policy raises the task of explaining the causes of the rapid growth of municipal activity in Germany after the end of hyperinflation. Widespread desire for recovery after war and inflation and concern over damage to public health provided clear motives for adopting new state tasks, yet such anxiety did not ensure state expansion. The complaints of housing reformers before the First World War did not, after all, lead to large-scale promotion of new housing construction in the absence of a political consensus in favor of government support for new housing settlements. What, then, were the political causes of the further growth of state activity on the local level during the Weimar Republic?

Since much of the growth of Weimar State activity occurred in social provision, histories of social policy might provide a useful approach for explaining the causes of Weimar State expansion; however, the vast field of inquiry into the history of social policy has yielded no single conclusive explanation of the origins and development of social states.[1] In the absence of agreement on any one model for the emergence of social states, analysis has instead sought to categorize major different types of social states.[2] Such variation in the causes for the growth of social welfare can also be noted in the history of social policy in an individual country. The German social state, for example, began its growth under very different political conditions from those found in the Weimar Republic or after the Second World War.[3]

In the case of the Weimar Republic, the influence of rapid democratization merits attention in analysis of the politics of social policy. The conjunction between democratization and the growth of state activity was particularly striking at the municipal level, but what precise role did democratization play in state expansion in Weimar Germany? The gains achieved by Social Democrats and other parties previously hampered by electoral restrictions might indicate that state expansion stemmed from political victories by advocates of an interventionist state, but much of the growth in municipal activity occurred after Social Democratic electoral losses in the immediate aftermath of hyperinflation and monetary stabilization. Taking into account such limits on Social Democratic power, political support for the expansion of municipal activity of the Weimar Republic can alternately be attributed to the emergence of consensus across party boundaries on the role of the state in an era of democratic politics.

To a certain degree, a case can be made that municipal recovery proceeded in response to mandates created by national political institutions. The national government delegated a number of tasks to local authorities. National laws established many municipal responsibilities for providing welfare, and the third emergency tax decree created the framework for financing the promotion of housing construction. Municipal leaders, for their part, commonly pointed to the burden of mandatory tasks when explaining that national political institutions helped to force the growth of municipal spending. Mayor Böß of Berlin, for instance, noted that the Reich had transferred numerous "burdens" to the cities.[4]

While German cities received more delegated tasks during the Weimar Republic, taking note of mandates for municipal action provides only a partial explanation of the political causes for the expansion of municipal policy. As analysis of municipal policy demonstrates, city governments commonly embarked on projects that no other political institution had mandated. No outside political institutions forced municipal administrations to carry out ambitious programs of economic promotion. There was no national legislative mandate to establish trade fairs and exhibitions. Nor, for that matter, did the Reichstag compel municipalities to build sports stadiums or rescue local theaters. In most cases, city governments acted alone to expand promotion of leisure, and municipal authorities also held enormous latitude in determining how to finance and organize the promotion of housing construction.

Local initiative to expand numerous areas of municipal activity beyond the parameters required by national legislation suggests the existence of some sort of political consensus in favor of state expansion, but any hint of such a trend raises a new set of historical problems. Stressing the prevalence of conflict and instability, political historians of the Weimar Republic, after all, note the fragility of governing coalitions in the Reichstag even between 1924 and 1928. These political cleavages evident in national politics marked the deep, long-term, political division of German society into groups alternately described by historians as political camps, political subcultures *(politischen Teilkulturen)* or "sociocultural milieus." These terms reflect the varied weight given to political enmity, political culture, and the appeal of institutional networks in creating Germany's political structure; yet however defined, the distinct, competing political groupings of the prewar era survived into the Weimar Republic.[5]

Despite the persistence of deep-seated political conflicts, the democratization of municipal politics created a structural basis for political convergence during the Weimar period of stabilization. Political fragmentation and the democratization of communal elections made it difficult for any single political party or narrow grouping of parties to exert unchallenged control over municipal affairs. There were few city governments where members of a single party dominated civic affairs throughout the entire Weimar Republic. The introduction of general, equal suffrage for communal elections in 1919 allowed the SPD and the Center Party to acquire a louder voice in civic affairs, and the emergence of splinter parties created greater diversity on the bourgeois political spectrum. Approving municipal initiatives in the new political climate often required cooperation between political parties.

The political consequences of the municipal democratic transition caused much unease among Germany's mayors. Many, if not most, mayors liked to think of themselves as experts standing above the fray of party politics. Düsseldorf's Mayor Lehr, for instance, described himself as an "unpolitical mayor" and remained unaffiliated with any political party until he joined the DNVP in either late 1928 or in 1929, but even mayors who belonged to political parties commonly stressed their independence from party motives. Berlin's Mayor Gustav Böß, a member of the DDP, saw himself as an expert who avoided party politics, and his expert qualifications appealed to Berlin's Social Democrats in the early 1920s.[6] Social Democratic mayors, for their part, also insisted on their expert qualifications. Hermann Heimrich, the Social Democrat who became mayor of Mannheim in 1928, shared the ideal of above-party administration.[7]

For all the appeal of the image of the mayor as an independent expert who steered clear of the potential entanglements of party politics, the office of mayor took on an increasingly political quality during the Weimar Republic. A number of mayors took part in national and regional politics. Mayor Jarres of Duisburg ran for president as candidate for the DVP and the DNVP in the first round of presidential elections in 1925. Konrad Adenauer of Cologne was an important figure in the Center Party, and Nuremberg's Mayor Hermann Luppe worked diligently, albeit fruitlessly, to reverse the declining fortunes of the DDP.[8]

Whether deeply involved in election campaigns or boasting of disdain for politics, few mayors could in practice ignore political parties in municipal governments. Even mayors who believed that municipal affairs should be the province of impartial experts realized that this was not the case. Robert Lehr, a mayor who derided party politics, disputed the accuracy of contemporary references to "autocratic mayors." "Is it actually a good time now for autocracy?" he asked. "We live in the age of parliamentarianism."[9] Mayors were still extremely powerful, but there was much truth to Lehr's complaint. From stadiums to housing construction programs, municipal initiatives required the backing of city parliaments. As Frankfurt's city planner Ernst May told his biographer, Frankfurt's administration could not have carried out its ambitious housing construction program without the support of Frankfurt's city parliament.[10]

The persistence of old political and confessional divisions made working with city councilors from different parties a difficult task for mayors and municipal officials. Mistrust between the SPD and bourgeois parties and between the SPD and the Center often obstructed cooperation on the local level. Nuremberg's Mayor Hermann Luppe recalled in his memoirs that working with the SPD, DDP, and Center required meetings devoted to avoiding mistakes and to the slow maturation of successes.[11] Luppe and mayors in other cities could not assume that city councilors would work smoothly together on the local level, overlooking divisive issues of national politics, for municipal politicians also engaged in bitter debates over highly-charged symbolic issues. Such topics as honoring monarchist heroes of aviation, naming a sports stadium, buying a bust of Hindenburg, and building a monument to Heine excited and enraged municipal politicians in Düsseldorf, Frankfurt, and Hanover, and city councilors elsewhere engaged in similar controversies.[12]

Recovery and Political Consensus

Given the volatile issues of Weimar politics, what political groupings could overcome mutual mistrust to cooperate in shaping programs of recovery? The strong identification between Social Democracy and the Weimar social state might suggest that "progressive" coalitions anchored by the SPD provided the political basis for the expansion of municipal activity. Anthony McElligott points to the role of "socialists and progressive liberal coalitions" in guiding municipal policy, and William McNeil notes the government of German cities by "progressive" coalitions.[13]

Though it is certainly logical to consider the political influence of Socialism as a cause of the expansion of state activity, recent research on European social policy has questioned the close identification of Social Democracy with the rise of social states.[14] In the specific case of municipalities of the Weimar Republic, arguably progressive groupings of political parties were active in some cities, but the municipal democratic transition of the Weimar Republic produced tremendous variation above all else. Fully democratic suffrage created political complexity rather than any clear trend towards a single type of coalition or loose alliance. On the political Left, the SPD was most often the strongest single party, but the SPD suffered severe losses to the KPD in many of the cities of the industrial region of the Ruhr and north Rhine. The large cities of western Germany were also strongholds of the Center Party, the political party founded as a representative for German Catholics in the nineteenth century, but the Center Party possessed negligible influence in cities in some parts of the country.

Variation in the fortunes of political parties was greatest among the bourgeois parties. Branches of the DDP, DVP, and DNVP were often active in municipal politics, but local parties also wielded influence in many city governments.[15] Groupings of house and property owners, which had dominated many civic assemblies until shortly before the First World War, regrouped in municipalities of Weimar Germany, often affiliating themselves with the emerging national Economic Party (Wirtschaftspartei). Regional parties made strong showings in some cities, particularly in Bavaria and in Hanover. Adding to the variety of bourgeois politics in municipalities of the Weimar Republic, bourgeois parties sometimes created political alliances that only existed locally.

In an extremely complex political environment, patterns of cooperation between political parties in city parliaments of the Weimar Republic varied from the highly sporadic to the fairly systematic. Though political parties seldom went so far as to create formal coalitions, cooperation in the interests of recovery began to erode prewar political divisions in cities with large Social Democratic and significant

Democratic contingents in municipal assemblies.[16] In Magdeburg, the only large city with a Social Democratic mayor throughout the entire period of stabilization, the SPD worked closely with the city's DDP after 1924. Praising the effectiveness of this arrangement, Magdeburg's Mayor Hermann Beims noted that "tasks in education, theater, art, economy, and transport [and] the organization of the budget could be fulfilled by both parties."[17] In cities outside of regions of heavy Catholic concentration, patterns of cooperation between the DDP and SPD could extend to include the Center Party. Thus, the SPD, DDP, and Center elected Hermann Heimrich Mayor of Mannheim in 1928. Other parties were less likely than either the DDP or Center to work with the SPD, but the DVP entered on occasion into loose arrangements with the DDP and the SPD. The SPD, DDP, and DVP cooperated in Hamburg's city parliament after the municipal election of 1924.[18]

While Social Democrats held considerable influence in municipal politics in several cities, it must be stressed that the Weimar Republic had no equivalent to "Red Vienna," the Austrian capital.[19] In none of Germany's largest cities did the SPD possess the same domination of civic affairs achieved by Austria's Socialists during the 1920s. The SPD won the office of mayor in only a few cities during the Weimar Republic including Magdeburg and Altona.

TABLE 2.1   Frankfurt's municipal election of 1924

Party	Percentage of Votes	Seats in City Parliament
KPD	11.3	8
USPD	2.3	1
SPD	24.7	19
DDP	10.2	7
Center	11.2	8
Arbeitnehmer (Employee Group)	6.0	4
DVP	8.1	6
DNVP	14.0	10
Economic Party	5.7	4
Völkisch (national/racist)	5.2	4

Source: Statistisches Jahrbuch deutscher Städte 23 (1928), 276, 282-83.

Democratization in Frankfurt am Main brought both a greater voice for the SPD and a broad political consensus in favor of expanding municipal activity. Frankfurt am Main fell into the category of cities where approval of policies of recovery required the support of both Social Democratic and bourgeois city councilors. Despite losing a sizeable block of support to the KPD among other parties in the aftermath of hyperinflation, Frankfurt's SPD retained its place as the largest single part in the city parliament during the period of stabilization. With 19 or 20 of the 71 seats in the city parliament between 1925 and 1928 (one seat was held by an Independent Social Democrat), Frankfurt's SPD, though not in a position to pass motions by itself, helped to approve virtually all major programs of recovery.[20] Along with the SPD, Frankfurt's DDP and Center joined in a loose consensus of recovery that also came to extend to the city's DVP for most of the period of stabilization.

This political consensus of recovery provided support for both social provision and economic promotion during the initial years of stabilization in Frankfurt. From 1924 to 1927, Mayor Ludwig Landmann won approval for most of his programs of economic promotion including transportation projects, the Summer of Music, and the trade fair. Speaking in 1925 for the city parliament's chief and economic committees, councilor Rebholz of the SPD expressed support for Frankfurt's trade fair in the "name of all parties."[21] Airport expansion was also popular among city councilors. Reporting to the city parliament in 1927, the economic committee of city councilors from the SPD, DDP, Center Party, DVP, and DNVP recommended that Frankfurt make improvements to its airport in order to keep pace with other cities.[22]

The political consensus of recovery in Frankfurt covered social provision as well as economic promotion. Of the major types of social provision, promotion of housing construction won the most enthusiastic support in the city parliament. Frankfurt's SPD regarded the city's new housing settlements as evidence of the success of its communal policy, but the thousands of new apartments of the "new Frankfurt" could not be identified as a purely Social Democratic achievement. Frankfurt's DDP, Center Party, and DVP also supported the promotion of housing construction through 1928.[23] Even members of the DNVP, the established bourgeois party farthest to the Right, approved of municipal promotion of housing construction, despite voicing misgivings about the building style and construction techniques championed by Frankfurt's city planner Ernst May. Councilor Dobler, of the DNVP, told the city parliament in 1928 that "we are of the opinion that we must carry out this housing construction program, or better simply the housing construction program, which will remove the housing shortage in the most rapid manner."[24] If

May's methods were not ideal, the DNVP, nonetheless, accepted support for housing construction as a necessary municipal activity.

Welfare programs, in contrast to the promotion of housing construction, gained more grudging support in Frankfurt's city parliament. Breaking ranks with bourgeois parties, Frankfurt's SPD competed with the KPD to win recognition as the true standard-bearer of the working class by calling for higher rates of welfare support. Such demands had a ritualistic quality since Social Democrats knew that the administration opposed any move to establish set rates of support for all welfare recipients.[25] Dispute over welfare intensified in 1927 when the SPD, noting that the economic downturn of early 1926 had exhausted previously-authorized spending for welfare, provoked a budget crisis by demanding an increase in the budget for welfare support for 1927 from RM 9 million to RM 12 million. The DDP, DVP, DNVP, and Center refused to go along with any motion that did not include revenue to cover higher expenditures. After a delay of several months, the city parliament finally passed a compromise budget, which provided for an increase from RM 9 million to RM 10 million in welfare support. City councilors from the Center and the established bourgeois parties, though unwilling to meet the SPD's targets for welfare support, had come to see a substantial commitment to welfare as a normal part of the city's budget.[26]

Shifting Majorities

The fairly consistent pattern of support for projects of recovery evident in Frankfurt and other cities where large Social Democratic parties cooperated with the DDP, on occasion, verged towards a second pattern of municipal politics in which major programs were approved by shifting majorities on a case by case basis. Berlin's budget majority of the SPD, DDP, DVP, and Center was similar to the grouping of parties that backed major municipal initiatives in Frankfurt, but Detlef Lehnert describes Berlin's budget majority as "brittle," and the biographer of Berlin's Mayor Böß suggests that conflict occurred more frequently in Berlin's city parliament than in other city parliaments.[27] The shifting nature of majorities was more clear in Altona where a loose alliance of the SPD and the DDP relied, alternately, on either the KPD or the parties of the Right to gain sufficient votes to pass new measures.[28]

A pattern of shifting majorities, if sometimes present in cities with large Social Democratic parties, was most striking in cities such as Cologne with a weak Social Democratic presence. Mayor Konrad Adenauer and Cologne's powerful Center Party cooperated with the local Social Democratic Party in the early years of the Weimar Republic, but Adenauer's relations with Cologne's SPD worsened after the municipal election of 1924 when the city's Social Democrats lost seats in the city parliament. Adenauer did not rely on any firm coalition of parties during the period of stabilization, but instead won approval of major municipal endeavors from shifting majorities. In 1927, Adenauer even relied on votes from Cologne's Communist city councilors to gain passage of his preferred plan for building a new bridge across the Rhine.[29]

North along the Rhine, a pattern of shifting majorities also emerged in Düsseldorf, but only after a firm majority of the Center Party and parties of the bourgeois Right dominated municipal affairs between 1924 and 1927. The communal election of 1924 left Düsseldorf's Center Party with 21 seats and the chief parties of the bourgeois Right, the DNVP and DVP, with 12 seats and 7 seats respectively in a city parliament of 75 city councilors. On the Left, Düsseldorf's KPD and relatively weak SPD were on hostile terms, and disputes over appointments to schools and confessional education blocked any systematic cooperation between the SPD and social reformers from the Center Party. With a weak SPD, a strong Center Party, and relatively healthy established parties of the bourgeois Right, the Center and DNVP were in a position to dominate Düsseldorf's city parliament. Peter Hüttenberger, the leading historian of modern Düsseldorf, concludes that "city politics resulted ... from the interaction of the city administration and the Right party spectrum in the city parliament – to the damage of the Left."[30]

TABLE 2.2   Düsseldorf's municipal election of 1924

Party	Percentage of Votes	Seats in City Parliament
KPD	24.3	19
USPD	2.0	1
SPD	8.8	6
DDP	4.1	3
Center	27.5	21
DVP	8.9	7
DNVP	16.0	12
Wirtschaftsbund	8.0	6

Source: *Statistisches Jahrbuch deutscher Städte* 23 (1928), 276, 282-83.

Düsseldorf's administration relied on the Center Party and the parties of the bourgeois right to back major initiatives during the early years of stabilization, but the pattern of support for municipal policy became much less consistent in 1927 and later years. The growing instability of municipal politics first became evident in the fall of 1927 when Mayor Lehr turned to a majority that included the SPD and the KPD to win approval for an increase in the surcharge to the trade tax on income above RM 3,000. When the Prussian District Committee refused to approve that measure, Düsseldorf's administration continued to display flexibility, gaining support for a more balanced package of temporary tax increases from a new majority that included the Center Party, DDP, DNVP, and the SPD.[31] Lehr, like Konrad Adenauer, sought majorities wherever he could find them when support was not forthcoming from his customary political allies.

The absence of any firm political alliance bridging the gap between the SPD and bourgeois parties in Düsseldorf did not prevent the emergence of a broad consensus of recovery in which political parties ranging from the SPD to the DNVP supported most major municipal programs during the period of stabilization. Lehr's initiatives of economic promotion faced persistent opposition only from the KPD and the Wirtschaftsbund (a local variation of the Economic Party), both of which objected to the costs of various projects, especially the permanent exhibition buildings constructed for the Gesolei exhibition of 1926. Lehr also found broad support for the construction of a new bridge across the Rhine.[32] When the Wirtschaftsbund charged in 1927 that the administration had exceeded its competence by failing to obtain approval for alleged cost-overruns for the construction of the second Rhine bridge, it found itself politically isolated. The DVP and DNVP joined the rest of the city parliament in dismissing the Wirtschaftsbund's claims as groundless.[33]

Despite the absence of a progressive coalition anchored by Social Democrats, Düsseldorf's consensus of recovery extended to the expansion of social provision, most notably in the area of housing construction. Calls for accelerating promotion of housing construction cut across class, party, and confessional boundaries in Düsseldorf as virtually the entire city parliament accused the city's administration of failing to grasp the gravity of the housing problem in 1925. "Build apartments, cost what it may!" councilor Liertz, a committed land reformer from the Center Party, told the administration. Belittling the administration's attempt to placate the city parliament by adding RM 2 million from the Sparkasse (municipal savings bank) to supplement RM 4 million in funds from the rent tax earmarked for housing construction, Liertz added, "One can not work with 6 million marks." On this issue, Mayor Lehr found little comfort in the attitude of the parties of the bourgeois Right that also pressed for more attention and funding for housing construction. The DVP urged the administration to prepare a motion for an additional RM 2.5 million for housing with the caveat that added spending be covered by loans rather than higher taxes.[34]

Confronted by disgruntled city councilors from all parties, Mayor Robert Lehr reminded his critics of the financial constraints on municipal action. The administration, he protested, would gladly increase promotion of housing construction if there were any more available funds. Lehr threatened to withdraw the entire housing budget for 1925 if the city parliament passed a motion raising spending for housing, without first detailing how to obtain additional funds. The mayor's tactics proved effective as the city parliament approved the housing budget for 1925.[35]

Düsseldorf's parties of the bourgeois Right and the Center Party continued, nevertheless, to identify themselves as strong supporters of plans to boost housing construction. Accusing the administration of inattention to the housing shortage, Düsseldorf's city councilors felt themselves vulnerable to charges of having done less than they could have to see that the city's inhabitants had apartments. City councilors from the Center Party and bourgeois parties took pains to defend themselves from criticism that they neglected housing in favor of the Gesolei exhibition. Approving funds for the construction of permanent exhibition buildings, the Center Party, DNVP, DVP, Wirtschaftsbund, and DDP issued a joint statement reaffirming their commitment to increasing the supply of housing. They wished to "avoid the appearance that the most urgent present task, the construction of apartments, should fall behind the large building projects important for Düsseldorf's future."[36]

Presenting a model for recovery, the Gesolei itself redoubled the force of demands for accelerating the pace of housing construction in Düsseldorf. The *Düsseldorfer Stadt Anzeiger*, a bourgeois newspaper, held that poor housing conditions embarrassed a city that ventured to hold an exhibition publicizing social policy. The city's mass quarters for the asocial were "unworthy of the city of the Gesolei."[37]

While the ideals of the Gesolei provided grounds for reproach of Düsseldorf's housing policy to date, the exhibition's success offered reason to believe that a solution to the city's housing shortage was possible if the administration approached the housing problem with the same energy it had brought to the organization of the exhibition of 1926. "We wish and it is our will …," declared councilor Drösser of the Center Party, "that Düsseldorf now also carry out its housing construction program with the same daring and the same enterprise with which we completed the great exhibition to the amazement of all." He hoped that the city of the Gesolei could become the "first German city without a housing shortage" and recommended, as a first step, expanding the housing construction program from the 1,400 apartments planned in 1926 to at least 2,500 to 3,000 apartments in 1927 by covering the costs of higher spending with loans.[38]

The widespread enthusiasm for promoting housing construction ultimately grasped Mayor Lehr, the onetime target of complaints that Düsseldorf was not doing enough to aid housing construction. After the Gesolei, Lehr chose to identify the municipal administration closely with efforts to end the housing problem. Introducing Düsseldorf's plan to help finance the construction of 4,000 apartments in 1927, he proudly announced that the city government planned to "decisively fight the housing shortage in Düsseldorf with all emphasis."[39]

The promotion of sports, if not nearly so high a priority for Düsseldorf's municipal leaders as the solution to the housing crisis, also won broad political support from the parties of the Left, the Center Party, and the established parties of the bourgeois Right. The DNVP's councilor Ellenbeck drew on the rhetoric of the Protestant Inner Mission movement to call for "inner colonization," to create "centers for relaxation," and Düsseldorf's KPD, DVP, and Center all urged the construction of additional swimming pools. The Center Party was not convinced that Düsseldorf had devoted sufficient resources to sports. True, the city had a resplendent new stadium, but statistics of sports facilities turned up the troubling fact that Düsseldorf stood below Cologne in a ranking of space for physical exercise per inhabitant. Further adding insult, Düsseldorf even lagged behind "a city like Gelsenkirchen," a relatively poor mining city in the center of the Ruhr coal belt.[40]

Manifested most dramatically in demands from nearly all quarters for the promotion of housing construction and leisure, the consensus of recovery in Düsseldorf yielded more halting approval of heightened municipal responsibility for welfare. As elsewhere, the SPD and KPD engaged in ritualistic calls for higher welfare rates – a member of the SPD even admitted on one occasion that his party was voting for a set of motions including a measure for higher welfare rates only because such positions could be taken as proof of "friendliness to workers."[41]

While the Center and DNVP refused to go along with what they regarded as agitatory motions by the SPD and KPD to raise welfare rates, they also declined to join the Wirtschaftsbund in moves to cut the city's welfare budget.[42] Attitudes towards welfare were ambiguous within the DNVP. Reflecting the lingering influence of mistrust of the moral effects of welfare, councilor Schwietzke, a leader of the conservative wing of the DNVP, lamented the damage that he believed welfare inflicted on the willpower of the unemployed. Such concerns, which could imply that the unemployed were partly to blame for their predicament, infuriated city councilors from parties of the Left, yet Schwietzke also admitted that higher social spending had become necessary since the First World War. He conceded that "the wounds of the lost war with its consequences, revolution and inflation have produced much innocent need."[43]

Political Competition and Convergence in Policy

A broad consensus of recovery in favor of new municipal programs emerged in cities such as Düsseldorf and Cologne where mayors resorted, when necessary, to shifting majorities, but what of cities where solid bourgeois blocks retained firm contours through ongoing competition with a Social Democratic opposition? Such a pattern of confrontation occurred in cities where brief episodes of Social Democratic influence in the early years of the Weimar Republic lent credence to bourgeois fears of the SPD's potential power and intensified preexisting animosity between bourgeois and Socialist political groupings. In Munich, for example, the tenure of the Social Democrat Eduard Schmid as mayor between 1919 and 1924 provided a backdrop for political reaction during the period of stabilization. The BVP, a Bavarian variant of the Center Party, cooperated in a de facto manner with the SPD in the early 1920s, but broke sharply with the SPD in the municipal election of 1924, warning in campaign rallies of the danger that Munich might become another "Red Vienna." Schmid resigned after the SPD suffered losses and was replaced as mayor by the BVP's Scharnagl.[44] Angered by the BVP's campaign tactics, the SPD refused to vote for the budget in ensuing years, but this rupture in municipal affairs did not preclude the possibility of any convergence between the BVP and SPD, which subsequently reached arrangements on a case by case basis to approve financing for individual municipal projects.[45]

TABLE 2.3   Hanover's municipal election of 1924

Party or Electoral List	Percentage of Votes	Seats in City Parliament
KPD	11.9	9
SPD	29.6	22
DDP	3.9	3
Bodenreformer Land Reform	2.6	1
Center	4.1	3
Deutsch Hannoveraner	15.4	11
Ordnungsblock	28.6	22
NSDAP	3.9	3

Sources: Statistisches Jahrbuch deutscher Städte 23 (1928), 276, 282; and Waldemar R. Röhrbein and Franz R. Zankl, eds., *Hannover im 20. Jahrhundert: Aspekte der neueren Stadtgeschichte* (Hannover, 1978).

Municipal politics in Hanover were almost as polarized as in Munich. Hanover, like Munich, had a Social Democratic mayor during the immediate postwar years. Though clearly on the Right of the SPD, Hanover's Mayor Robert Leinert still met with persistent hostility from bourgeois municipal politicians and Communists in Hanover. United by opposition to Leinert, a bourgeois block known as the Ordnungsblock won a plurality of 22 seats in Hanover's municipal election of 1924. The Deutsch Hannoveraner won 11 seats and the Center Party, loosely allied with the Deutsch Hannoveraner in Hanover, won 3 seats in the city parliament. The Ordnungsblock and the Deutsch Hannoveraner anchored a slim but solid majority in the city parliament that ensured approval of the administration's motions between 1924 and 1929. Hanover's Social Democrats and Communists with 22 and 9 seats respectively remained almost powerless in the municipal arena until 1929.[46] Reducing the SPD's ability even to comment on municipal policy in a formal setting, Menge cut meetings of the city parliament to the bare minimum. Committees of the city parliament assumed many of the functions once exercised by the entire institution.[47]

Nothing resembling a progressive coalition anchored by the SPD or the Center Party existed in Hanover, yet the Weimar trend towards convergence in municipal policy was evident even in a city like Hanover where hostility between bourgeois and Social Democratic civic leaders continued unabated throughout the period of stabilization. Persistent animosity between Mayor Menge and Hanover's

Social Democrats gave a static quality to Hanover's municipal politics that obscured the administration's changing relationships with both its allies and enemies.

Tensions within the bourgeois Right first emerged after the 1924 election in a feud between the administration and a vocal member of the city's House and Property Owners' Association. House owners had made up a majority of those entitled to vote in prewar municipal elections – 6,502 of the 11,348 men with full rights as citizens of Hanover in 1912 were house owners – but lost substantial power with the introduction of universal equal suffrage in communal elections. A house owners' list won 9,106 votes in the first postwar municipal election, a large showing by prewar standards, but only a small fraction of the approximately 144,000 votes cast in 1919.[48] Despite their diminished influence, house owners took a leading role in the bourgeois campaign against Mayor Robert Leinert during the early years of the Weimar Republic. Ernst Demmig, a Hanover architect and member of the House and Property Owners' Association, vilified Leinert and Hanover's administration. Criticizing the growth of administration, supposed extravagance in city offices, and state intervention in the housing market, Demmig represented a house owner ideology of opposition to public spending and the growth of state activity.[49]

An ensuing conflict between Demmig, despite his service as a publicist in the bourgeois campaign against Leinert, and the Ordnungsblock soon revealed the sharp limits of the influence of organized house owners in the era of democratic municipal politics. Demmig fell out with the Ordnungsblock almost immediately after the municipal election of 1924. Claiming that all traces of Socialism had yet to be rooted out of the administration, Demmig attacked the lingering influence of the "Leinert spirit" in Hanover's municipal government. He soon discovered that his one-time allies on the bourgeois Right no longer had much use for his brand of polemics against spending, extravagance, and municipal activity after Leinert's resignation.[50] Carrying out a political about-face that struck Hanover's small Communist party as noteworthy after Demmig's previous performance as the "lackey of the Ordnungsblock," both the Ordnungsblock and the Deutsch Hannoveraner condemned Demmig's renewed claims of municipal extravagance. A series of speakers for the administration, chief bourgeois parties and the SPD rejected Demmig's charges of municipal corruption and extravagant expenditures on items such as telephones and travel expense, and the city parliament concluded by passing a resolution refuting Demmig's indictment of the city government.[51]

Primarily a reaction against a political gadfly deemed to have outlasted his usefulness, the administration's break with Demmig also marked the very tentative beginnings of Mayor Arthur Menge's own move away from the principles of municipal policy that he had advanced during the Ordnungsblock's struggle with Leinert. Rather than emphasizing the need to undertake new programs of recovery, Menge and his chief ally, Heinrich Tramm, the city's chief municipal official up until the end of the First World War, attributed Hanover's postwar problems to what they regarded as Socialist deviation from sound principles of administration of Tramm's almost three decades in office as Hanover's Stadtdirektor from 1891 and 1918. The Ordnungsblock called for a return to order under thrifty, expert administrators. Campaign advertisements urged potential voters to "create order here for the coming years," and Tramm, taking campaign pronouncements as a guide for future action, told a Social Democrat in April 1925 that the Ordnungsblock had been elected "to create order" and "to make our finances healthy again."[52]

Creating order, the goal of the Ordnungsblock, did not, as it turned out, provide a clear guide for municipal action under Mayor Arthur Menge. Condemning what they took as the effects of excessive Social Democratic influence, bourgeois civic leaders yearned for some approximation of prewar stability. Idealization of municipal government under Tramm implied that prewar municipal policy offered a suitable model for regaining the benefits associated with the past. If so, Hanover would forge its own path to recovery, refraining from the expansion of state activity that occurred in other cities. However, neither nostalgia for prewar order nor the unchallenged grasp of the bourgeois Right over municipal affairs in Hanover prevented the growth of pressure for more aggressive policies of recovery, including the expansion of social provision. As elsewhere, municipal leaders became convinced that a solution to the housing problem required new forms of state intervention. Ernst Demmig of Hanover's House and Property Owners' Association failed to persuade even bourgeois city councilors that abolishing rent control and the rent tax could end the housing shortage. Noting the lack of capital available to private industry to construct apartments, councilor Eggers of the Deutsch Hannoveraner argued that "it is necessary that the ... alleviation of the housing shortage be born on broad shoulders, namely by the state and by the communities."[53]

With the appointment of Elkart, previously a housing official in Berlin, as Hanover's Stadtbaurat in 1925, Hanover's administration gained an advocate for increased promotion of housing construction. Informing Menge that only massive public support for housing construction over a period of several years could solve the housing problem, Elkart projected in 1925 that it would take the construction of 2,200 apartments per year for five years or 1,700 per year over ten years to satisfy demand for housing. Menge, who still associated recovery with a return to prewar social conditions, countered that Elkart's use of the average household size of 3.55 rather than the prewar average of 4.0 yielded an exaggerated estimate of the housing shortage.[54] Ultimately shedding his skepticism about the dimensions of the housing shortage, Menge himself came to concede the need for new forms of state intervention in the housing market. In March 1926, he told Hanover's city parliament that housing construction at the present time required public funding from the rent tax. It was, he conceded, unfortunate "that the public hand accumulates immense amounts of capital from a tax, the rent tax, on the impoverished people," but Menge saw no alternative. "A revival of housing construction activity … can not otherwise be achieved under the current conditions."[55]

Reaction to a small typhus epidemic that struck Hanover in the fall of 1926 reinforced the trend towards more concerted municipal action for improving housing conditions in Hanover. Hanover's Social Democratic newspaper, *Der Volkswille*, charged, shortly after the onset of typhus in September 1926, that housing conditions in many parts of the city did "not meet modern requirements."[56] More embarrassing still, the official investigation by a committee of experts into the causes of the epidemic found that poor housing conditions had helped to spread infection. The typhus outbreak most probably stemmed from substandard conditions at Hanover's oldest water filtration station, but victims of typhus were also more likely to infect others when they lived in crowded dwellings. The committee warned that, "disorder and dirtiness are unfortunately frequently unavoidable where people live close together in crowded inferior rooms."[57]

Never a major concern for Hanover's city government during Heinrich Tramm's long career as Stadtdirektor before the war, the promotion of housing construction became a central component of municipal policy in Hanover during a period of renewed control by the bourgeois Right over municipal affairs during the Weimar period of stabilization. In the aftermath of Hanover's typhus epidemic, Menge spoke of the importance of aiding housing construction with enthusiasm equal to that displayed by the mayors of Germany's other large cities. Describing the management of the housing shortage as "our most urgent and foremost task," he said in 1928 that "without its elimination, all other measures that aim at the recovery of the health and strengthening of our people must remain ineffective."[58]

Pressure for the expansion of social provision in Hanover carried over from housing to sports. Enthusiasm for increased municipal assistance for sports first surfaced in the city parliament before reaching Menge's administration. Proposals by the SPD in 1926 to raise subsidies for sports clubs and by the Deutsch Hannoveraner to enlarge a swimming pool met with a cold reception from the Magistrat, and Menge even claimed that "demands in the area of sport are... in part extraordinarily exaggerated." However by 1927, both Menge and the Ordnungsblock spoke with favor of new sports projects.[59] The Ordnungsblock vied with the SPD to take credit for introducing a motion to enlarge Hanover's stadium, and Menge, for his part, agreed that the stadium, which lacked covered stands for spectators, sufficient changing rooms, and even toilets connected to sewers, "did not satisfy modern standards." He also recommended increased funding for the swimming pool in order to make it suitable for "holding large sporting swim meets." Hanover's budget for 1927 included RM 250,000 for improvements to the stadium, a sum later increased by another RM 100,000.[60]

While Menge remained noticeably more cautious in taking up large-scale projects than his counterparts in Berlin, Cologne, Düsseldorf, and Frankfurt, his support for projects like the expansion of Hanover's stadium and his commitment to promoting housing construction on a large scale marked a shift towards a conception of civic duties that went beyond the parameters established by Heinrich Tramm. In 1927 and 1928 Menge adopted a new tone, speaking less of obstacles and more of new plans. Boasting of his administration's devotion to "reconstruction," he noted sums spent for housing construction, sports facilities, aviation, health care, and sanitation.[61] Eager to restore the order that the Ordnungsblock had associated with prewar administration, Menge did not confine himself to prewar instruments of municipal policy. By the late years of the period of stabilization, Menge identified a set of municipal duties that coincided, to a surprising degree, with lists of civic obligations drawn up by Hanover's Social Democrats in criticism of Hanover's administration.

The contribution of democratization to state expansion in Hanover became most evident as the municipal election of 1929 approached. Broad agreement on the proper goals of municipal policy in Hanover generated continued competition between the SPD and the city's administration and bourgeois allies over which political grouping was best suited to improving living standards for the urban population. While the SPD rebuked Menge's administration for insufficient attention to housing construction, sports, and social programs for children, the Vereinigte Bürgerschaft (United Citizens), the bourgeois electoral list that succeeded the Ordnungsblock, boasted that the Hanover had made great strides in satisfying precisely those public needs identified as critical areas for municipal activity by Social Democrats. The same programs dismissed as inadequate by the SPD served in advertisements for the Vereinigte Bürgerschaft as evidence of the wisdom of entrusting municipal government to a bourgeois majority. The Vereinigte Bürgerschaft celebrated the achievements in the areas of housing, physical exercise, and public health made during Menge's administration.

The Vereinigte Bürgerschaft argued that the Ordnungsblock and Menge had provided the public goods demanded by the SPD without the harmful effects associated with Social Democratic power. The Ordnungsblock worked to remove housing misery by constructing 12,000 apartments, but avoided injury to the construction trade by refraining from direct sponsorship of housing construction. The Ordnungsblock promoted sports by completing the stadium and creating sports fields, playgrounds, and a public bath all the while maintaining "unpolitical physical training of youth."[62] In short, voters did not need Socialists to gain new housing, sports facilities, and better sanitation. Bourgeois political leaders provided the same benefits without excessively high taxation, irreligion, political influence over sport, discrimination against private construction firms, or threats to property.

Drawing public attention to accomplishments of Hanover's city government since 1924, the Vereinigte Bürgerschaft tried to fend off the very real threat of Social Democratic revival in a region with a long history of success by the SPD in elections for the Reichstag, but the Vereinigte' Bürgerschaft's commitment to social policy amounted to more than an election strategy. Menge had occasion to restate his support for social policy shortly after the election when his proposal that Hanover purchase part of the treasure of the Welfs, the medieval dynasty with roots in Lower Saxony, met with fierce opposition. Angered by Social Democratic accusations that he neglected more pressing social tasks to propose a "luxury expenditure," Menge insisted that his record in social policy was beyond reproach, referring to the RM 40-50 million spent for housing construction and to the large sums spent for building sewers.[63]

Democratization, State Expansion, and Bourgeois Politics

Across a varied group of cities, analysis of municipal politics of the Weimar Republic confirms the limitations of explaining the politics of state expansion in terms of a struggle between progressive alliances anchored by Social Democrats and conservative opponents. The influence of Social Democrats helps to account for some of the variation in municipal policy.[64] Cities like Frankfurt, for example, where Social Democrats retained a strong voice in civic affairs, often undertook particularly ambitious recovery programs. However, expansion of municipal activity also occurred even where Social Democrats lacked local power.

A broad array of civic leaders helped to carry out the expansion of municipal activity in Düsseldorf, Frankfurt, Hanover, and other German cities during the Weimar period of stabilization. Both mayors and city councilors gathered support for initiatives of recovery. Mayors such as Robert Lehr and Ludwig Landmann generally took the lead in calling for economic promotion, assuring city councilors that the long-term benefits of economic development outweighed the short-term costs of trade fairs, exhibitions, and transportation projects, but mayors did not invariably push city councilors into expanding social provision. Indeed, in Hanover and particularly in Düsseldorf, city councilors urged mayors to increase the pace of promotion of housing construction. The enthusiasm of many mayors and city councilors for extensive programs of recovery confirmed that civic leaders, despite all their complaints about the burdens of tasks delegated by national authorities, helped to create pressure for the growth of state activity during the Weimar period of stabilization.

The mayors and city councilors who championed ambitious programs of recovery and new municipal tasks came from a wide variety of political groupings. The comparison between "Red Vienna" and large German cities of the 1920s is instructive in revealing how support for the expansion of municipal activity extended far into the bourgeois sections of the political spectrum in Germany. The record of municipal policy was not identical in Germany and Austria. Vienna, unlike German cities, instituted a special housing tax to fund housing construction and directly sponsored the construction of new housing blocks that became closely identified with the power of the working class in Austria's capital. Yet for all the fear of Vienna voiced in many bourgeois circles in Germany, German cities and Vienna engaged in many of the same tasks: welfare, and promotion of housing construction and leisure. In many respects, German city governments without Social Democratic majorities proved to be as ambitious and as effective as "Red Vienna" in undertaking new municipal initiatives.[65]

Though bourgeois and Social Democratic municipal leaders in German cities might have preferred to govern by themselves, they were usually able to reach compromises, if only on a case by case basis, when no political alternative existed. Mayors such as Düsseldorf's Lehr and Cologne's Adenauer were willing to take votes where they could find them, and Social Democrats followed a pragmatic course in cities like Frankfurt, knowing from simple calculations of political power that there would be no "Red Vienna" in Germany.

The German pattern of broad support for the expansion of municipal activity was the product of complex interaction between two forms of politics. Prewar fragmentation into milieus, political camps, or subcultures continued into the Weimar Republic on the local level. Highly charged symbolic disputes demonstrated the survival of political and confessional cleavages from the imperial era, and the revolution of 1918-1919 even intensified divisions between the political Left and the Right in cities such as Munich and Hanover. The example of Hanover, indeed, reveals that anti-Socialism remained a prime organizing principle of bourgeois politics on the local level into the late 1920s.

Despite the continued salience of prewar political cleavages in delineating lines of conflict, rapid democratization simultaneously influenced the politics of state expansion at the local level during the Weimar Republic. The democratic transition of municipal politics created structural pressure for tentative cooperation between parties of the Left and the Right. With the onset of monetary stabilization, municipal leaders from virtually all political camps proclaimed their desire to undertake recovery programs. Given the broad variety of political actors produced by democratization, municipal leaders generally had to cooperate across party lines if they wished to advance the programs they identified as so critical for recovery.

Democratization created structural pressure, not only for political cooperation, but also for convergence between the policies of parties of the Left and the Right. Facing demands for recovery in an era of mass democracy, bourgeois parties emphasized their support for expanding social provision. Established bourgeois parties in Düsseldorf, Frankfurt, and Hanover all pressed in particular for expanding municipal efforts to ensure a suitable supply of housing for the urban population. In similar fashion, the bourgeois parties in Berlin complained about the city's housing shortage, and even many opponents of the administration supported municipal promotion of housing construction.[66] Advocating the promotion of housing construction and leisure, established bourgeois parties presented themselves as suitable representatives of mass need for social assistance.

Democratization and the politics of expanding municipal activity shifted the boundaries between bourgeois parties and their opponents on the Left. Supporting most major municipal initiatives and cooperating, if only when necessary, with their counterparts from the SPD, bourgeois mayors and city councilors reshaped their own political identity. In the complex environment of Weimar municipal politics, there were bourgeois groupings which consistently opposed municipal policies of recovery, but despite isolated cases of firm bourgeois opposition to major civic initiatives and assertions of political independence by mayors, the support of established bourgeois parties for the chief municipal programs of recovery and the confident leadership of mayors placed a bourgeois stamp upon the expansion of state activity at the local level during the Weimar period of stabilization. In so doing, they reinforced the identification of bourgeois parties with the rapid expansion of the state.

Municipal politics of the period of Weimar stabilization therefore incorporated both an emerging form of modern politics and severe political contradictions. After the democratic transition of 1918-1919, the pursuit of recovery during the period of stabilization encouraged further movement toward a modern form of politics. Whereas prewar politics was based on a fractured foundation of rival milieus, political camps or subcultures, the politics of recovery cut across party, class, and confessional boundaries. For municipal leaders evaluating many key state functions, the politics of recovery created broad convergence on state duties with limited disagreements over the exact boundaries of state activity. In the politics of recovery, parties of the Left and Right both stressed their capacity to represent demands for state assistance by a broad cross section of the urban population.

Though there may be no single path to modern politics, this politics of democratization, incorporating broad convergence on state duties and appeals to diverse groupings across the boundaries of milieus or subcultures, represented a major form of modern politics in the German context.[67] Yet despite providing a political foundation for an important phase of state expansion, the politics of recovery did not replace prewar political structures during the Weimar Republic. Analyzing the Weimar Republic, it is entirely possible to find ample evidence of both intense ideological conflict between multiple rival blocks and the growth of consensus across much of the political spectrum. Overall, in politics as in other areas, Weimar Germany's encounter with "classical modernity" produced severe contradictions.

Notes

1. Christopher Pierson, *Beyond the Welfare State? The New Political Economy of Welfare* (University Park, Pennsylvania, 1991); and Peter Baldwin, "The Welfare State for Historians: A Review Article," *Comparative Studies in Society and History* 34 (1992): 695-707.

2. Gosta Esping-Andersen, *The Three Worlds of Welfare Capitalism*, Princeton, 1990.

3. Gerhard A. Ritter, *Sozialversicherung in Deutschland und England: Entstehung und Grundzüge im Vergleich* (Munich, 1983); Volker Hentschel, *Geschichte der deutschen Sozialpolitik 1880-1980: Soziale Sicherung und kollektives Arbeitsrecht* (Frankfurt am Main, 1983); and Hermann Beck, *The Origins of the Authoritarian Welfare State in Prussia: Conservatives, Bureaucracy, and the Social Question, 1815-70* (Ann Arbor, Michigan, 1994).

4. Böß, *Wie helfen wir uns? Wege zum wirtschaftlichen Wiederaufstieg* (Berlin, 1926), p. 66.

5. Karl Rohe, *Wahlen und Wählertraditionen in Deutschland: Kulturelle Grundlagen deutscher Parteien und Parteiensysteme im 19. und 20. Jahrhundert* (Frankfurt am Main, 1992), pp. 9-29, 121-24; Detlef Lehnert and Klaus Megerle, *Politische Teilkulturen zwischen Integration und Polarisierung: Zur politischen Kultur in der Weimarer Republik* (Opladen, 1990); and M. Rainer Lepsius, "Parteiensystem und Sozialstruktur. Zum Problem der Demokratisierung der deutschen Gesellschaft," in *Wirtschaft, Geschichte und Wirtschaftsgeschichte: Festschrift Zum 65. Geburtstag von Friedrich Lütge*, ed. W. Abel (Stuttgart, 1966), pp. 37-93; Lepsius, "From Fragmented Party Democracy to Government by Emergency Decree and National Socialist Takeover," in *The Breakdown of Democratic Regimes*, ed. Juan J. Linz and Alfred Stepan (Baltimore, 1978), pp. 41-42.

6. StA Düsseldorf, Nachlass Lehr 4, Lehr to Mulert, 6 December 1927; Hüttenberger, *Die Industrie- und Verwaltungsstadt*, pp. 310-11; and Engeli, *Gustav Böß*, pp. 39-40.

7. Hermann Heimrich, *Lebenserinnnerungen eines Mannheimer Oberbürgermeisters*, ed. Jörg Schadt (Stuttgart, 1982), p. 63.

8. Luppe, *Mein Leben*, pp. 143-45.

9. StVV Düsseldorf, 1926, p. 228.

10. Hofmann, *Zwischen Rathaus und Reichskanzlei*, p. 171; and Justus Buekschmitt, *Ernst May* (Stuttgart, 1963), pp. 53-55.

11. Luppe, *Mein Leben*, pp. 53-54.

12. StA Hannover, Finanzkommission, 1925-1926, pp. 119-24; StVV Düsseldorf, 1928, pp. 238-40, 277-93; and StVV Frankfurt, 1928, pp. 1054-58, 1312-18. See also Lehnert, *Kommunale Politik*, p. 109.

13. Anthony McElligott, "Crisis in the Cities: The Collapse of Weimar," *History Today* 43 (1993): 19; and McNeil, *American Money and the Weimar Republic*, pp. 77-78.

14. Baldwin, *The Politics of Social Solidarity*.

15. Fritzsche, *Rehearsals for Fascism*, p. 105.

16. Dieter Rebentisch, "'Die treusten Söhne der deutschen Sozialdemokratie:' Linksopposition und kommunale Reformpolitik in der Frankfurter Sozialdemokratie der Weimarer Epoche," *Archiv für Frankfurts Geschichte und Kunst* 61 (1987): 340.

17. Büttner, *Politische Gerechtigkeit*, p. 189; and *Die rote Stadt im roten Land*, pp. 28, 30.

18. Schadt, *Lebenserinnerungen*, pp. 60-61; and Büttner, *Politische Gerechtigkeit*, p. 189.

19. Detlef Lehnert, "Das 'rote' Berlin: Hauptstadt der deutschen Arbeiterbewegung?" in *Studien zur Arbeiterbewegung und Arbeiterkultur in Berlin*, ed. Gert-Joachim Glaessner, Detlef Lehnert and Klaus Sühl (Berlin, 1989), pp. 1-35.

20. Rebentisch, "'Die treusten Söhne,'" p. 340.

21. StVV Frankfurt, 1925, p. 870.

22. Ibid., 1927, p. 918.

23. Rebentisch, "'Die treusten Söhne,'" p. 344.

24. StVV Frankfurt, 1928, p. 1023.

25. Ibid., 1925, pp. 684-86, 787; and 1926, p. 511.

26. Ibid., 1927, pp. 407-10, 434-42, 608, 723-27.

27. Lehnert, *Kommunale Politik*, pp. 164-65; Gough, *Die SPD in der Berliner Kommunalpolitik*, pp. 23-29; and Engeli, *Gustav Böß*, p. 214.

28. Christoph Timm, *Gustav Oelsner*, pp. 119-20.

29. Stehkämper, ed., *Konrad Adenauer*, pp. 266-71, 288-91; and Schwarz, *Konrad Adenauer*, p. 205.

30. StVV Düsseldorf, 1926, p. 136-37; and 1927, pp. 127-30, 142-46, 226-29; and Hüttenberger, *Die Industrie- und Verwaltungsstadt*, p. 319.

31. StVV Düsseldorf, 1927, pp. 282, 298-300; and 1928, pp. 2-14.

32. Ibid., 1925, pp. 215-16 and 1926, pp. 187-93.

33. Ibid., 1927, pp. 208-11.

34. Ibid., 1925, pp. 87-88, 90.

35. Ibid., pp. 92, 168, 172.

36. Ibid., p. 214.

37. StA Düsseldorf III 11614, *Düsseldorfer Stadt Anzeiger*, 30 August 1926.

38. StVV Düsseldorf, 1926, p. 173.

39. Ibid., 1927, p. 2.

40. Ibid., 1925, pp. 232-35; 1926, p. 198; and 1927, pp. 132-33.

41. Ibid., 1925, pp. 99, 313, 318-20, 379; and 1926, p. 100.

42. Ibid., 1926, pp. 55, 105; and 1929, pp. 117-18.

43. Ibid., 1927, pp. 75-6.

44. Steinborn, *Münchener Kommunalpolitik*, pp. 267-69, 349.

45. Ibid., p. 402.

46. *Statistisches Jahrbuch deutscher Städte* 23 (1928), pp. 276, 282.

47. BVK Hannover, 1927-1928, p. 57; and 1928-1929, pp. 50, 63-64.

48. Röhrbein and Zankl, eds., *Hannover im 20. Jahrhundert*, pp. 34, 77.

49. BVK Hannover, 1921-1922, p. 294; and 1923-1924, pp. 1574-76. See also Ernst Demmig, *Das System Leinert* (Hanover, 1924).

50. BVK Hannover 1925-1926, pp. 358-68.

51. Ibid., pp. 809-918.

52. *Hannoverscher Anzeiger*, 2 May 1924; and BVK Hannover, 1925-1926, p. 83.

53. BVK Hannover, 1925-1926, p. 26.

54. StA Hannover, Baukommission, 22 October 1925, pp. 4-11.

55. BVK Hannover, 1925-1926, pp. 1299-1300.

56. StA Hannover XXIII D2 6a 1, *Volkswille*, 19 September 1926.

57. Ibid., XXIII D2 6a 2 III, Die Typhusepidemie in Hannover," pp. 208-11.

58. *Hannoverscher Anzeiger*, 7 March 1928.

59. BVK Hannover, 1925-1926, pp. 1625-27, 1748.

60. Ibid., 1926-1927, pp. 696-97, 724-25, 784; and 1927-1928, p. 150.

61. *Hannoverscher Anzeiger*, 7 March 1928.

62. Ibid., 12 November 1929, 13 November 1929; and *Volkswille*, 17 November 1929.

63. BVK Hannover, 1929-1930, pp. 107-8, 113-14, 116.

64. Harvey, *Youth and the Welfare State*, p. 176.

65. Helmut Gruber, *Red Vienna: Experiment in Working Class Culture 1919-1934* (New York, 1991), pp. 9, 47-49, 66, 102; and von Saldern, "Sozialdemokratie und kommunale Wohnungsbaupolitik," pp. 198-99.

66. Lehnert, *Kommunale Politik*, pp. 225, 244.

67. Social scientists now dispute the assumption that modernization necessarily leads to democratization. See Rainer Zitelmann, "Die Totalitäre Seite der Moderne," in *Nationalsozialismus und Modernisierung: Mit einem aktuellen Nachwort zur Neuauflage*, ed. Michael Prinz and Rainer Zitelmann (Darmstadt, 1994), pp. 3-12.

Chapter 3

MUNICIPAL FINANCE AND DESTABILIZATION

*I*f historians' comments about illusions of stabilization suggest the difficulty of evaluating the middle years of the Weimar Republic, analysis of municipal policies and politics of recovery underscores the problem of accounting for stabilization in a period best known for disaster. In place of the traumas of stabilization outlined by historiography of the Weimar Republic, a focus on the municipal level reveals remarkable local activism in the aftermath of hyperinflation. Instead of the political strife described by studies of national politics, a municipal perspective shows that the conjunction of recovery with democratization yielded a broad political consensus in favor of expanding municipal activity.

Despite the achievements of civic leaders during the period of Weimar stabilization, municipal pursuit of recovery yielded contradictory results. The growth of municipal activity met with both broad approval and mounting criticism. Indeed, reaction against municipal policy, civic leaders, and established political parties steadily gathered force on the local and national levels between 1926 and 1929, well before the 1930 national electoral breakthrough of the National Socialists. By the end of the period of Weimar stabilization, many of the municipal leaders who had taken a leading part in organizing recovery found themselves on the defensive, facing charges that city governments had actually crippled recovery.

How did city governments come to face multiple waves of attack despite the broad base of support for municipal policies of the period of stabilization? It is no more convincing to identify a single cause of reaction against Weimar municipalities than it is to find a single cause for the collapse of the Weimar Republic.[1] Criticism of municipalities arose from a wide variety of political, cultural, and economic discontents and conflicts. Of all of the explanations of the roots of opposition to municipal programs, the simplest attributes reaction to financial burdens. Local pressure for recovery manifested itself in municipal budgets through rising spending and borrowing, and at least part of the criticism of Weimar city governments centered on the rising costs of municipal activism.

Recovery and Municipal Finance

Municipal spending during the Weimar period of stabilization was divided into two separate categories, ordinary and extraordinary budgets. An ordinary budget consisted of expenditures that were covered by annual income: transfers of revenue from the national and state governments, profits of municipal companies, and taxes.[2] An extraordinary budget, the rough equivalent of a capital budget, consisted of spending to be covered by loans or funds obtained over a number of years, such as returns on real estate.[3]

Both extraordinary and ordinary spending rose during the Weimar period of stabilization. The Association of German Cities calculated that ordinary municipal spending in 1925 had increased between 82 percent and 110 percent from prewar levels.[4] Measuring the precise rate of increase in ordinary spending was complicated by the distinction made in municipal budgets between total spending and *Zuschußbedarf* (sometimes referred to as *Fehlbetrag* in the 1920s), a term which referred to spending that was not covered by administrative revenue such as income from fees.[5] Average ordinary spending in cities with more than 200,000 residents continued to rise during the period of stabilization, growing from RM 130 per resident in 1925 to RM 177 per resident in 1929, an increase of 36 percent almost identical to the 35 percent increase in average Zuschußbedarf per resident during the same time period (see Tables 3.1 and 3.2).

Though more difficult to track than ordinary expenditures, extraordinary spending also rose after 1925. Statistics compiled by the Association of Cities indicated sharp growth in extraordinary spending in Frankfurt from RM 7,718,000 in 1925 to RM 16,164,000 in 1927. Extraordinary spending increased even more swiftly in Düsseldorf and Hanover, rising from RM 2,585,000 in 1925 to RM 21,760,000 in 1927 in Düsseldorf and from RM 2,060,000 in 1925 to RM 15,134,000 in 1927 in Hanover (see Table 3.3).

TABLE 3.1 Average ordinary expenditures per resident for major types of municipal spending between 1925 and 1929 in cities with more than 200,000 residents (Money Amounts in RM)

	Total	General Admin.	Welfare and Health	Housing	Education and Culture	Building Admin.	Other
1925	131	23.98	37.29	13.07	30.07	11.13	15.36
1927	155	24.69	50.93	18.44	33.09	9.85	17.64
1928	166	25.98	50.92	20.27	39.00	10.79	19.47
1929	177	20.74	57.75	22.01	42.40	11.77	22.13

Source: Statistisches Jahrbuch deutscher Städte 26 (1931), 356. Note that the figures for table 3.1, 3.2, and 3.4 do not include Berlin, Bremen, and Hamburg, and that the Association of German Cities did not compile comparative financial statistics for 1926.

TABLE 3.2 Average Zuschussbedarf per resident for major types of municipal spending between 1925 and 1929 in cities with more than 200,000 residents (Money Amounts in RM)

	Total	General Admin.	Welfare and Health	Housing	Education and Culture	Building Admin.	Other
1925	83	20.15	26.22	1.33	20.42	8.39	6.86
1927	97	21.87	36.15	1.22	24.11	6.58	7.47
1928	105	23.25	35.49	1.27	28.19	8.07	8.61
1929	111	18.01	39.95	2.45	31.55	8.87	9.75

Source: Statistisches Jahrbuch deutscher Städte 26 (1931), 356.

TABLE 3.3 Extraordinary spending in Düsseldorf, Frankfurt, and Hanover(Money Amounts in RM)

	1925	1927	1928	1929
Düsseldorf	2,585,000	21,760,000	8,150,000	11,150,000
Frankfurt	7,718,000	16,164,000	—	—
Hanover	2,060,000	15,134,000	12,998,000	13,488,000

Sources: Statistisches Jahrbuch deutscher Städte 22 (1927),19; Ibid., 1928, 308; Ibid., 1929, 194; and Ibid., 1930, 179.

As municipal expenditures rose during the Weimar period of stabilization, civic leaders faced a financial predicament. Municipal authorities could not simply increase the surcharge to the income tax, the chief source of municipal revenue before the First World War, for Finance Minister Erzberger's tax reforms of 1919 and 1920 had rescinded municipal power to set this surcharge. Returns from the income tax, though still an important source of funds for city governments during the Weimar Republic, fell from 53.3 percent of all municipal tax revenue in 1913 to 28.0 percent of municipal tax revenue in 1925.[6] As returns from the income tax fell as a proportion of total municipal revenue, city governments relied heavily on the surcharges to the state trade tax and state property tax, two surcharges that municipal authorities could still adjust during the Weimar Republic. Surcharges to the state trade and property taxes provided over 75 percent of revenue from municipal taxes in Düsseldorf, Frankfurt, and Hanover in 1928 (see Table 3.5). Municipal governments supplemented these and other smaller taxes and fees with profits from municipal utilities, especially electrical power plants, which provided over 50 percent of total earnings from city firms in 1927.[7]

Aside from the temporary palliative of estimating higher returns from existing taxes, municipalities could cover deficits in ordinary budgets either by raising surcharges to the state trade and property taxes or by increasing earnings from utilities through higher gas, water, and electricity rates. Both solutions were unattractive. Proposals to raise utility rates roused the ire of Social Democrats and Communists who decried the regressive impact of relying on profits from utilities, while moves to increase the surcharge to the trade tax troubled bourgeois councilors who warned of damage to commerce.

Table 3.4 Sources of revenue as a percentage of Zuschußbedarf in 1928

	Profits of Municipal Firms	Transfers from Reich Taxes	Transfers from State and Municipal Taxes
Düsseldorf	28.6	29.5	41.7
Frankfurt	18.8	31.4	46.6
Hanover	25.6	26.5	46.5
Municipal Average	19.9	31.3	46.9

Source: Statistisches Jahrbuch deutscher Städte 24 (1929), 185, 200.

Table 3.5   Income from property and trade taxes in 1928
(Money Amounts in RM)

	Income from Property Taxes	Income from Trade Tax	Total Income from Municipal Taxes
Düsseldorf	7,502,000	11,853,000	24,857,000
Frankfurt	12,064,000	22,051,000	42,847,000
Hanover	11,065,000	8,254,000	22,984,000

Source: Statistisches Jahrbuch deutscher Städte 25 (1930), 441.

Municipal governments struggled to avoid raising taxes during the period of stabilization. Frankfurt's surcharge to the property tax rose from 150 percent in 1925 to 200 percent by 1928 and 1927, but the city government managed to hold the surcharge on the trade tax on profits at 400 percent from 1925 to 1928, with the exception of a temporary increase to 460 percent in 1926 to cover the deficit caused by the decline in revenues during the economic slump of the winter of 1925-1926.[8] Frankfurt's trade tax, argued City Treasurer Asch, required businesses to pay significant, but not crushing sums. He calculated in 1928 that the surcharge to the trade tax on profits exacted RM 138 from income of RM 5,000, RM 536 from income of RM 10,000, and RM 1,336 RM from income of RM 20,000. These sums were not "catastrophic."[9]

No matter how much they stressed their allegiance to low taxes, mayors found it difficult to avoid tax increases during the Weimar period of stabilization. In the case of Düsseldorf, Mayor Robert Lehr wished to hold down tax rates as did Düsseldorf's bourgeois parties, and Dr. Joseph Wilden of the Chamber of Industry and Commerce warned against any "one-sided overload" of the economy with municipal and other taxes. However when the city parliament actually cut the surcharge to the state trade tax on profits in 1926 from 500 percent to 400 percent, the administration soon began to consider raising taxes.[10] Bowing to pressure from bourgeois parties, the administration postponed making any changes to the major municipal taxes until November 1927 when Lehr shocked the DNVP by turning to a majority consisting of the Center Party, the SPD, and the KPD that voted to raise the surcharge to the trade tax on income above RM 3,000 from 1,250 percent to 2,250 percent. After the Prussian District Committee blocked this measure as unbalanced, Lehr pulled together a new majority of the DNVP, Center, DDP, and SPD that voted to cover the deficit with temporary retroactive increases of 30 percent in the surcharge to the trade tax on profits, and 15 percent in the surcharge to the property tax along with a temporary increase of 800 percent in the surcharge to the trade tax on income. Düsseldorf never returned to the lower tax rates of 1926 as the administration drafted budgets with a 420 percent surcharge to the trade tax on profits and a 190 percent surcharge to the property tax in 1928 and 1929.[11]

Hanover's mayor and municipal officials, though no more disposed than their counterparts in Düsseldorf to raise taxes, also succumbed to budgetary pressure to increase taxes. The administration's chief political allies, the Ordnungsblock and the Deutsch Hannoveraner, recommended increasing revenues from municipal companies as an alternative to higher taxes, a strategy condemned by the SPD and KPD as a form of regressive taxation. However earnings from municipal companies could not balance Hanover's budgets, and in 1926 the city parliament and Magistrat raised the surcharge to the trade tax on profits from 200 percent to 300 percent and the surcharge to the property tax by 50 percent.[12] Facing a deficit in early 1927, Mayor Arthur Menge again found himself compelled to support both higher taxes and utility rates. The Magistrat initially failed to gain the city parliament's approval for a tax increase, prompting demands from the SPD that Menge resign, but the bourgeois parties finally agreed to raise the surcharge to the trade tax on profits to 450 percent and the surcharge to the property tax to 365 percent.[13]

Increasing ordinary revenue, whether through higher taxes or higher utility rates, was unpopular, and municipalities were hard-pressed to cover the rising costs of items such as welfare, let alone of other major programs of recovery, through ordinary income. Turning to loans was an attractive financial option for municipal officials and politicians during the Weimar period of stabilization. As Mayor Arthur Menge noted, borrowing reduced the financial burden placed on tax payers.[14] Menge and his counterparts in other cities had little reason to avoid borrowing during the early years of stabilization, for revaluation of debts reduced preexisting debt to a small fraction of pre-inflation book value. As providers of social services, German cities suffered from inflation, but as borrowers, they were among the winners of inflation. City governments seeking loans presented potential lenders with financial statements that showed substantial existing assets and very limited debt.

Relying heavily on credit to finance programs of recovery, municipal authorities turned to a variety of lenders and types of loans. The

Association of Cities estimated that cities of more than 200,000 residents had borrowed RM 565 million in long-term domestic credit by the end of March 1928; however, domestic capital was insufficient to satisfy municipal demand for long-term loans. Banks that agreed to lend to cities sometimes found themselves unable to place bond issues on the German market. The Direction of the Frankfurt Bank concluded in 1927 that the response to a 6 percent Frankfurt municipal loan of 1926 had not been "favorable." Frankfurt's offering shared the fate of other 6 percent domestic public loans when interest rates rose in 1926 as German investors shied away from long-term public credit offerings.[15] In 1927 domestic capital became scarce when the national government borrowed RM 500 million. And after negotiations collapsed in 1927 between Düsseldorf and a consortium of banks led by the Deutsche Bank, Düsseldorf's administration concluded that banks were unable to offer the city "a long-term domestic loan at any acceptable conditions under the present condition of the money market," and Frankfurt's Finance Deputation described conditions on the domestic capital market in the summer as "extremely unfavorable at the moment." Frankfurt's City Treasurer Asch also cautioned Mayor Landmann that it "could be practically impossible" to obtain loans at "favorable conditions" for a long period.[16]

Municipalities pursued credit on both foreign and domestic fronts. By March 1928, cities of more than 200,000 residents had borrowed at least RM 488 million in long-term foreign loans, chiefly from the United States. With the stabilization of the German currency in 1924, agents acting on behalf of German public institutions and private companies flooded the American capital market with inquiries. Despite considerable success in gaining American loans, German municipal authorities were unable to obtain as much American credit as they wished.[17] To control municipal access to foreign credit, the Reich government created an Advisory Board for Foreign Credit (Beratungsstelle für Auslandskredit) in late 1925, empowered to screen municipal applications for loans. Composed of representatives from the Finance Ministry, the Reich Economic Ministry, the Reichsbank, the Prussian State Bank, the Bavarian State Bank, and a representative from the state making a particular loan application, the Advisory Board approved only RM 927,000,000 out of the total of RM 2,038,000,000 in applications for loans submitted by municipalities between 1925 and 1928 before waning American interest in lending abroad finally shut the American credit market for German cities in 1928 and 1929.[18] Hanover was the last German city to obtain a sizable long-term American loan during the period of stabilization, borrowing $3.5 million from Brown Brothers & Co of New York in October 1929.[19]

City governments used foreign and domestic loans to cover a large part of the costs of major recovery programs including new utilities, housing settlements, and numerous other projects. Long-term foreign credit most often went for utility projects – some 55 percent of foreign long-term credit was invested in electrical power plants (see Table 3.6). One of the more successful cities in the competition for foreign loans, Frankfurt applied most of its $4 million 1925 loan from Speyer & Company and its $6.25 million 1927 loan from E.H. Rollins to pay for renovation and expansion of its electrical power utility.[20]

Domestic long-term borrowing by cities paid for several types of projects including the promotion of housing construction. City governments received substantial revenue from the state rent tax; Düsseldorf and Hanover spent between RM 8 million and RM 10 million a year in rent tax revenue on housing construction, and Frankfurt spent over RM 15 million annually in rent-tax revenue on new housing, but the rent tax did not cover the full costs of promoting housing construction, and municipalities turned to loans to complete financing for annual housing construction programs.[21] Complying with widespread political pressure for larger housing construction programs increased municipal borrowing. Düsseldorf's housing program for 1927 required RM 14 million in loans, and Hanover borrowed RM 3,900,000 in 1926, RM 4,000,000 in 1927, and RM 4,500,000 in 1928 to help pay for the promotion of housing construction.[22] Overall, some 22 percent of municipal domestic long-term borrowing in large cities went to pay for housing construction programs.

Reliance on loans to pay for the promotion of housing construction was actually higher than the Association of Cities' statistics suggested. A significant portion of the 4 percent of domestic long-term borrowing employed to pay for sewers, the 13.3 percent that paid for streets and bridges, and the 11.75 percent that financed land purchases helped cover costs associated with housing construction. The extra costs of building new housing settlement often appeared in plans for individual loans. A 1928 domestic loan obtained by Frankfurt included RM 8.4 million to pay for street and sewer extension associated with the city's housing program, along with RM 10 million to pay for housing construction; Düsseldorf obtained RM 3 million in 1926 to pay for new streets and sewer extensions associated with housing construction.[23]

Borrowing to cover the costs of major programs of recovery, municipal governments also paid for numerous other projects with loans. Municipal financial officials periodically listed projects that had been approved in expectation of gaining credit. By 1926, Düsseldorf's city parliament had already approved RM 450,000 for a women's swimming pool, RM 1,240,000 for a stadium, and RM 4,050,000 for permanent exhibition buildings among other expenses to be paid for with future loans.[24] A Hanover motion of 1927 listed RM 19 million in expenditures to be paid for with future loans, including RM 193,500 for a public bath.[25] As late as 1930, Frankfurt's city government noted past approval of expenditures to be paid for with future loans including RM 592,500 for cemetery expansion and RM 186,000 added to the Palm Garden Company's capital.[26]

TABLE 3.6 Use of municipal long-term loans as of 31 March 1928 in cities with more than 200,000 residents

Domestic credit (Money amounts in thousands of RM)

	Amount	Percentage of Total
Total	565,792	100
Electricity	34,847	6.2
Transportation	67,851	12.0
Sewers	24,199	4.3
Housing Construction	125,300	22.2
Streets and Bridges	75,126	13.3
Land Purchases	66,803	11.7
Hospitals	22,167	3.9
Gas	14,928	2.6
Schools	13,044	2.3
Other	121,527	21.5

Foreign credit (Money amounts in thousands of RM)

	Amount	Percentage of Total
Total	488,809	100
Gas	34,526	7.1
Water	39,877	8.2
Electricity	270,867	55.4
Transportation	131,055	26.8
Other	12,484	2.5

Source: StA Frankfurt U190 IV, Herbert Martin, "Die Anleiheverschuldung der deutschen Städte," p. 4. Note that these figures do not include Bremen and Hamburg.

The many motions approved by city parliaments that included the clause "to the burden of future loans" signalled that municipal authorities would probably draw on the proceeds of short-term loans to begin work on projects in question. Unable to obtain sufficient long-term credit from either domestic or foreign sources to cover the full costs of projects of recovery, municipal governments resorted to short-term credit. Exact and convincing statistics for municipal short-term borrowing were unavailable during the Weimar period of stabilization. The Association of Cities placed total short-term debt as of March 1928 at RM 373,122,000 for large cities and RM 664,690,000 for all cities.[27] In answers to surveys in late 1927, Frankfurt's administration calculated Frankfurt's short-term debt at RM 32.8 million, and Düsseldorf's administration placed Düsseldorf's total short-term debt at RM 27.2 million.[28] Relatively cautious in contracting short-term debt, Hanover's administration claimed that the city's total short-term debt as of March 1928 consisted of a $2 million (RM 8,400,000) American short-term loan.[29]

The municipal appetite for all available types of loans from short-term credit to long-term loans provided dramatic evidence of local activism for recovery. Levels of municipal debt varied, but in all cases municipal authorities, struggling to hold down tax increases, took advantage of low debt burdens to take out new loans. In sum, the pursuit of credit to cover the costs of expensive projects such as new utilities and housing settlements or to provide smaller sums for sports facilities showed the financial results of widespread local demands for programs of recovery.

Municipal Finance and Communal Politics

Although a broad range of political groupings supported recovery programs, the financial consequences of municipal activism had the potential to damage the political consensus of recovery. Rising ordinary expenditures forced municipal authorities to select between the unpopular alternatives of raising taxes or utility rates; often city governments did both. Borrowing to cover the costs of major programs of recovery meanwhile raised municipal debt. Struggling to balance ordinary budgets and pursuing loans, civic leaders across Germany confronted a common set of financial problems. Emerging concern about problems of municipal finance did not in and of itself ensure collapse of local consensus, but financial disagreements between major political groupings could splinter the political consensus of recovery.

As total municipal spending grew, the rising cost of individual programs began to worry municipal politicians. Surveying ordinary budgets, mayors and city councilors had particular reason to take note of the rising costs of social provision, in particular, of social welfare. Already 453 percent higher in 1925 than in 1911, average welfare expenditures grew steadily during the period of stabilization.[30] Between 1925 and 1929, higher expenditures for welfare and health care accounted for RM 20 of the average increase of RM 46 in ordinary spending per inhabitant in cities with more than 200,000 residents (refer to Table 3.1). The contribution of welfare to higher municipal spending was even more pronounced on uncovered ordinary expenditures. Spending for welfare and health care made up RM 13 of the RM 28 increase between 1925 and 1929 in Zuschuß-bedarf per inhabitant (see again Table 3.2).[31]

On the local level, alarm at the cost of welfare reached a first peak during the economic slump of the winter of 1925-1926 when high unemployment forced many to seek assistance from municipal welfare offices. At this point, rising welfare costs shaped politics chiefly by exposing tensions between city governments and national and local authorities. Municipal leaders, troubled by swelling expenditures for welfare, charged that the national and state governments had forced an excessive burden on city governments. Düsseldorf's Mayor Lehr voiced a common complaint when he told city councilors in March 1926 that "we have not received the consideration and support from the Reich and state that we must receive according to the situation." In similar fashion Frankfurt's Mayor Landmann noted the "greatest strain of our finances because of the care for the unemployed" and complained about the "costs supported by the city administration alone" for the unemployed who had exhausted their benefits.[32] Meanwhile Hanover's Mayor Menge, in March 1926, stressed the pressure on expenditures of "the new tasks, which have been assigned to the communities in the area of welfare etc." A year later, Menge again complained that "Reich and state continually place new large tasks on the communities, especially in the area of welfare work."[33]

Expenditures for welfare fell during 1926, but then increased again during the transition from stabilization to depression. From late 1928 onward, soaring unemployment multiplied the burden of spending for welfare. Unemployment in Frankfurt, for example, rose sharply from 15,242 on July 1928 to 24,782 on 15 December 1928, a disturbing trend that drove up the costs of providing welfare. Frankfurt's spending for welfare for the unemployed increased from RM 630,048 in 1927 to RM 3,158,042 in 1928.[34] Other German cities suffered similar experiences.

Though dissatisfaction with the readiness of national and state authorities to shift costs of welfare to city governments crossed party lines at the local level, the rising expense of welfare also caused particular discontent among political groupings seeking to represent the bourgeois Right. Calculating the economic impact of mounting outlays for welfare, city councilors with ties to economic interest groups suspected that the economy suffered from the costs of extending welfare to the unemployed. Councilor Schwietzke, founder of the Economic Committee of Düsseldorf's DNVP, conceded in late 1925 that the "necessity of unemployment support is generally recognized," but asked "Where does the money come from? Ultimately it comes from the economy." Two years later, as Düsseldorf's city parliament tried to cover the city's budget deficit, councilor Köngeter, a member of the DVP and Düsseldorf's Chamber of Industry and Commerce, cautioned against the creation of a "pure welfare state": the costs of social policy had reached a level that could not be supported by the private economy.[35]

Among other major social expenditures of the Weimar period of stabilization, spending for housing construction prompted isolated grumbling, chiefly from advocates of landlords' interests. Düsseldorf's *Lokal Zeitung*, a newspaper sympathetic to the Wirtschaftsbund, asked in 1928 "What would one have said before the war to an administration which felt it had a mission to spend RM 13.5 million for housing purposes?" Still, even the harshest critics of municipal spending in city parliaments seldom called for reducing support for housing construction. Düsseldorf's Wirtschaftsbund preferred to attack methods used to distribute funds for housing construction rather than the level of spending. Councilor Stein of the Wirtschaftsbund was quite willing to see the rent tax used for rent subsidies, a policy that would put more money into the hands of landlords.[36]

Though hardly the chief item in municipal budgets, rising subsidies for cultural institutions also worried city councilors. In 1927 cities with more than 200,000 residents spent at least RM 39 million in subsidies for theaters and orchestras.[37] Despite this generosity, subsidies approved by city parliaments seldom covered theater deficits. Thus, Frankfurt's city parliament approved a RM 800,000 subsidy for the 1925 budget, but added RM 700,000 in February

1926. A member of Frankfurt's DNVP, city councilor Lüttke, warned in August 1926 that the city parliament could not continue to underwrite large deficits indefinitely. He described a "feeling ... amongst the city's inhabitants that a lasting maintenance of the high theater subsidy stands outside of the sphere of possibility." Impossible though a higher subsidy might be, the city parliament consented to raise the subsidy for 1926 from RM 1,200,000 to the RM 1,500,000 originally proposed by the Magistrat, and city councilors again approved additional funds for the theater at the end of 1927, though the DNVP opposed a larger subsidy on this occasion.[38]

Concern over the level of municipal social and cultural spending was not exclusively the property of parties of the bourgeois Right. In Frankfurt, the Center Party, a party that had backed virtually all of the administration's major initiatives, suggested in 1929 that expensive social and cultural programs injured the city's finances and the private economy. Councilor Kercher of the Center Party referred to the "favor which we bring to cultural questions and to social demands, but warned, "We must still demand that by the raising of means the economy does not bleed itself but remains healthy."[39]

Even as the rising costs for welfare and theater subsidies worried many city councilors, so too did the expense of municipal economic promotion. In cities such as Düsseldorf and Frankfurt where mayors championed high-profile projects designed to stimulate economic development, the costs of economic promotion created friction between mayors and city parliaments.

Resentment among city councilors over the costs of economic promotion frequently surfaced in the aftermath of trade fairs and exhibitions when administrations asked city parliaments to pick up the bill for undertakings that had gone over budget. Municipal politicians typically praised exhibitions when the first visitors arrived, only to take a more critical line as they later learned of the swelling deficit of the exhibition in question. Yesterday's civic triumphs caused irritation as bills kept on coming in long after the crowds left. Effusive in their praise of the Summer of Music exhibition in 1927, city councilors in Frankfurt voiced displeasure with the exhibition's deficit in 1928. Councilor Kirchner of the SPD asked "whether the cultural values" created by the exhibition "are too highly paid for."[40] In Düsseldorf, cost overruns for the permanent exhibition buildings constructed for the Gesolei exhibition of 1926 became a sore point, not only for the Wirtschaftsbund, but also for the DVP, which accused Düsseldorf's administration of failing to inform the city parliament of the cost overruns. A meeting of the

DVP's party agents (*Vertrauensleute*) was devoted to "a passionate and excited discussion of the costs of the permanent buildings."[41]

Irritated by one-time cost-overruns for exhibitions, city councilors logically objected to the persistent deficits incurred by trade fairs. The recurrent deficit of Frankfurt's trade fair was a major cause of deteriorating relations between Mayor Ludwig Landmann and city councilors. Landmann struggled for years to convince reluctant city councilors to continue to underwrite the city's trade fair. Confidence in the fair was already shaky in 1925 when the DVP opposed a proposal to fund the construction of a House of Fashion.[42] Landmann persuaded the city parliament on this occasion to approve a loan of RM 1,300,000, but disappointing financial results for the first trade fair in 1926 led Frankfurt's SPD to reconsider its support.[43] After years of complaint, the city parliament passed a motion in 1928 to abolish the trade fair when the small National Socialist Party added its votes to those of the SPD and KPD. Landmann resorted to administrative means to preserve a specialized fair before the enterprise finally collapsed in 1929.[44]

City councilors also came to regret the RM 13 million price of Frankfurt's new market hall, another of Landmann's major initiatives of economic promotion. Although the city parliament approved the project in 1926, even supporters of the administration wondered whether the towering structure, which contained apartments, offices, and restaurants along with storage space, could have been built on a smaller scale for less money. Councilor Kercher of the Center Party noted popular irritation with the market hall captured in references to the building as the "vegetable church."[45]

Both Landmann's nominal allies and foes decided that the administration's complex array of economic projects overextended the city government. Social Democratic resistance to the costs of economic promotion surfaced in 1925 when the SPD opposed Frankfurt's purchase of the Bad Homburg Spa. In 1926 and 1927 the SPD, though convinced of the economic value of promoting aviation, called for cutting the budget for aviation from the levels requested by the administration. City councilors of the DDP, for their part, joined the DVP in December 1928 in recommending a reduction in the number of municipal companies.[46]

Among the parties of the bourgeois Right, opposition to Landmann's plans of economic promotion began to build in 1927 when the DNVP and DVP objected to the costs of incorporating the town of Höchst, a measure which Landmann argued, with reason, would make Frankfurt the undisputed center of the German chemical industry. The DVP subjected Landmann's economic initiatives to increasingly harsh scrutiny in 1928 and 1929, focusing in particular on the Frankfurt Gas Company's acquisition of a coal field. The DVP held Landmann responsible for the Gas Company's debts and for losses caused by water damage to the coal field.[47]

The costs of Ludwig Landmann's ambitious programs of economic promotion created general concern within Frankfurt's city parliament but did not rupture the consensus of recovery at any distinct point on the political spectrum until 1929. Both parties of the Left and the Right, despite choosing different targets for their most intense criticism, objected to the costs of particular programs of economic promotion. Such pervasive unease with the expense of economic promotion was common to cities with ambitious mayors. Thus, Cologne's Konrad Adenauer found himself on the defensive by the late 1920s as the expense of the new Mülheim bridge and the city's Pressa exhibition caused alarm among broad sectors of civic opinion.[48]

Despite concerns by city councilors at the costs of various social, cultural, and economic programs, it was not clear that the overall course of municipal finance gave cause for any broad reaction against municipal policies of recovery. Much of the cost of recovery was covered by loans, and levels of municipal debt were not particularly high for most of the period of stabilization. Even taking into account possible discrepancies between actual and declared municipal short-term debt, levels of municipal debt fell well below the book-value of assets owned by cities. Düsseldorf, for instance, claimed to possess net assets of nearly RM 320 million in July 1927, and other cities also held assets well in excess of debts.[49]

Why, then, did municipal reliance on loans begin to cause alarm during the Weimar period of stabilization? Local critics of municipal borrowing charged that city governments increased their debt at a reckless rate. Groups with close ties to organized landlords were among the early foes of municipal borrowing. Thus, Düsseldorf's Wirtschaftsbund, though initially encouraged by municipal use of loans as an alternative to taxes, criticized the city's financial practices without respite from 1926 until the end of the period of stabilization.[50] "We must express our sharpest disapproval of the public finances of the city of Düsseldorf," declared Otto Stein, a city councilor of the Wirtschaftsbund and head of the House and Property Owners' Association. In 1927 he called Mayor Lehr's financial policy "unsolid ... because the debts have been contracted at an unbelievably quick pace."[51]

If organized landlords offered the most vocal local criticism of the risks of borrowing, municipal officials were themselves troubled by the difficulty they faced obtaining loans at favorable conditions. In Frankfurt, City Treasurer Asch noted in 1927 that the construction of a new market hall, utilities, and housing had already required Frankfurt to take out large loans. Asch cautioned that the city should avoid being forced "through financial restriction to loan transactions, which burden us heavily for years." Ever-more concerned as credit grew scarce, Asch described the capital market in 1929 as "really completely unproductive at present." Scrambling to find credit of any sort, Asch vainly tried to acquire foreign short-term credit in June of 1929 to cover RM 21,026,043 in short-term debt, though he at least managed to obtain a RM 30 million three-year bearer bond in the summer of 1929.[52]

In 1929, Frankfurt's DVP, a party that had long supported most of the administration's measures, turned against municipal borrowing of the period of stabilization. Projects should not begin, the DVP argued, without secure funding. Warning against completing new housing settlements without first obtaining sound financing, councilor Merton of the DVP acknowledged the importance of housing construction from a "social standpoint," but asserted that Frankfurt could no longer afford to pay for projects with future loans. We may not "carry out a pure expenditure policy," he told the city parliament.[53] Depicting dire consequences to this pattern of spending, the DVP concluded that paying for the promotion of housing construction and other projects with short-term credit had damaged credit markets. A motion issued by the party in September 1929 charged that: "the communal financial policy previously pursued here and elsewhere which consisted of financing building plans of all types in the largest measure almost exclusively with short-term credit has unfavorably contributed to shaping money conditions in Germany and in connection with foreign countries, and to raising interest rates."[54]

By late 1929, Mayor Landmann and his closest remaining ally, the city's faltering DDP, accepted the need for greater financial restraint. Arguing that economic conditions mandated a pause before starting on new municipal projects, councilor Korff, the DDP's chair in the city parliament, compared Frankfurt to a mountain climber who had just reached a peak. Frankfurt now needed to rest and catch its breath before climbing other summits or beginning work on new projects. Landmann agreed that conditions on capital markets and the policies of the Reichsbank and Advisory Board left Frankfurt with no choice but to take such a rest.[55]

As the examples of Düsseldorf and Frankfurt am Main indicate, many of the most vocal critics of rising debt during the last years of stabilization came from parties of the bourgeois Right, but Social Democrats, for their part, were not averse to pointing out the risks of reliance on short-term credit in cities where the SPD stood in firm opposition to the administration. In Hanover, a city with comparatively low short-term debt, delay in transforming an American short-term loan into a long-term loan gave the city's Social Democrats cause to charge Mayor Arthur Menge with financial mismanagement. Menge claimed that Hanover had only briefly paid more than 7 percent interest on short-term credit, but total interest, including all charges, on the city's American loan rose to 8.5 percent by late 1928, and Menge was himself concerned by the delay in converting Hanover's short-term debt. In 1928, he informed the Prussian government of Hanover's pressing need for approval of a long-term foreign loan.[56]

Accused by Hanover's Social Democrats of dangerous delay in converting short-term into long-term debt, Menge also confronted criticism of Hanover's financial policy from a surprising source, his long-time ally Heinrich Tramm, who repeatedly called for fiscal caution. In January 1928, Tramm recommended that Hanover refrain from beginning projects placed in the extraordinary budget until it had acquired secure funding. Tramm specifically cautioned against Stadtbaurat Elkart's proposal to pay for part of the city's 1928 housing construction program with future loans, and the same advice held good for emergency work projects that were not already funded by ordinary revenue.[57] Revealing his differences with Menge during a session of the city parliament in 1929, Tramm made similar complaints to Social Democrats about Hanover's delay in converting short-term debt into a long-term loan.[58]

The dispute between Tramm and Menge centered on the risks of optimism. Menge and other architects of municipal recovery programs were optimistic. The pursuit of recovery, after all, presumed that public institutions could respond to severe economic and social traumas, and this optimism of recovery extended, as Menge himself admitted, to financial policy. Asking whether it was responsible to begin work on projects to be paid for with future loans, he replied "that it can not be denied, that one can only answer this question positively with a certain courage and optimism." Tramm found this line of reason unsettling and "too optimistic." The mayor expected interest rates to sink, but Tramm feared that they might just as well rise.[59]

Financial Crisis and the Loss of Self-Administration

With the onset of depression, municipal finances in cities across Germany rapidly deteriorated, setting off a crisis of municipal self-government.[60] Ordinary budgets, not debt, produced the initial collapse of municipal finance in 1930. Soaring expenditures for the welfare unemployed combined with sinking revenues to create continual deficits. From 1930 onward, municipal officials and politicians struggled and frequently failed to bring order to municipal budgets.[61] Mayors and city councilors faced an extremely unappealing choice during the depression: municipal authorities could either raise taxes during a deep economic slump or hand over effective control of municipal finances to the state and national governments.

The vacillations of municipal authorities confronting the unpalatable alternatives of raising taxes or abandoning self administration were particularly striking in Düsseldorf in 1930. Düsseldorf's Mayor Lehr spent months in 1930 trying to obtain any majority in the city parliament for a budget. To limit tax increases, Lehr accepted improbable revenue estimates, which cut RM 500,000 for estimated interest payments and added RM 300,000 to estimates of tax transfers from the Reich and Prussia. The entire city parliament, nonetheless, rejected Lehr's proposal, which included increases in the surcharges to the trade tax and the property tax. The Center Party and the parties of the bourgeois Right, including the Wirtschaftsbund, drafted a budget without any tax increase by projecting further increases in revenue transfers from Prussia and the Reich and additional cuts in debt service payments, but this fanciful scheme went too far for Lehr. Rejecting the budget proposal, Lehr explained that he would be subject to disciplinary measures from Prussia if he approved such a budget.[62]

While the Wirtschaftsbund and its allies celebrated the city parliament's refusal to raise taxes as evidence of the "formation of a *Bürgerblock* (bourgeois block)," the risk of subjecting Düsseldorf to the budgetary dictates of Prussian authorities brought the city parliament to reconsider tax increases.[63] The Center Party called on the city parliament in May to approve a budget with some tax increase in order to preserve self-administration, and Lehr managed to patch together a majority in July of the Center, SPD, DVP, and DDP to raise the surcharge to the property tax by 35 percent to 225 percent, the surcharge to the trade tax on profits by 35 percent to 455 percent, and the surcharge to the trade tax on income by 170 percent to 1,530 percent.[64] This tax package demonstrated the desire of the city parliament to preserve self-administration but did not come close to balancing the budget. By late October 1930, Lehr reported an increase in the welfare budget of RM 5.5 million and a decline of RM 1.8 million in tax revenues transferred from the Reich.[65]

Municipal authorities ultimately failed to preserve self-administration during the depression. A series of emergency laws created conditions for reducing self-administration. The first emergency decree of 26 July 1930 limited the right of communes to raise surcharges to the property and trade taxes unless communal authorities simultaneously levied a beer tax, an alcohol tax, and a head tax (*Bürgersteuer*). Other emergency decrees cut the trade tax and placed controls on communal access to domestic credit.[66] From late 1930 onward, authorities of the German states pressed municipalities to levy emergency taxes to balance budgets. In the most dramatic cases, states appointed savings commissars. Prussia instituted tax raises recommended by a savings commissar in Frankfurt in 1930, and other cities began to fall under the dictates of savings commissars including Berlin and Breslau.[67] In other cases such as in Düsseldorf, the Prussian government simply approved tax increases agreed to by the Magistrat without obtaining the approval of the city parliament.[68]

The final act in the collapse of municipal finance came with the banking crisis of 1931. The collapse of the central European banking system set off a run on municipal savings banks. Düsseldorf's Mayor Lehr noted on 17 July 1931 that the run on the savings bank had left the city in the position of bridging a RM 8 million gap in short-term credit per month to cover daily obligations.[69]

From Finance to Destabilization?

Causing a crisis of self-administration, the collapse of municipal finance between 1930 and 1932 marked a momentous turn in the history of German cities, but the deterioration of municipal finance during the depression offers only a partial explanation of the transition from recovery to destabilization. Municipal reliance on short-term credit exacerbated the effects of the banking collapse of 1931, yet the municipal contribution to financial crisis was only a coda to the reaction against municipal policies and politics of recovery. During the period of stabilization, cities served as chief targets of early moves of reaction against programs and political arrangements of stabilization. By 1931, city governments were scarcely salient objects for attack by the enemies of the Weimar Republic.

The complex political responses to municipal budgetary troubles once again reveal that local politics of the Weimar Republic cannot be analyzed solely in terms of any conflict between the political Left and Right. Financial pressures could create cleavages, not only between parties of the Left and Right, but also between local and national governments and between city parliaments and municipal administrations. Thus, rising welfare expenditures brought expressions of resentment from civic leaders of all parties against state and national authorities who failed to provide sufficient revenue for tasks delegated to municipalities. Within municipal governments, city councilors from the Left and Right came to look with unease on the costs of programs of economic promotion advocated by ambitious mayors. Reservations about soaring expenditures for ambitious projects of economic promotion created serious divisions between Frankfurt's Mayor Landmann and his nominal allies in the city parliament, and other prominent mayors including Düsseldorf's Robert Lehr faced similar criticism.

By the end of the period of stabilization many of the most vociferous critics of municipal finances were found on the bourgeois Right, particularly in splinter parties like Düsseldorf's Wirtschaftsbund; however, budgetary shortfalls and the difficulty of converting short-term debt into long-term loans caused concern across much of the political spectrum. By 1929, the German Association of Cities, hardly an organization dominated by Socialists, called for more cautious financial policy by its member cities. The Board of the Association of Cities advised retrenchment, urging all cities "that every individual municipal administration be guided by still greater thrift ... and avoid further short-term debt."[70]

Even Social Democrats offered little opposition to the movement towards municipal financial retrenchment. Hanover's Social Democrats, though victorious in municipal elections in November 1929, made little effort to increase municipal spending for any tasks. Despite accusing the administration of using the need for savings as an excuse to limit cultural and social tasks, councilor Westphal of the SPD acknowledged that the Social Democrats took difficult financial conditions as grounds to restrict motions for new projects. To take one example, the SPD decided to delay introducing any motion to build a new professional school. Mocking the SPD for having introduced proposals for only minor alterations in the budget for 1930, Hanover's KPD taunted its Social Democratic rivals for inaction. The KPD's councilor Sedat stated that "nothing is done for the worker in reality."[71]

If there was comparatively little disagreement over proper municipal financial policy at the end of the period of destabilization, how did budgetary trends contribute to political destabilization? Constructing a case for a close relationship between financial troubles and political crisis, Knut Borchardt suggests that a sick economy left politicians with few options other than an authoritarian political solution to economic crisis.[72] Whatever the possible drawbacks to arguing that financial crisis narrowed the range of political options, Borchardt offers useful suggestions about financial roots of reaction to Weimar democratization.

Even as budgetary woes fed a wide variety of political conflicts, discontent with municipal finance bolstered attacks against the democratization of municipal government. It was not surprising that organized landlords, political losers of municipal democratization, often joined in reaction against democratization. Analyzing the politics of organized landlords in Berlin, Detlef Lehnert observes that "the democratization of communal representation was included among the strictly rejected elements of the Weimar System" prior to the municipal election of 1929.[73] In Düsseldorf, *Haus und Grund*, the newspaper of Düsseldorf's House and Property Owners' Association, assigned guilt for "financial mismanagement" to the "communal representation" and observed that "the unfortunate party spirit governs here ... since the postwar era."[74]

Local reaction against democratization created an unusual alliance between splinter parties of the bourgeois Right with populist aspirations and commercial and industrial interest groups. Local splinter parties and industrial interest groups both attributed excessive spending to the politicization of government and competition for votes, a diagnosis which encouraged proposals to reduce the influence of parliaments. In Düsseldorf, the Chamber of Industry and Commerce recommended increasing the power of corporate representatives of economic interests or, alternately, requiring the approval of the mayor for any proposal to increase the ordinary budget.[75]

Criticism of municipal finance not only bolstered critiques of democracy, but also confronted most established parties with a political dilemma. For all the widespread acceptance of an imperative for retrenchment by city governments, few municipal political groupings were in a position to profit from calls for spending cuts. Attacking municipal financial practices suggested that past municipal policy was at least partly to blame for budgetary troubles, and very few municipal politicians or officials could truthfully claim to have opposed most large-scale municipal initiatives of the period of stabilization.

Notes

1. Kolb, *The Weimar Republic*, pp. 193, 196.
2. *Statistisches Jahrbuch deutscher Städte* 22 (1927), p. 5.
3. In the great majority of cities, loans provided over 80% of extraordinary revenue. See Ibid. 25 (1930), p. 179.
4. Ibid. 22 (1927), pp. 15-18.
5. Wells, *German Cities*, pp. 228-30.
6. LA Berlin STB 1533/I, Städte, Staat und Wirtschaft, p. 64.
7. Gerold Ambrosius, *Die öffentliche Wirtschaft in der Weimarer Republik: Kommunal Versorgungsunternehmen als Instrumente der Wirtschaftspolitik* (Baden-Baden, 1984), pp. 123-31.
8. StVV Frankfurt, 1925, p. 324; 1926, pp. 7, 795, 978; 1927, p. 345; 1928, pp. 513, 843.
9. Ibid., 1928, p. 360.
10. StVV Düsseldorf, 1925, pp. 114-16; Josef Wilden, "Das Verhältnis der Wirtschaft zur Stadtverwaltung," *Wirtschaft und Verkehr* 3 (1925): 43; and StVV Düsseldorf, 1926, p. 117.
11. StVV Düsseldorf, 1926, pp. 156-59; 1927, pp. 69-70, 158, 198, 282, 298-300; 1928, pp. 2-13, 83-95, 104; StA Düsseldorf XXIV 1013, *Düsseldorfer Nachrichten*, 17 December 1927; and StVV Düsseldorf, 1929, pp. 134-37.
12. BVK Hannover, 1925-1926, pp. 209, 1434-35, 1821, 1857-67; and 1926-1927, pp. 509, 571, 590.
13. Ibid., 1926-1927, pp. 677, 702, 737, 740, 906, 998, 1080-81.
14. Ibid., 1926-1927, p. 689.
15. StA Frankfurt U190 IV, Dr. Herbert Meyer, "Die Anleiheverschuldung der deutschen Städte;" Theo Balderston, *The Origins and Course of the German Economic Crisis 1923-1932* (Berlin, 1993), p. 254; and StA Frankfurt Stadtkämmerei 116, Frankfurter Bank Direktion, 5 September 1927.
16. NWHStA 31318 Regierung Düsseldorf, Oberbürgermeister, 13 July 1927; StA Frankfurt Stadtkämmerei Zugang 3/75 170, Beschluß der Finanzdeputation, 31 August 1927; and StA Frankfurt U190 IV, Asch to Landmann, 2 July 1927.
17. McNeil, *American Money and the Weimar Republic*, p. 48.
18. BA Koblenz R2/2002, Übersicht über die Tätigkeit der Beratungsstelle; and McNeil, *American Money and the Weimar Republic*, pp. 216-18.
19. StA Hannover VII B 2D 127.
20. StA Frankfurt U237; and StA Frankfurt U240.
21. *Statistisches Jahrbuch deutscher Städte* 23 (1928), p. 68; 24 (1929), p. 53; 25 (1930), p. 220; and 26 (1931), p. 80.
22. StVV Düsseldorf 1927, 1-2, 18; and BVK Hannover 1929-1930, 24 March 1930, Wohnungsbauprogramm 1930.
23. StA Frankfurt U241, Inlandsanleihe 20 Mill. RM; and NWHStA Düsseldorf 31318, Oberbürgermeister to Regierungspräsident, 5 November 1926.
24. NWHStA Regierung Düsseldorf 31318, Bezirksausschuß, 4 March 1927.
25. BVK Hannover, 1926-1927, p. 986.
26. StA Frankfurt, U246, Aufnahme einer Anleihe, 2 July 1930.
27. Ibid., U190 IV, Herbert Meyer, "Die Anleiheverschuldung der deutschen Städte," p. 7.
28. StA Frankfurt Stadtkämmerei 144, Fragebogen, 28 November 1927; and NWHStA 31318 Regierung Düsseldorf, Fragebogen, 21 December 1927.

29. StA Hannover VII B 2D 127, Übersicht über das Stand das Vermögen und die Schulden Hannover, 31 March 1928.

30. *Statistisches Jahrbuch deutscher Städte* 22 (1927), p. 18.

31. Welfare accounted for most of the increase in total expenditures for welfare and health care. Total welfare expenditures per inhabitant in cities with a population of over 200,000 residents rose by RM 16 between 1925 and 1929. Uncovered welfare expenditures rose by nearly RM 13 per inhabitant in the same period. See *Statistisches Jahrbuch deutscher Städte* 26 (1931), p. 357.

32. StVV Düsseldorf, 1926, p. 27; and StVV Frankfurt, 1926, p. 145.

33. BVK Hannover 1925-1926, p. 1290; and 1926-1927, p. 679.

34. StVV Frankfurt, 1929, p. 125; and 1930, p. 185.

35. StVV Düsseldorf, 1925, pp. 307-8; and Stadtverordneten Köngeter, "Der Nachtragsetat der Stadt Düsseldorf," *Wirtschaft und Verkehr* 5 (1927): 546.

36. StA Düsseldorf XXIV 1113 *Düsseldorfer Lokal Zeitung*, 11 November 1928; and *Haus und Grund*, 29 December 1928.

37. *Statistisches Jahrbuch deutscher Städte* 25 (1930), pp. 37-39, 51.

38. StVV Frankfurt 1925, p. 1109; 1926, pp. 139, 787, 794, 1159; 1927, pp. 1088, 1252; and 1928, pp. 146-71.

39. Ibid., 1929, p. 187.

40. Ibid., 1928, pp. 1187-1206.

41. StA Düsseldorf, Nachlaß Lehr 3, Stadtverordnetenfraktion der DVP to städtische Verwaltung, 11 November 1926; and DVP Düsseldorf to Lehr, 10 December 1926.

42. StVV Frankfurt, 1925, pp. 870, 876.

43. Ibid., 1926, p. 657 and; Rebentisch, *Ludwig Landmann*, pp. 238-39.

44. StVV Frankfurt, 1928, pp. 813-28; and Rebentisch, *Ludwig Landmann*, pp. 238-42.

45. Rebentisch, *Ludwig Landmann*, pp. 188-90; and StVV Frankfurt 1929, p. 187.

46. StVV Frankfurt, 1925, p. 317; 1926, pp. 205, 306; 1927, pp. 370, 377; and 1928, pp. 1425-29.

47. Ibid., 1927, p. 1213; 1928, pp. 31-48; 1929, pp. 629-30; and Rebentisch, *Ludwig Landmann*, pp. 181-84.

48. Schwarz, *Adenauer*, pp. 208-9.

49. NWHStA 31318 Regierung Düsseldorf, Oberbürgermeister, 13 July 1927; StA Hannover VII B 2D 127, Übersicht, 31 March 1928; StA Frankfurt Stadtkämmerei 176.

50. StVV Düsseldorf, 1925, p. 93.

51. Ibid., 1926, p. 222; and 1927, p. 84.

52. StA Frankfurt U 190 IV, Asch to Landmann, 2 July 1927; StVV Frankfurt, 1929, p. 772; StA Frankfurt Stadtkämmerei 145, 18 June 1929, 9 July 1929; and StA Frankfurt U244, 9 August 1929, 15 August 1929.

53. StVV Frankfurt, 1929, pp. 837-38.

54. Ibid., 1929, p. 894.

55. Ibid., 1929, pp. 216-17, 242.

56. BVK Hannover, 1928-1929, pp. 35-36, 39; StA Hannover VII B 2D 116 II; StA Hannover VII B 2D 124, Magistrat to Regierungspräsident, 12 June 1928.

57. StA Hannover, Finanz Kommission, 1927-1928, pp. 102-5; Baudeputation, 11 January 1928, p. 7; and Finanz Kommission, 1928-1929, pp. 68-9.

58. BVK Hannover 1928-1929, p. 230.

59. BVK Hannover, 1928-1929, pp. 187-88, 230.

60. Arnold Köttgen, *Die Krise der kommunalen Selbstverwaltung* (Tübingen, 1931).

61. LA Berlin STA 397, Niederschrift ... des engeren Vorstand, 21 December 1929.

62. StVV Düsseldorf, 1930, pp. 96, 98, 212-13.

63. *Haus und Grund*, 3 May 1930.

64. StVV Düsseldorf, 1930, pp. 237, 275.

65. Ibid., 1930, p. 362.

66. Adelheid von Saldern, "Kommunale Verarmung und Armut in den Kommunen während der Große Krise (1929 bis 1933). Am Beispiel der Finanz- und Wohnungs(bau)politik," *Soziale Bewegungen* 3: 72-73.

67. StVV Frankfurt, 1930, p. 1181; Wells, *German Cities*, p. 147; von Saldern, "Kommunale Verarmung," p. 86; and McElligott, "The Collapse of Weimar," p. 23.

68. StVV Düsseldorf, 1931, pp. 145-46.

69. James, *The German Slump*, pp. 100, 104-5; and StVV Düsseldorf, 1931, p. 198.

70. LA Berlin, STA 163, Deutscher Städtetag, der Vorstand, 5 November 1929.

71. BVK Hannover, 1929-1930, pp. 315, 339, 509, 566-78, 594.

72. Borchardt, "Wirtschaftliche Ursachen," pp. 183-205; and "Zwangslagen und Handlungsspielräume," pp. 165-82.

73. Lehnert, *Kommunale Politik*, p. 307.

74. *Haus und Grund*, 19 November 1927.

75. *Veröffentlichungen des Reichsverbandes der deutschen Industrie*, Nr. 42 (Berlin: 1928), p. 20; Wilden, "Das Verhältnis der Wirtschaft zur Stadtverwaltung," *Wirtschaft und Verkehr* 43; and Köngeter, "Der Nachtragshaushalt der Stadt Düsseldorf," *Wirtschaft und Verkehr* 5 (1927): 548.

Chapter 4

CITIES AND DISTRIBUTIONAL CONFLICT

Far more than an internal matter for debate by city councilors and mayors during the Weimar Republic, municipal policies of recovery became the subject of controversy at the national and even international level during the Weimar period of stabilization. Contemporary belief in the importance of the municipal role in recovery, for good or for ill, can be detected, not only in the promises of mayors or in the titles of books and magazines commemorating civic deeds, but also in the vociferous attacks of powerful critics against municipal policy. Well before the economic collapse of the 1930s or the National Socialist political breakthrough, municipal authorities served as chief targets of early reaction against policies of recovery. After taking up ambitious recovery programs, mayors and city councilors found themselves accused of both having damaged municipal finances and of having hampered overall German recovery.

The product of local pressure for recovery, the expansion of municipal activity, encountered fierce resistance at the national level. As city governments sought revenue to cover the costs of recovery, so too did other levels of government and the private economy. The ensuing competition for resources between sectors of the private economy and city governments provoked intense criticism of cities in many economic circles. Gerhard Schulz, noting the conjunction of the growth of social policy with limited resources, suggests that "the controversy between the free economy and public finance was unavoidable."[1] Municipal authorities, for their part, paid a high political price for their entrance into national distributional conflicts.

Distributional conflict of the Weimar period of stabilization set off a multi-sided struggle between several major public and private actors. The Association of Cities, the central lobbying organization for cities, spoke as the chief advocate for municipal interests, but individual mayors also defended municipal access to resources. Both the Association of Cities and mayors encountered attacks led by major economic interest groups, including the German Association of Industry and the Langnamverein, and by banking authorities, most notably Hjalmar Schacht, the President of the Reichsbank. While the lines of distributional conflict often ran between private and public actors, public institutions did not invariably act in concert. To a significant degree, municipalities, state governments, and the national government all took independent parts in distributional struggles. Even as they faced criticism of public spending from advocates of the private economy, public authorities simultaneously competed among themselves for sources of public revenue.

Distributional Conflict: Cities and the Private Economy

Throughout the period of Weimar stabilization, leading economic interest groups charged that public authorities in general and city governments in particular spent an excessive portion of national income. The German Association of Industry, for example, called repeatedly for reductions in public spending. In December 1925 the German Association of Industry recommended an across-the-board 20 percent cut in public spending. Convinced that all levels of government damaged the economy, the German Association of Industry singled out communal taxation for attack, charging that "the financial management of the communes is felt as especially heavy in the framework of the entire tax burden." Communal taxation amounted to "nothing other than the expropriation of private assets in favor of the public hand."[2]

Despite simmering discontent regarding the levels of communal taxation, credit markets were the chief battle grounds for distributional conflict at the national level between cities and the private economy during the Weimar period of stabilization. Increases on surcharges to the state trade tax and state property taxes might anger business organizations in a particular city, but municipal pursuit of loans created competition for credit between local authorities and the private economy at the national and even international level. Economic interest groups and financial authorities took note of the municipal appetite for credit. As William McNeil observes, "the ability of the cities to attract American capital unleashed a multi-sided power struggle within Germany."[3] For leading economic interest groups, municipal borrowing showed the costs of excessive state activity for a private economy short of capital for economic reconstruction.

Municipal representatives, for their part, consistently maintained that cities deserved the same access as all other borrowers to all types of credit. Amidst debates over the role of the Advisory Board for Foreign Credit set up to review municipal applications for foreign loans, the Association of Cities opposed any special restrictions on municipal access to loans. The committee of the Association of Cities resolved in October 1925 that the "acquisition of loans for the productive aims of the public economy is of the same economic importance as the borrowing of the private economy."[4] Resisting calls for restrictions on municipal borrowing, the Association of Cities shared the belief of its critics in the private economy that cities and sectors of the private economy were engaged in a distributional struggle for credit. When the Advisory Board for Foreign Credit moved to postpone hearings on municipal requests for loans in the winter of 1927-1928, the committee of the Association of Cities voiced fears that "circles of the economy or of agriculture" would claim foreign credit for themselves, leaving cities empty-handed.[5]

From the early years of the period of stabilization, cities engaged in the pursuit of loans faced their most steadfast single opponent in Reichsbank President Hjalmar Schacht. Alarmed by municipal pursuit of all sources of credit, Schacht worked to reserve credit for investment in production. Schacht viewed production as the key to recovery. "The most important problem of the present," he declared, "consists of the promotion of production with all means." Recognizing the shortage of domestic capital, Schacht acknowledged that German industry required foreign loans. He told representatives of the state governments in February 1926 that "foreign credit must first flow to industry, which cannot complete its reconstruction without foreign capital."[6]

Eager to limit foreign loans to the level required for production, Schacht sought to preserve domestic capital for investment in production. Placing highest priority on satisfying the capital needs of private industry, he called for holding down state consumption.[7] The Reichsbank President boasted that his efforts to restrict consumption were not calculated to make him popular in all quarters. "A warning to reduced consumption," he said, makes no one popular, especially if this warning is directed to individual people," but added that savings by all levels of the state would enable individuals to avoid the hardships of cutting consumption.[8]

Schacht's stance against government borrowing concurred closely with the views of leading industrial interest groups, which agreed that domestic capital should flow to industry rather than to public authorities such as city governments. Speaking to the chief committee of the German Association of Industry in October 1928, Geheimrat Kastl repeated charges that municipal borrowing reduced industrial access to capital, thereby crippling the entire German economy. Noting the decline of American lending to Germany, Kastl decried continued communal borrowing from German lenders. The communes, he claimed, "exhaust the domestic capital market to a large degree." He accused city governments of hindering the ability of industry to obtain credit "in a very regrettable manner for economic development."[9] As the period of stabilization drew to an end, the German Association of Industry thus accused cities of having crowded the private economy out of the capital market, charging in 1929 that municipal borrowing practices had damaged "issue possibilities for all rightful borrowers." Municipalities had "pushed the private economy ... out of the capital market," causing unemployment and new burdens for the communes. These consequences made necessary the creation of central controls over municipal access to all forms of credit.[10]

The chief municipal programs of recovery played a major part in generating the intense distributional conflict between city governments and German industry. Looking over municipal budgets, opponents of municipal borrowing had particular reason to take notice of municipal economic promotion and support for housing construction, both of which presented other economic sectors with competition for capital. Between 1925 and 1929, total investment in housing accounted for 17.8 percent of domestic gross investment.[11] Virtually all of the investment in housing construction came from domestic sources. Blocking the use of foreign credit for housing construction, the Advisory Board made one significant concession, offering in 1928 to approve RM 100 million in foreign loans for private mortgage banks, but this ruling had little effect in practice as mortgage banks only managed to obtain about RM 9 million by early 1929.[12]

Economic interest groups objected to massive investment of domestic capital, either from loans or from the rent tax, in housing construction. During the early years of stabilization, after hyperinflation had wiped out a large part of German savings, municipal investment of capital from savings banks in building projects, including housing construction, alarmed industrial and commercial interest groups. A 1925 declaration issued by leading economic interest groups of the northern Rhine and Westphalia, including the Chambers of Industry and Commerce of Düsseldorf, Solingen, Cologne, Essen, Bochum, Dortmund, Duisburg, and Münster, as well as the Langnam Verein, noted that cities and other communities had become the "greatest customers of the construction trade." The interest groups asserted that there was "nearly no capital formation outside of the savings banks… ," and complained that capital from savings banks was not being supplied "mainly to the capital-poor economy to raise productivity." Logically enough, they demanded that any "newly formed domestic capital" should also be "supplied mainly to the productive economy."[13]

Envious of municipal control of capital in savings banks, industrial and commercial interest groups also opposed the investment of the proceeds of the HZS (Hauszinssteuer) in housing construction. Demanding an end to the use of the HZS for mortgages, the German Association of Industry, the Langnam Verein, and the Congress of German Industry and Commerce contended that HZS mortgages permitted public authorities to build up capital holdings.[14] In 1929 the German Association of Industry repeated its strictures against investing public funds in housing construction: spending public money for housing construction had "greatly hampered capital formation."[15]

Calling for an end to HZS mortgages left economic interest groups to answer the obvious question of how German communities would then be able to promote housing construction. The Congress of German Industry and Commerce, the German Association of Industry, and the Langnam Verein advised that the proceeds of the HZS should be used for interest subsidies, a step actually taken in Prussia in 1927 to supplement direct investment of the HZS in housing construction.[16] In theory, interest subsidies would attract private capital for investment in housing construction, but was there really enough private capital available to finance housing construction programs? The Langnam Verein admitted that it was uncertain whether the private capital market could supply the funds necessary for housing programs. If private credit was unavailable, the construction of new housing would have to wait for more favorable conditions on the capital market.[17] A committee set up by the German Association of Industry to study housing policy reached similar conclusions. The German Association of Industry's housing committee recognized that private capital and the sale of mortgage bonds might not yield sufficient funds to finance housing programs, but insisted that a shortage of readily available capital did not justify withdrawing capital with a tax, the HZS, from the economy. A solution to the housing shortage would only be possible if the "necessary free capital is available."[18] If pursuit of recovery fostered competition between public and private investment plans, industrial interest groups advocated giving priority to the private economy.

Alarmed by the level of investment of domestic capital in housing construction, industrial and commercial interest groups received reinforcement from the Reichsbank. A Reichsbank memorandum of June 1927 accepted the estimate that the total bill for housing construction would reach approximately RM 3 billion by the end of September 1927, a sum which the Reichsbank thought stretched acceptable limits in an economy suffering from rationalization difficulties and capital shortages. The housing shortage simply could not be ended in "a couple of years." Until the "crisis" on the capital market ended, expenditures for housing construction would have to "comply with the ability to pay of the capital market."[19]

The Boundary of Economic Activity: Cold Socialization

Perturbed by massive public investment in the promotion of housing construction, leading economic interest groups and the Reichsbank also criticized the flow of credit towards investment in municipal economic promotion. Through the spring of 1928, cities with over 200,000 residents spent more than RM 30,000,000 in long-term foreign credit on gas supply, nearly RM 40,000,000 in long-term foreign credit on water supply, and more than RM 270,000,000 in long term foreign credit on electricity supply. This last sum amounted to 55 percent of all long-term foreign credit spent by large cities by 1928.[20]

Opposition to the level of investment in the communal economy fed conflict over the proper boundaries of public and private activity. Noting the high levels of spending on municipal economic promotion, the foes of municipal borrowing charged that city governments interfered in areas best left to the private economy. The battle against communal economic activity reached a first peak during the Weimar period of stabilization with the campaign against "cold socialization" of the winter of 1925/26, a term reportedly coined by Schacht which referred to public interference in the private economy. Leading economic interest groups including the Central Association of German Banks and Bankers, the Association of German Industry, the Congress of German Industry and Commerce, and numerous local chambers of industry and commerce threw their weight behind the struggle against "cold socialization." The Association of German Industry maintained in December 1925 that communes and their firms "have expanded to areas that are to be regarded as purely private economic activity."[21]

Countering the campaign against cold socialization, representatives of municipalities stressed the long-term continuity in communal economic activity. The operation of the core firms of the communal economy had, after all, been established as suitable tasks for city governments long before the war. The Association of Cities noted in October 1926 that "in the course of development it has become a matter of course that gas, water, electricity, and transit firms lie in the hand of the communes."[22]

Amidst the debate over cold socialization, municipal authorities saw a new economic threat to the core firms of the communal economy in plans to create long-distance gas and electricity distribution networks. Administrations of cities such as Düsseldorf and Frankfurt responded to the campaign against "cold socialization" by vigorously defending the boundaries of the communal economy against private utilities. Thus, Frankfurt sought to fend off gas supply by the Ruhr Coal Syndicate, and Düsseldorf's administration became embroiled in a dispute with the Rheinisch-Westfälisches Elektrizitätswerk (RWE), a private electricity distribution network. Asserting that it possessed sufficient generating capacity to supply Düsseldorf with electricity, RWE tried to block approval of a loan in 1925 to cover the expansion of Düsseldorf's electricity plant, but Düsseldorf's Mayor Lehr countered that RWE could not meet Düsseldorf's peak demand. Düsseldorf's administration subsequently began to purchase shares of RWE in order to try to win influence over the city's chief private rival.[23]

The municipal defense of core economic activities extended to the communal savings banks under attack from private banks during the campaign against cold socialization. A report for the committee of the Association of Cities advised instruction of member cities "about the attack by the banks ... in order to organize a comprehensive resistance." Joining in the municipal response to the cold-socialization campaign, savings banks issued a statement referring to "cold socialization" as a "slogan." The German savings banks charged that their private counterparts had adopted the term "cold socialization" in order to win allies from other private economic associations.[24]

Gathering widespread support from leading economic interest groups at the national level, the campaign against "cold socialization," in turn, presented a threat to the political consensus of recovery at the municipal level, but attacks by economic interest groups did not suddenly erode support for the communal economy in city

parliaments on either the political Left or Right. Bourgeois city councilors generally did not see long-established elements of the communal economy as evidence of a wave of "cold socialization." The
rationale for municipal control of utilities was seldom at issue during the period of stabilization. While voicing doubts about the suitability of communal enterprises such as the supply of wine for
Düsseldorf's music hall, Dr. Wilms of Düsseldorf's DVP expressed a
common view when he noted that bourgeois politicians were not
uniformly opposed to the communalization of firms and defended
communal ownership of utilities as well as slaughter houses.[25]

Though it did not sweep away political backing for the communal economy, the campaign against "cold socialization" found some
resonance in municipal politics. Bourgeois city councilors, in particular, displayed a mixed response to the campaign, continuing to
back core communal firms while advising limits on the expansion of
communal economic activity. Speaking in 1926 during the first campaign against "cold socialization," councilor Schwietzke of Düsseldorf's DNVP praised Mayor Lehr, a staunch advocate of communal
economic promotion, yet also declared that "we oppose any progress
towards communal socialization."[26]

The misgivings about communal economic promotion fostered by
the campaign against "cold socialization" grew towards the end of
the era of stabilization. Local reaction against communal economic
activity was most pronounced in cities such as Frankfurt where
municipal economic promotion was most ambitious. In December of
1928, Frankfurt's bourgeois parties joined in calling for an investigation of the expansion of Frankfurt's communal economic activity.[27] Attacks against municipal interference in the private economy
became a regular feature of the campaign by the bourgeois Right
against Mayor Landmann in 1929. The booklet, *Wie Oberbürgermeister Dr. Landmann regierte*, a vitriolic assault on Landmann published
for the communal election of November 1929, asserted that the proliferation of city firms presented private companies with unfair competition. Emboldened by victory, city councilors from the bourgeois
Right in the new city parliament continued to attack the over-exten-
sion of Frankfurt's communal economy.[28]

Distributional Conflict between Public Authorities

While economic interest groups and the Reichsbank saw municipal
spending and economic activity as particularly egregious examples

of mistreatment of the private economy by government or the public hand, the very conception of a conflict pitting the "public hand" against the private economy gave a false impression of government unity. Municipal authorities, for their part, saw themselves as fighting to defend the autonomy of city government against pressure from both the private economy and from other levels of government, namely the Reich and state governments. As Konrad Adenauer observed in 1926, "the struggle against self-administration starts from the economy and from the Reich and state."[29] Adenauer had reason to identify other levels of government as opponents of cities. Defending municipal access to credit and operation of communal firms from attacks emanating from the private economy and Reichsbank, city governments simultaneously took part in struggles over the distribution of revenue and assignment of duties between the different levels of the Weimar State.

Without exception, municipal leaders charged that the Reich and state governments unfairly burdened cities by assigning new duties to cities while cutting municipal control over sources of revenue. Having lost the ability to levy a surcharge to the income tax with Erzberger's finance reform of 1919, city governments subsequently saw the Reich and states further restrict municipal control over taxes during the early years of the period of Weimar stabilization. During 1925 and 1926, the Reich and states cut the wage tax, amusement tax, and land purchase tax, and eliminated the drink tax. Subsequent losses of municipal revenue from these taxes, concluded Oskar Mulert, President of the Association of Cities, placed pressure on city governments to raise the trade tax.[30] Analyzing the impact of tax cuts and delegated burdens on one city's taxes, Essen's Mayor Bracht calculated that the increased expenditures and decreased income resulting from Reich and state measures amounted to either 95 percent of Essen's income from the property tax or to 65 percent of Essen's income from the trade tax.[31]

Dismayed by the continuing encroachments on municipal control over revenue, the Association of Cities lobbied persistently for at least a partial reversal of Erzberger's income tax reform. Oskar Mulert of the Association of Cities called for reintroducing the communal surcharge to the income tax. The Association of Cities maintained in October 1926 that the communal surcharge was the "prerequisite for a truly responsible communal thrift."[32]

Despite the Association of Cities' persistent support for a return to a communal surcharge to the income tax, some municipal leaders actually doubted whether a surcharge adjustable by cities actually offered the best means to increasing communal revenue. The introduction of a surcharge would carry both financial and political risks. A communal surcharge to the income tax might come at the cost of a reduction in transfers from other taxes to the communes, and municipal control over the surcharge to the income tax might also create new political disputes within municipal governments. Setting the level of the communal surcharge to the income tax had, after all, created conflicts within municipal governments in the past.[33]

Whatever the merits or disadvantages of a communal surcharge to the income tax, the obstacles to any imminent return to such a surcharge compelled municipal authorities to look for other methods to increasing municipal revenue. Municipal leaders intent on gaining a larger share of tax revenue for cities sought to adjust the *Finanzausgleich*, the agreement for redistributing revenue between the Reich, states, and local authorities. Municipal representatives seldom found either the Prussian or the Reich Finanzausgleich satisfactory. The provisional Reich Finanzausgleich of 1927 actually raised the guaranteed communal share of revenues from taxes including the income tax, but the Association of Cities saw this measure as inadequate compensation for the elimination of a special guarantee covering the communal share of the turnover tax revenue. The Committee of the Association of Cities concluded that the provisional Reich Finanzausgleich of 1927 brought "significant deterioration" of municipal finances.[34]

Frustrated by the readiness of the Reich and state governments to delegate duties to cities while restricting municipal control over revenue, many municipal leaders advocated plans for administrative reform of the relationship between the different levels of the German State. Complaining of the duplication of Reich and state competency in local matters, President Mulert of the Association of Cities favored the creation of a decentralized unitary state. This proposal, though not supported by all mayors, appealed to many influential municipal leaders as a means to recapturing a greater degree of self-administration for city governments. "Only in a unitary state … which will be a decentralized unitary state," argued Frankfurt's Mayor Landmann, "can the self-administration gain its rights."[35]

Municipal favor for proposals to create a unitary state increased tension between mayors and the state governments, most notably Prussia. Looking to end the duplicity of Reich and state competency in local affairs, municipal leaders suggested that municipal interaction with other levels of government should be concentrated at the interface between city government and the national government.

State governments, in contrast, would, at the very least, have reduced authority in a unitary state. While municipal supporters of a unitary state did not go so far as to call for abolition of the state governments, they did speak critically of the state governments. President Mulert referred to "a hollowing out of the communes by the states."[36]

Mistrust between Prussia and city governments surfaced in a dispute between Prussian Interior Minister Grzesinski and Mayor Gustav Böß of Berlin in 1927 and 1928. At the 1927 convention of the Association of Cities, Grzesinski denied that state oversight constituted an impediment to the free activity of local administration."[37] Informing the 1928 annual meeting of the Association of Cities that the free initiative of communal administration was not obstructed, but warning that he would not approve all municipal incorporation plans, Grzesinski earned a public rebuke from Mayor Böß who told the Association of Cities that the Prussian Interior Minister's speech contained "confirmation of our most serious anxiety about the restriction of self-administration." Frankfurt's Mayor Landmann felt compelled to assure Grzesinski of the absence of resentment by Prussian cities against the Prussian Ministry of the Interior, but Grzesinski subsequently informed the leadership of the Association of Cities that Böß's criticism caused him to reconsider whether he should take part in the meeting for 1929.[38] Although Mulert again invited Grzesinski to address the Association of Cites and Böß, embroiled in the Sklarek scandal, absented himself from the annual meeting in September 1929, the very public dispute between the mayor of Germany's largest city and the Prussian Minister of the Interior revealed persistent tensions between Prussia and Prussian city governments. (For more discussion of the political impact of the Sklarek scandal, see chapter 7.)

Conflict over the distribution of duties and revenue occurred, not only between different levels of the German State, but also between city governments. Prussian municipal leaders agreed that the 1927 Finanzausgleich did not provide sufficient revenue for city governments, but they struggled among themselves to come up with an alternative proposal that would treat all Prussian cities fairly. Neither population nor prewar tax revenue provided a fair measure for distributing tax revenue between cities.[39]

In 1927, Berlin went so far as to threaten to leave the Association of Cities on the grounds that the Association was not considering Berlin's financial needs in proposals to revise the Finanzausgleich. Berlin's municipal officials maintained that the measures used to distribute tax revenues discriminated against Berlin. As Berlin's city treasurer Dr. Lange explained to the committee of the Prussian Association of Cities, the use of prewar tax revenue figures in the formula for postwar tax revenue redistribution had the effect of lowering Berlin's share of the income tax. Noting Berlin's special burdens as a destination for internal migration and as the capital city, Berlin's administration insisted that tax income gathered in Berlin should not be redistributed to any other community unless it was previously determined that the community in question had relatively higher burdens than Berlin.[40]

Although the Association of Cities managed to keep Berlin in its fold, German cities never managed to resolve exactly how they wished to see the Finanzausgleich revised. When Hanover's Mayor Menge told the committee of the Prussian Association of Cities that his city could not afford to pay the taxes of cities in the Ruhr, Essen's Mayor Bracht reminded him that coal and iron producers of the Ruhr had to face competition on the world market. The committee agreed to approve a motion submitted by its own financial committee calling for raising the communal share in the income tax and for considering local tax revenue in to determine how to redistribute tax revenue.[41] Unable to reach a consensus on a new plan for distributing tax revenue, the Prussian Association of Cities turned over the dilemma to a specially-created subcommittee of its financial committee.

Distributional Conflict and Reaction

Social stabilization and economic promotion, though supported by a broad consensus locally, produced intense distributional conflicts and criticism of municipal governments at the national level. The multiplication of local pressure for recovery transformed cities as a group into a major participant in competition for loans during the Weimar period of stabilization. In a climate of rivalry for resources to pay for varied public and private programs of recovery and rationalization, municipal pursuit of loans fostered reaction against city governments by other actors in distributional competition as well as by financial authorities.

Conflict over the distribution of resources between public institutions and the private economy provoked repeated assaults against municipalities by influential economic interest groups and financial authorities. In 1924 and 1925, as stabilization began, representatives of industry voiced fear that spending and borrowing by public institutions including city governments impeded economic recovery. In 1925 and 1926, the leading economic interest groups made city governments one of the chief targets of the campaign against cold socialization. The year 1927 saw renewed attacks against municipal borrowing by the President of the Reichsbank, and economic interest groups charged that city governments bore much of the blame for allegedly driving private industry out of credit markets as stabilization drew to a close in 1928 and 1929. In sum, these repeated attacks cast municipal recovery programs as major obstacles to German recovery.

Distributional reaction against municipal authorities fits into a broader interpretation of Weimar political strife as an example of intense conflict over the proper boundaries of state intervention. In this explanation of Weimar destabilization, the rapid expansion of state activity prompted a broad critique of new forms of state intervention that culminated in attacks against socialization and the welfare state.[42] Though conflict over the proper limits of the state came to focus on unemployment insurance, municipal programs of recovery provided important targets for enemies of an expansionist state long before Chancellor von Papen's critique of the welfare state in 1932.

Creating broad reaction against city governments in industrial and financial circles, distributional conflict at the national level in turn placed strain on the consensus of recovery at the local level. Though reaction against the expansion of municipal activity by economic interest groups and the Reichsbank did not suddenly cause city councilors to turn against central municipal programs, distributional conflict could gradually weaken the local consensus of recovery. Thus, the campaign against "cold socialization" reinforced the unease of bourgeois parties with the expansion of communal economic activity in cities like Frankfurt whose mayors pressed for ambitious and expensive projects of economic promotion.

Even as municipal authorities defended themselves against the attacks of economic interest groups and the Reichsbank, wide-ranging conflicts over the distribution of tax revenue between the different levels of the German State weakened the effectiveness of municipal lobbying organizations. United in decrying the Reich and states for delegating burdens to cities while reducing municipal control over revenue, municipal leaders agreed that cities deserved a higher proportion of tax revenue, but could not arrive at a consensus on how to divide up revenue fairly between cities. Proposals for adjusting the distribution of tax revenue set off infighting between city governments, most notably between Berlin and other cities. These internal distributional conflicts exposed rifts within the very organizations entrusted by municipalities with representing the municipal case against critics from the private economy.

Notes

1. Schulz, *Zwischen Demokratie und Diktatur*, vol. 2, p. 91.
2. Reichsverband der Deutschen Industrie, *Deutsche Wirtschafts- und Finanzpolitik* (Berlin, 1925), pp. 14, 29-30.
3. McNeil, *American Money and the Weimar Republic*, p. 77; and Schulz, *Zwischen Demokratie und Diktatur*, vol. 2, p. 90-91.
4. LA Berlin STA 654, Niederschrift über die Vorstandssitzung, 9 October 1925.
5. Ibid., STA 302, Niederschrift über die Sitzung des Vorstandes, 23 January 1928, p. 6.
6. *Akten der Reichskanzlei Weimarer Republik: Die Kabinette Luther I und II*, vol. 1, ed. Karl-Heinz Minuth (Boppard am Rhein, 1977), p. 504; and BA Potsdam 25:01 Reichsbank 6629, Besprechung mit den Vertretern der Länderregierungen, 10 February 1926.
7. *Akten der … Kabinette Luther*, vol. 1, p. 504.
8. Hjalmar Schacht, *Eigene oder geborgte Währung* (Leipzig, 1927), p. 15. Note that the economic historian Knut Borchardt also identifies state spending as consumption. Borchardt, "Wirtschaftliche Ursachen," pp. 188, 195.
9. *Veröffentlichungen des Reichsverbandes der deutschen Industrie*, Nr. 42 (Berlin, 1928), p. 26.
10. Reichsverband der deutschen Industrie, *Aufstieg oder Niedergang?* (Berlin, 1929), p. 43.
11. Michael Ruck, "Der Wohnungsbau-Schnittpunkt von Sozial- und Wirtschaftspolitik," in *Die Weimarer Republik als Wohlfahrtsstaat*, ed. Abelshauser, p. 114.
12. *Westfälisches Wohnungsblatt*, 18 (1928), pp. 96-97, 398; BA Koblenz R2/2128, Sitzungsprotokolle der Beratungsstelle, 23 March 1928, pp. 1-2; R2/2129, Sitzungsprotokolle der Beratungsstelle, 30 April 1928, p. 16; and R2/4065, Sitzungsprotokolle der Beratungsstelle, 20 February 1929, p. 6.
13. StA Frankfurt, T862 XIII, Einfluß der Bautätigkeit der öffentlichen Körperschaften auf die Wirtschaftslage, 27 July 1925; and *Wirtschaft und Verkehr* 3 (1925), pp. 474-76.
14. Westfälisches Wirtschaftsarchiv K2 Nr. 1547, Deutscher Industrie und Handelstag Entwurf: Leitsätze für die Finanzierung des Wohnungsbaus, 1927; *Mitteilungen des Vereins zur Währung der gemeinsamen wirtschaftlichen Interessen in Rhineland u. Westfalen* (1927), nr. 5, p. 54; and Westfälisches Wirtschaftsarchiv, K2 Nr. 1542, Zusammenstellung der Arbeiten des Auschusses für Wohnungspolitik des Reichsverbandes der Deutschen Industrie, pp. 19, 25, 32.

15. Ruck, "Der Wohnungsbau," p. 121; Abraham, *Collapse of the Weimar Republic*, 2d ed., pp. 225-228; and RDI, *Aufstieg oder Niedergang?* p. 22.

16. BVK Hannover 1927-1928, pp. 1-13.

17. *Mitteilungen des Vereins zur Währung der gemeinsamen wirtschaftlichen Interessen in Rheinland und Westfalen* (1927), nr. 5, pp. 54-55.

18. Westfälisches Wirtschaftsarchiv K2 Nr. 1542, Zusammenstellung der Arbeiten des Auschusses für Wohnungspolitik des Reichsverbandes der Deutschen Industrie, pp. 27-28.

19. BA Potsdam 25:01, Reichsbank 6630, Zur Frage der Finanzierung des Wohnungsbaus mit Auslandsanleihen, 28 June 1927, pp. 4-5.

20. StA Frankfurt am Main, U 190 IV, Dr. Herbert Meyer, Die Anleiheverschuldung der deutschen Städte, p. 4.

21. Carl Böhret, *Aktion gegen die `kalte Sozialisierung' 1926-1930: Ein Beitrag Zum Wirken ökonomischer Einflussverbände in der Weimarer Republik*, (Berlin, 1966), pp. 28, 38-45, 59-67; and RDI, *Deutsche Wirtschafts- und Finanzpolitik*, p. 30.

22. LA Berlin STB 1533/I, Städte Staat Wirtschaft, p. 55.

23. Hüttenberger, *Die Industrie- und Verwaltungsstadt*, p. 383; and Rebentisch, *Ludwig Landmann*, pp. 206-14.

24. LA Berlin STA 619, Vorbericht für die Vorstandssitzung ... am 14. Mai 1926; and Um das Kreditgeschäft der Sparkassen. Antwort auf die Denkschrift des Centralverbandes des deutschen Bank- und Bankiergewerbes.

25. StVV Düsseldorf, 1926, p. 48.

26. Ibid., 1926, p. 43.

27. StVV Frankfurt, 1928, pp. 1425-28.

28. *Wie Oberbürgermeister Dr. Landmann regierte*, p. 16; and StVV Frankfurt, 1929, p. 1285.

29. Adenauer, "Der Kampf gegen die Selbstverwaltung," *Kommunalpolitische Blätter* 17 (1926), p. 217.

30. LA Berlin STA 467, Vorbericht Vorstandssitzung, 10 December 1926; and STA 264, Jahresversammlung des deutschen Städtetages, 17-18 September 1926, p. 26.

31. Oberbürgermeister Bracht, "Die deutschen Städte an der Wende des Jahres," *Der Städtetag* 21 (1927): 503-4.

32. LA Berlin, STA 264, Jahresversammlung des deutschen Städtetages, 17-18 September 1926, p. 32; and STB 1533/I, Städte Staat Wirtschaft, p. 71.

33. Hansmeyer, ed. *Kommunale Finanzpolitik*, pp. 133-34.

34. LA Berlin STA 398/I, Vorbericht für die Vorstandssitzung des deutschen Städtetages, 9 May 1927; and STA 398/II, Niederschrift über die Vorstandssitzung, 9 May 1927.

35. Ibid. STA 396, Jahresversammlung des deutschen Städtetages, Breslau, 25 September 1928, pp. 28-29, 35, 41, 64; and STA 27/II, 7. deutscher Städtetag in Magdeburg, 28 October 1927, pp. 19-21.

36. Ibid. STA 396, Jahresversammlung des deutschen Städtetages, 25 September 1928, p. 29.

37. Ibid. STA 27/II, 7. deutscher Städtetag, p. 34.

38. Ibid. STA 396, Jahresversammlung, 25 September 1928, pp. 51-58, 61-63; and STA 603/I, Notiz zum engeren Vorstand, 29 June 1929.

39. Hansmeyer, ed., *Kommunale Finanzpolitik*, p. 133.

40. LA Berlin, STA 398/II, Niederschrift über die Vorstandssitzung des deutschen Städtetages, 9 May 1927; and STA 186/II, Vorstandssitzung des preussichen Städtetages, 22 September 1927.

41. Ibid. STA 186/II, Vorbericht für die Vorstandssitzung des preussischen Städtetages; Vorstandssitzung, 22 September 1927; and STA 634, Vorstandssitzung des preussischen Städtetages, 26 November 1927.

42. See for example: Borchardt, "Wirtschaftliche Ursachen;" James, "Economic Reasons," p. 32; Abelshauser, "Die Weimarer Republik – ein Wohlfahrtsstaat?," pp. 10, 31; Mommsen, *Verspielte Freiheit*, p. 493; and Schulze, *Weimar Deutschland*, p. 66.

Chapter 5

CITIES AND THE
WEIMAR PRODUCTIVITY DEBATE

As conflicts over the distribution of resources provoked reaction against municipal policies of recovery of the Weimar period of stabilization, so too did debate over the utility or productivity of municipal spending. For all of the vehemence of critiques of city governments issued by the Reichsbank and leading economic interest groups, municipal leaders were no less adamant in asserting the importance of municipal policy for recovery. Municipal leaders described their programs of recovery as comprehensive, functional, and complementary with economic rationalization. If, in fact, municipal governments had taken up critical tasks for both social and economic recovery, how could their critics maintain that cities obstructed stabilization?

Setting forth the economic arguments against municipal policy, Harold James argues that city governments exemplified the ills of public finance in the Weimar Republic: "The communes demonstrated in an especially extreme form that rather intractable problem we have diagnosed elsewhere in German public finance in the 1920s: high spending without adequate revenue, meaning a dependence on borrowing, coupled with widespread doubts about the value or purpose of public activity."[1]

There are two separate elements to James's critique of Weimar municipal policy. He points to the high level of municipal borrowing and to uncertainty over the value of municipal activity. Indeed, municipal governments certainly relied on loans to fund recovery programs, but did they also squander credit on projects of dubious value? The reference to "widespread doubts" about the purpose of public activity suggests that reaction against the growth of the state was not simply the result of high expenditures.

During the Weimar period of stabilization, disdain for the value of public activity both magnified antagonism against the state and undermined the arguments in favor of municipal policy. Claims that city governments wasted funds on useless projects suggested that the comprehensive functional policy favored by many municipal leaders was not, in fact, functional. In a period in which mayors and city councilors stressed the utility of municipal initiatives, the assertion that programs of recovery served no useful purpose emerged as one of the most damaging critiques of municipal activity.

The Case Against Municipal Utility

The case against the productivity of municipal spending found support during the period of stabilization among both financial authorities and small splinter parties. On the local level, the loudest and most persistent criticism came, not from established political parties, but from splinter parties of the bourgeois Right, the small parties, often organized to represent a single constituency that competed to win votes from the established bourgeois parties: the DDP, DVP, and DNVP. While the National Socialists, only one of many splinter parties during the 1920s, often denied the value of municipal policy, small parties that claimed to represent house owners and small business engaged in the most persistent criticism of the utility of state activity during the period of stabilization. Nationally the most prominent of these parties during the period of stabilization was the Economic Party.

One local splinter party that engaged in especially vigorous criticism of the utility of municipal spending was Düsseldorf's Wirtschaftsbund, a local variant of the Economic Party with strong ties to Düsseldorf's House and Property Owners' Association and to tavern owners. The Wirtschaftsbund maintained that Düsseldorf wasted scarce credit on a series of expensive and unnecessary projects, most notably the permanent exhibition buildings constructed for the Gesolei exhibition of 1926. Adopting an unaccustomed moderate tone, councilor Stein of the Wirtschaftsbund and House and Property Owners' Association wrote in 1927 "that we all made the mistake at the time, not to examine the necessity of the permanent exhibition buildings more thoroughly than happened."[2]

Criticism of the permanent exhibition buildings set a pattern for attacks by the Wirtschaftsbund and sympathetic newspapers against numerous municipal projects: Stein warned that German cities were in danger of falling victim to "project makers."[3] For *Haus und Grund*, the newspaper of the House and Property Owners' Association, Düsseldorf's new stadium illustrated the lack of purpose of many expensive municipal projects. Echoing complaints about the stadium's remote location, *Haus und Grund* asked whether it was not possible to choose a more central location "if one absolutely wanted to squander the apparently plentiful tax pennies of Düsseldorf's citizens in order to simply not fall behind other cities."[4] Recovery, the Wirtschaftsbund and its allies maintained, had become an excuse for conspicuous consumption by public authorities that saddled urban residents with the cost of paying for prestige projects.

If charges of municipal waste and extravagance by splinter parties such as the Wirtschaftsbund were an annoyance to municipal leaders during the early years of stabilization, German mayors and the Association of Cities faced powerful foes including Reparations Agent Parker Gilbert and Reichsbank President Hjalmar Schacht. Questioning spending choices by all levels of government, Schacht singled out municipal governments for special opprobrium. He derided the utility of municipal expenditures, claiming that city governments had squandered the proceeds of loans on luxury expenditures. In a highly-publicized speech at Bochum in November 1927 he asserted that city governments could probably have avoided borrowing a single foreign loan if they "had refrained from ... luxury expenditures." Schacht's list of "luxury expenditures" included sums spent for stadiums, swimming pools, parks, land purchases, fair buildings, festival halls, hotel buildings, office buildings, planetariums, airports, theater and museum buildings, credit guarantees, and participation in the private economy.[5]

Schacht argued that unproductive public spending threatened to reignite inflation. Subscribing to the theory, rejected by some contemporary economists, that capital imports increased inflation by raising monetary supply, Schacht asserted that the types of expenditures made by public authorities aggravated this inflationary pressure. He maintained that public authorities made investments that did not earn foreign exchange, thereby forcing the Reichsbank to obtain foreign exchange to cover interest payments for these unproductive public investments.[6]

As might be expected, attacks against the utility of municipal spending by leading financial authorities reinforced the campaigns by local splinter parties and their backers against municipal programs. Schacht and the Reparations Agent Parker Gilbert received rave reviews from Düsseldorf's Wirtschaftsbund and its supporters. Hailing the disclosure of a memorandum by Parker Gilbert criticizing public finance, Düsseldorf's *Lokal Zeitung,* a newspaper that accorded some measure of respect in local affairs only to the Wirtschaftsbund, asserted that 60-70 percent of Düsseldorf's expenditures were "dead investments." When Schacht made his Bochum speech, the *Lokal Zeitung* praised the Reichsbank President for holding up a mirror before those responsible for endangering the economy, Germany's mayors, and *Haus und Grund* commended Schacht for informing the general public of dangers that it had already noted.[7]

Encouraged by Schacht's stance against public spending decisions, splinter parties stepped up their own critique of the utility of municipal policy over the next several years. Throughout 1928 and 1929, Düsseldorf's Wirtschaftsbund and its allies rebuked municipal luxury, continuing to harp on the permanent exhibition buildings constructed for the Gesolei as favorite examples of municipal extravagance, but also finding new evidence of waste in such items as the construction of water works, baths, a school building, the purchase of land and of part of the Sigmaringen art collection, and the "pompous written works about the great deeds of the city," probably referring to the large official catalog of the Gesolei. Luxury might lurk anywhere. Councilor Schöpke of the Wirtschaftsbund asked that plans to build a new ape house at Düsseldorf's zoo "avoid unnecessary luxury."[8] Frankfurt's Economic Party, though less vigorous than Düsseldorf's Wirtschaftsbund, issued a similar stream of sarcastic remarks about municipal extravagance, seeing evidence of "the so-often rebuked megalomania of Frankfurt am Main" in the city's new stadium and claiming to spot extravagance in the central heating and baths of apartments in Frankfurt's new housing settlements.[9]

Schacht's tirade against luxury expenditures encouraged splinter parties but infuriated municipal leaders across the political spectrum. Leaders of the Association of Cities and most mayors angrily rejected the Reichsbank President's claim that city governments wasted scarce funds on unnecessary projects. And criticism of Schacht was by no means restricted to mayors with ties to the political Left. Expressing views common to his colleagues, Mayor Lehr of Düsseldorf accused Schacht of "exaggeration" and cautioned that anyone who wished to evaluate municipal spending would do well to consider that so many tasks had to be delayed during and immediately after the world war. Speaking for large cities, Oskar Mulert, President of the Association of Cities, asserted that "no dollar, Guilder or pound of foreign loans is spent for so-called unproductive purposes."[10]

The Productivity Debate

How did mayors, city councilors, and bankers, sharply divided in their assessments of the value of municipal activity, determine the utility of expenditures? At least for projects funded with foreign credit, a formal process existed to evaluate the utility of spending proposals. Required to submit applications to take out foreign loans to the Advisory Board for Foreign Credit, municipal governments had to demonstrate that they required foreign credit for urgent, necessary, and productive investments. The Advisory Board's original guidelines stipulated that a "necessary" investment was one that could not be postponed until such a time when domestic capital was available. The chair of the Advisory Board, Geheimrat Norden of the Reich Finance Ministry, explained that investments could be necessary without being urgent, but amended guidelines in 1927 also indicating that "urgent" referred only to those investments that could not be postponed.[11]

The Advisory Board's adoption of productivity as a guide to the utility of expenditures reflected the widespread belief that Germany could only hope to recover from war, while paying some portion of reparations, by making the most productive use of resources. Leading industrialists, politicians, and officials all committed themselves to productive spending. Weimar pursuit of productivity helped give rise to the rationalization "mania" of the 1920s, a phenomenon that also occurred in other European states. If gains in production seldom met expectations raised by the rhetoric of efficiency and expertise, productivism dominated European managerial thinking during the interwar years.[12]

Rather than creating an objective standard for making spending decisions, selection of productivity as a key measurement of utility intensified debate in Germany over the definition of productivity. Productivity promised to combat human fatigue and improve efficiency, but what, precisely, was productivity itself? The Advisory Board's own definition of productivity required that investments yield sufficient earnings to cover debt service, a standard that Schacht found too flexible. Modified guidelines of February 1926 made the capacity of investments to cut imports or raise exports a supplementary measure of productivity, though Geheimrat Norden, Chair of the Advisory Board, assured his colleagues that the impact of a given investment on exports or imports would provide only a secondary test of productivity.[13]

From puzzling over the productivity of expenditures, it was a short step to the closely-related quandary of identifying consumption.[14] Widespread acceptance of productivity as a key to economic recovery stood in sharp contrast to contemporary dispute over the economic impact of consumption. The Fordist model of mass consumption won admirers in unions and among a minority of economists, but financial authorities and economic interest groups warned that Germany could not yet afford a high level of consumption.[15] American conditions, they insisted, did not apply to Germany.

The municipal thirst for credit to pay for recovery programs made mayors, city councilors, and the Association of Cities participants in the ongoing debate of the Weimar era to define productivity. This productivity debate took place in the press, in city parliaments, and in meetings of the Advisory Board. Controversy over municipal borrowing brought civic leaders and their critics to examine the utility of public spending for items including the modernization of utilities and the promotion of housing construction and leisure. The productivity debate focused at length on municipal economic promotion. Virtually every city making an application to the Advisory Board wished to borrow foreign credit to pay for utility projects, and municipal officials believed that they had a strong case for taking out foreign loans to pay for electrical power plants. The profitability of municipal power plants was not in question. Rising consumption of electricity after 1924 assured municipal governments of gaining sufficient earnings from sales of electrical power to cover the costs of debt service.

However, those mayors and city treasurers who expected proposals of investment of foreign loans in utilities to sail through the Advisory Board were soon disappointed. Geheimrat Norden, Chair of the Advisory Board, and the Directors of the Reichsbank suspected cities of exaggerating their need for credit for gas and electricity plants.[16] Norden found it "surprising" that all cities claimed that their water supply and gas and electricity capacity were insufficient. The Directors of the Reichsbank accused public authorities of using foreign loans "to create further new installations whose economic necessity is not absolutely proven."[17] The true reason for municipal construction of utilities, according to the Reichsbank, was not any absolute shortfall in the supply of electrical power and gas, but the lure of guaranteed profits. An internal Reichsbank analysis of the response by the President of the Association of Cities to Schacht's 1927 Bochum speech concluded that the "rationalization of municipal firms" chiefly benefitted "public finance."[18]

Critical of plans to modernize municipal utilities, the Reichsbank conceded that investments in municipal supply firms were profitable, but contended that such investments were only productive in a "formal" sense, for monopoly control of rates actually made production more expensive. Reinforcing advocates of privatization, the Reichsbank insisted that rising demand for electricity and gas could best be met by private utilities and distribution systems, especially by long-distance distribution systems. The emergence of long-distance gas and electricity supply made the "usefulness" of expanding individual municipal firms "extremely disputed."[19]

Despite the Reichsbank's efforts to dispute the utility of improvements to communal gas and electricity plants, mayors managed to defend the productivity of investment in the core firms of the communal economy. On a number of occasions the Reichsbank's representative on the Advisory Board and Geheimrat Norden failed to eliminate or reduce proposals to spend foreign credit on improvements to gas works and electrical power plants. In frustration, the Reichsbank issued a list in 1927 of instances where a majority of the Advisory Board had voted against the Reichsbank; these included applications by Nuremberg and by groups of towns from Thuringia, the Pfalz, and the Rhineland.[20] Nonetheless, the Advisory Board did hold most other forms of municipal economic promotion to be unproductive. Transportation projects seldom won the Advisory Board's approval: plans to renovate harbors fared poorly, and the Advisory Board flatly denied that construction of city streets was a productive investment.[21] Proposals to invest foreign credit in street car lines and local railways yielded more involved debate. Prussian representatives to the Advisory Board maintained that loans for street cars lines could be productive, but the Reichsbank questioned whether construction of street car lines truly promoted production. Over time, the Advisory Board became less willing to approve of the use of foreign credit to pay for local transportation projects, though the Reichsbank was not able to prevent the Advisory Board from making an exception to allow Berlin to borrow abroad to help pay for the U-Bahn.[22]

Both the Reichsbank and the Advisory Board denied the productivity of exhibition halls and market halls, not to mention the events held in these structures. The Advisory Board did not content itself with simply cutting funds designated to be used for market and exhibition halls from loan applications (the fate of a loan proposal from Breslau in 1926), but also penalized a number of cities for having built halls financed with domestic sources, taking such expenditures as evidence that the cities in question did not truly need foreign loans. The mayor of Mulheim found himself interrogated by members of the Advisory Board who wanted to know why his administration had seen fit to spend money for such a project when it claimed to need a loan to pay for a shipping facility and its electrical power work. Drastically reducing a 1925 application by Düsseldorf for an American loan from $6 million to $1.75 million, the Advisory Board criticized the city for having built permanent exhibition halls for the Gesolei, advising that such expenditures must "be postponed for better times."[23]

Disputing the utility of municipal economic promotion, the Reichsbank and other opponents of municipal policy also questioned the productivity of spending for the promotion of housing construction. Resisting making foreign credit available to pay for the promotion of housing construction, Reichsbank President Schacht told representatives of the state governments in 1926 that he could think of no more unsuitable use for foreign credit than investment in housing construction.[24]

Why did the Reichsbank decide that housing construction should not receive the highest priority for investment? Calls for limiting funding for housing construction were controversial at a time when numerous politicians and planning professionals described the housing shortage as one of the chief obstacles to recovery. In the face of widespread demands for support for housing construction, even the Reichsbank conceded some slight utility to housing. An internal memorandum admitted that housing construction stimulated the economy and even acknowledged that the effects of housing on "efficiency" made spending on housing construction "indirectly productive."[25] However, the Directors of the Reichsbank and members of the Advisory Board saw such benefits as negligible in comparison to the injury caused to production by shifting scarce resources away from investment in productive capacity into investment in housing construction. The Advisory Board decided that only housing for workers in the immediate vicinity of industry might possibly meet the guidelines for productivity. Exceptions to the Advisory Board's policy of rejecting foreign credit for housing construction, explained Geheimrat Norden, were possible "if the construction of housing for the work force of an industrial firm is an absolute requirement."[26]

To explain why spending for housing was not a critical investment, the Reichsbank identified housing as a form of consumption. The "predominantly consumptive character" of housing construction, contended the Reichsbank's Directors, made the use of foreign capital for housing programs "erroneous."[27] Differentiating between housing construction and productive investments with rapid capital turnover, the Reichsbank pointed out that while machines, factories, and mines produced new value continuously, housing construction demanded the use of capital for a single purpose over a long period of time and did not promote exports or yield foreign exchange.[28]

The status of housing as a form of consumption made advocates of municipal housing construction programs uneasy. Like many housing professionals, Stadrat May of Halle underscored the benefits of housing: he told a meeting of public health officials that housing construction was "necessary in order to preserve and to strengthen the capacity for work and enjoyment of work of our fellow citizens who suffer from housing privation," but May still worried that housing construction might be identified as consumption. "It is not correct," he stated, "that housing construction only serves purely consumptive ends."[29] Proponents of housing construction tried to distinguish spending for housing from other forms of consumption. "The purchase of a new dwelling," explained Eberhard Wildermuth, an official in the Reich Labor Ministry, could not be placed "on the same level economically with the purchase of a woman's hat," presumably the epitome of superfluous consumption. Stadrat Binder of Bielefeld drew a more general distinction between housing and other consumer goods, cautioning that it "would be irresponsible to use ... capital only for the goods of daily consumption."[30]

Although critics of municipal policy questioned the utility of costly activities such as support for housing construction and economic promotion, the productivity debate was not confined to the municipal projects of power plants and housing developments that presented other economic sectors with serious competition for capital. Thus, sports stadiums, though far less expensive than the expansion of electrical power plants, for example, acquired curious prominence during the height of the productivity debate, attracting more publicity during the 1920s than most other municipal projects. Convinced that spending on these sports facilities represented particularly egregious misuse of capital by communal authorities, the critics of municipal activity made the new stadiums into symbols of the errors of German city governments.

Condemning stadiums as the least productive of municipal expenditures, the epitome of misguided civic luxury, the Reichsbank tried to prove the folly of municipal policy by telling cautionary tales of cities and their stadiums. In 1926 the Directors of the Reichsbank informed the Reich Chancellor of a city that had constructed a stadium while applying for a foreign loan of RM 25.6 million. Another city had supposedly built a stadium at a cost of RM 27 million (this sum could only have been calculated from the cost at some point during the inflation). For the Reichsbank's Directors, these and other new stadiums offered the clearest evidence that municipal governments, despite all protests to the contrary, made unproductive investments.[31]

Reichsbank President Schacht, who disapproved of all manner of municipal projects, reserved special scorn for stadiums. Frankfurt's City Treasurer Bruno Asch learned from the American banker James Speyer of a conversation between Speyer and Schacht, in which Schacht claimed that Frankfurt had financed construction of its stadium with American credit (the stadium had in fact been built before Speyer & Company's 1925 loan to Frankfurt).[32] In his diatribe at Bochum in November 1927 against municipal luxury, Schacht sarcastically stated that "the famous stadiums" always appeared among municipal luxury expenditures.[33]

Even more sympathetic observers of projects of recovery thought that expenditures for sports facilities went well beyond the bounds of useful spending. Alfred Lansburgh, editor of the journal *Die Bank*, criticized municipal expenditures "for certain sanitary and cultural purposes touching on luxury (sports places, museums, planetariums!)… In a needy economy one may not carry out prestige policies."[34] The banker Max Warburg told the Enquete Ausschuß of the Reichstag in 1927 that housing was at least indirectly productive but added that this should not be said too loudly lest mayors build not only housing but also stadiums.[35]

Most municipal leaders, for their part, rejected charges that expenditures on sports facilities and leisure gave proof of mistaken priorities. Representatives of the Association of Cities suggested that the construction of stadiums and sports places provided work and boosted public health. The "strengthening of youth," explained President Mulert, "amounts at the same time from a financial standpoint to immediate savings from costs of illness and care." Employing similar logic, Düsseldorf's Mayor Lehr told his city parliament that projects that Schacht mocked created opportunities for work and "served the physical training of the population," worthy goals given the "regrettable decline of public health."[36] When the German Association of Industry met in Frankfurt in 1927, Frankfurt's Mayor Landmann tried to persuade a skeptical audience of the economic value of a broad municipal approach to recovery that included the promotion of leisure. Cities built facilities for physical exercise in the "service of the German nation that can only prosper if the German people are the best in the world."[37]

The dispute over the utility of promoting sport clearly exposed a deep division between Germany's municipal leaders and the Reichsbank. Municipal explanations of the productivity of sports facilities made little impression upon Schacht. The Reichsbank President ridiculed municipal stadiums with a vitriolic and satirical edge absent from the Reichsbank's communications objecting to excessive investment in housing construction. Identifying stadiums as a form of public conspicuous consumption, Schacht cut the close relationship that many mayors drew between social provision and production.

Productivity and Human Capital

Analysis of the Weimar productivity debate reveals the limits to interpreting reaction against municipalities as the product of conflict over economic and social priorities. It is admittedly appealing to describe the dispute between municipalities and their critics from industrial and financial circles as a conflict between advocates of social stabilization and economic recovery. Industrial interest groups and the Reichsbank sometimes described their conflict with municipalities in these terms, and economic historians have adopted similar logic to describe Weimar reaction against state expansion.[38] Yet while the rate of growth of social spending troubled industrial interest groups and the Reichsbank, the conflict over municipal programs of recovery was not simply a dispute between social stabilization and economic rationalization for either civic leaders or for many industrialists.

To a large degree, disputes over the utility of municipal social provision stemmed from the choice of different criteria for determining productivity. Schacht and the Directors of the Reichsbank defined productivity chiefly as a measure of industrial capacity, but municipal officials and politicians advocated a broader definition of productivity. Mayors and city councilors defended the productivity of investments in housing construction or in sports facilities by measuring productivity in terms of benefits to human capital.

Mayor Ludwig Landmann of Frankfurt outlined the importance of human capital for German economic recovery in a speech to the assembly of the German Association of Industry in 1927. By working to create "quality people," German cities cooperated with industry "in the effort to win back the world through quality work." Arguing that technology alone could not guarantee quality work without development of human capital, Landmann drew attention to the contrast between the United States, the land of technical progress and Russia which, following liberal tradition, he still saw as a symbol of backwardness. "You will never be able to achieve quality work," Landmann claimed, "if you put an American machine in the hands of Russian *Muschiks* (peasants)." German workers had the education to surpass their Russian counterparts, and municipal expenditures for recreation and exercise further raised the ability of the German work force to supply quality work.[39]

Convinced that developing human capital was the key to quality work, civic leaders argued that Reichsbank President Schacht overlooked the productivity of expenditures that maintained and improved capacity for work. In his public response to Schacht's speech at Bochum, Oskar Mulert, the President of the Städtetag, declared: "The capacity for work of German workers forms the most valuable foundation of our economic productivity." Economic caution caused by concern for German ability to pay reparations did not justify neglecting capacity for work. On the contrary, the "preservation and promotion" of capacity for work was "the prerequisite for the ability of Germany to fulfill its reparations obligations."[40]

While municipal authorities never managed to persuade Schacht of the utility of their policies, the municipal emphasis upon improving human capital did win endorsement from some economists. Adolf Weber, Professor at the University of Munich, acknowledged the wisdom of establishing a central organ to examine the use of foreign credit by public institutions, but chided Schacht for overlooking the economic value of improving capacity for work. Weber described capacity for work as our "main wealth." According to him, "the development of physical strength and the preservation of public health" was an "urgent problem of productivity."[41]

Though Weber's recognition of both the need for caution in borrowing and the utility of many public expenditures suggested a possible path towards reconciliation between the public authorities and the Reichsbank, the tone of the productivity debate remained bitter and acerbic. Direct discussions between the Reichsbank and German mayors were rare and acrimonious. A delegation from the Association of Cities consisting of Mulert, Böß, Adenauer, Landmann, and Scharnagl among others met with the Reich Finance Minister and Schacht on 28 September 1927, but became so enraged by Schacht's stream of insults and interruptions that they threatened to break off any further discussions, and consented to continue talks on the following day only at the request of the Finance Minister.[42]

The chief participants in the productivity debate thus tended to talk past one another. Municipal officials and their critics in the Reichsbank and on the Advisory Board never arrived at a common understanding of the definition of productivity. While mayors lauded improvements to human capital, the Directors of the Reichsbank and the members of the Advisory Board ultimately discounted the contribution of human capital to production. Human capital, the vital link between social provision and production in the municipal conception of recovery, was largely absent from the Reichsbank's discussion of recovery. Arthur Norden, the Chair of the Advisory Board, asked if the need to reduce spending "should also apply ... to expenditures, whose non-fulfillment could be seen as low regard for capacity for work?" Noting the massive demand for credit, Norden implied that there was little choice but to assign a low priority to spending on improving human capital.[43]

Going beyond criticism of the utility of social provision, Schacht implied that the type of investor determined the productivity of a given investment. In Schacht's case, unrelenting hostility towards municipal recovery programs revealed a monetarist disdain for public investment. Refusal to approve of any municipal undertaking left the impression that public investment was inherently unproductive.[44] Even the Advisory Board did not follow Schacht to this conclusion.

If the Reichsbank and Advisory Board generally viewed improvements to human capital as a peripheral standard for determining productivity, many industrialists actually agreed with municipal officials that the development of human capital was vital for recovery.[45] Ernst Poensgen of the Vestag steel conglomerate praised the Gesolei for providing information about "preserving and raising the ability to work," and even industrialists who criticized municipal policies of recovery did not entirely deny the possible importance of human capital. Carl Duisberg, the Chair of the German Association of Industry, protested to Frankfurt's Mayor Landmann that industry regarded people as its "most important part."[46]

Beyond how to balance social stabilization with economic rationalization, industrialists and municipal leaders also disputed how best to develop human capital. While industrialists and municipal officials both wished to develop human capital, they often argued about how to go about raising the ability of workers to supply "quality work." Industrial initiatives for the development of human capital overlapped in some respects with the municipal model of recovery: both mayors and DINTA (Deutsches Institut für technische Arbeitsschulung), an organization which received support from industrialists in the Ruhr, favored the promotion of sports, but industry's exponents of human rationalization favored a more carefully targeted and less expensive approach to improving human capital.[47]

Weimar debates over the significance of human capital and methods for improving capacity for work reveal the complexity of politics of social reproduction. Widespread concern over threats to national health and capacity for work did not lead inexorably to any single set of policies or programs of recovery. For all the contemporary anxiety that damage to the capacity for work had lowered the quality of the labor force, requirements for social reproduction were difficult to determine. The inability of the Reichsbank and municipal leaders to discuss, let alone arrive at, a common understanding of the relationship between social provision and social reproduction blocked planning for recovery and transformed important public institutions into enemies.

If Reichsbank President Schacht deserved much of the blame for the breakdown of dialogue between Germany's central bank and large cities, the municipal approach to developing human capital was not the only possible solution to the task of protecting social reproduction. From the perspective of later eras of recovery, the faith of Weimar municipal leaders in the influence of housing and sports on the capacity for work, while not discredited, betrayed a certain naiveté.

Notes

1. James, *The German Slump*, p. 92.
2. *Haus und Grund*, 8 January 1927.
3. StVV Düsseldorf, 1927, p. 87.
4. *Haus und Grund*, 23 April 1927.
5. Schacht, *Eigene oder geborgte Währung*, p. 22.
6. Ibid., pp. 12-13. Contemporary economists, most notably Adolf Weber, disputed Schacht's theory of inflation, but the historian William McNeil argues that disinclination to devalue the German currency created real currency transfer problems for German fiscal authorities. See Adolf Weber, *Hat Schacht Recht? Die Abhängigkeit der deutschen Volkswirtschaft vom Ausland* (Munich, 1928), pp. 13-16; and McNeil, *American Money and the Weimar Republic*, pp. 98-101.
7. *Düsseldorfer Lokal Zeitung*, 12 November 1927; *Düsseldorfer Lokal Zeitung*, 26 November 1927; and *Haus und Grund*, 3 December 1927.

8. StVV Düsseldorf, 1928, pp. 21, 253; 1929, p. 242; *Haus und Grund*, 21 April 1928; 22 September 1928; and StA Düsseldorf XXIV 1013, *Haus und Grund*, 29 December 1928.

9. StA Frankfurt StVV 1.593, 15 February 1929; and StVV Frankfurt, 1929, p. 838.

10. StVV Düsseldorf, 1927, pp. 280-81; and Mulert, "Der deutscher Reichsbankpräsident gegen die deutschen Städte," *Der Städtetag* 21 (1927): 387.

11. BA Koblenz R2/2126, Sitzung der Beratungsstelle, 2 February 1926, Sitzung der Beratungsstelle, 3 February 1926; and Hansmeyer, *Kommunale Finanzpolitik*, pp. 214-15. Note that guidelines were also amended in 1926, adding the ability of investments to raise exports or to cut imports as additional measures of productivity, but these standards were only used as secondary tests for determining the suitability of loans.

12. Mary Nolan, *Visions of Modernity: American Business and the Modernization of Germany* (New York, 1994); Anson Rabinbach, *The Human Motor: Energy, Fatigue, and the Origins of Modernity* (New York, 1990), p. 272; James, *The German Slump*, pp. 148-49; Joan Campbell, *Joy in Work, German Work: The National Debate, 1800-1945* (Princeton, 1989), pp. 131-57; and Peukert, *Die Weimarer Republik*, pp. 116-18.

13. *Akten der ... Kabinette Luther*, vol. 1, pp. 623-24; BA Koblenz R2/2126, Sitzung der Beratungsstelle, 3 February 1926; and R2/2002, Enquete Ausschuß, Unterausschuß für Geld-, Kredit-, und Finanzwesen, Die neue Reichsbank, pp. 141-44.

14. See Borchardt, "Wirtschaftliche Ursachen," p. 191. Borchardt refers to the consumptive and investive use of resources.

15. Mary Nolan, "The Infatuation with Fordism: Social Democracy and Economic Rationalization in Weimar Germany," in *Change and Illusion Labor in Retreat: Studies on the Social Crisis in Interwar Europe*, ed. Wolfgang Maderthaner and Helmut Gruber (Vienna, 1988), pp. 156-57; and RDI, *Aufstieg oder Niedergang?* p. 8.

16. BA Potsdam 25:01, Reichsbank 6629, Besprechung mit den Vertretern der Länderregierungen, 10 February 1926.

17. BA Koblenz R2/2126, Sitzung der Beratungsstelle, 8 March 1926; and *Akten der...Kabinette Luther*, vol. 2, pp. 1053-54.

18. BA Potsdam 25:01, Reichsbank 6630, Nachprüfung der Festellungen des Präsidenten Mulert, 26 November 1927, p. 14.

19. Ibid., pp. 14-15.

20. BA Potsdam 25:01, Deutsches Reichsbank 6630, 14 September 1927.

21. The Advisory Board was more inclined to approve applications for loans for ocean harbors than for river harbors. See Hansmeyer, *Kommunale Finanzpolitik*, p. 209.

22. BA Koblenz R2/2047, Der Preußische Minister des Innern, 19 September 1927, and R2/2026, Sitzung der Beratungsstelle, 29 June 1927.

23. BA Koblenz R2/2127, Sitzung der Beratungsstelle, 13 April 1926, and R2/2044, Gutachten, 16 November 1925.

24. BA Potsdam 25:01, Reichsbank 6629, Besprechung mit den Vertretern der Länderregierungen, 10 February 1926, p. 1.

25. Ibid., Reichsbank 6630, Zur Frage der Finanzierung des Wohnungsbaues mit Auslandsanleihen, 28 June 1927, pp. 2-3.

26. "Wohnungsbau und Auslandsanleihe," *Westfälisches Wohnungsblatt* 18 (1928): 96-97; and "Auslandsanleihen für den Wohnungsbau," *Westfälisches Wohnungsblatt* 18 (1928): 399.

27. *Akten der Reichskanzlei Weimarer Republik: Die Kabinette Marx III und IV*, vol. 2, ed. Günter Abramowski (Boppard am Rhein, 1988), p. 823.

28. BA Potsdam 25:01, Reichsbank 6630, Zur Frage der Finanzierung des Wohnungsbaus mit Auslandsanleihen, 28 June 1927, pp. 2-3.

29. Stadtrat May, "Wohnungsnot und Wohnungsbau," *Bauamt und Gemeindebau* 9 (1927): 25.

30. Eberhard Wildermuth, "Grundzüge der Wohnungspolitik," *Der deutsche Volkswirt* 1 (1927): 1542; and Stadrat Binder, "Probleme des Wohnungsbaus in städtischen Eigenhäusern," *Bauamt und Gemeindebau* 8 (1926): 174.

31. *Akten der...Kabinette Luther*, vol. 2, p. 1054.

32. StA Frankfurt, Stadtkämmerei Zugang 3/75 170, Asch to Dr. Picard, 1 October 1927. Note that Schacht denied having had such a conversation with Speyer.

33. Schacht, *Eigene oder geborgte Währung*, p. 22.

34. Alfred Lansburgh, "Die Währung und die Wirtschaftskrise; Folgen für die Kommunalwirtschaft," *Zeitschrift für Kommunalwirtschaft* 16 (1926): 330.

35. BA Potsdam 25:01, Reichsbank 6630, Bericht über die Sitzung des V. Unterausschußes des Enqueteausschußes am 5. Juli, 7 July 1927, pp. 5-6.

36. LA Berlin STB 1533/1, "Städte, Staat, und Wirtschaft," 1926, p. 49; Mulert, "Der deutsche Reichsbankpräsident gegen die deutsche Städten," *Der Städtetag* 21 (1927): 389-90; and StVV Düsseldorf, 1927, p. 281.

37. *Mitglieder Versammlung des Reichsverbandes der Deutschen Industrie* (Berlin, 1927), p. 15.

38. McNeil, *American Money and the Weimar Republic*, p. 276.

39. *Mitglieder Versammlung des Reichsverbandes der Deutschen Industrie* (Berlin, 1927), p. 15.

40. Dr. Mulert, "Der deutsche Reichsbankpräsident gegen die deutschen Städte," *Der Städtetag* 21 (1927): 390.

41. Weber, *Hat Schacht Recht?* pp. 16-17.

42. LA Berlin, STB 2784/II, Besprechung ... Zwischen den Vertretern des deutschen Städtetages, dem Reichsfinanzminister und den Reichsbankpräsidenten, 28-29, September 1927.

43. Arthur Norden, "Einschränkung des kommunalen Anleihebedarfs," in *Kommune und Wirtschaft: Sondergabe der Kölnischen Zeitung* (Cologne, 1929), pp. 31-32.

44. Note that Harold James recognizes that public investment is not inherently unproductive. See James, "Municipal Finance in the Weimar Republic," in *The State and Social Change in Germany, 1880-1980*, ed. W.R. Lee and Eve Rosenhaft (New York, 1990), p. 253. For an analysis of the argument that only private investment is productive see Robert Heilbroner and Peter Bernstein, *The Debt and the Deficit: False Alarms/Real Possibilities* (New York, 1989), pp. 57-67, 106-9.

45. Nolan, "Housework Made Easy: The Taylorized Housewife in Weimar Germany's Rationalized Economy," *Feminist Studies* 16 (1990): 558-67.

46. Schloßmann, ed., *GE-SO-LEI*, p. 16; and *Mitgliederversammlung des Reichsverbandes der deutschen Industrie*, 1927, p. 21.

47. Nolan, "The Infatuation with Fordism," pp. 158-159; and Rabinbach, *The Human Motor*, pp. 284-85.

Chapter 6

DEFINING THE CIVIC PUBLIC

For all of the vehemence of the attacks at the national level by economic interest groups and financial authorities against municipal
policies of the Weimar Republic, urban residents at the local level
shared a common interest in the benefits of municipal programs of
recovery. Municipal appetite for capital might have created unwanted
competition in credit markets for the private economy, but city governments sought to provide urban residents with housing, green
space, and cultural institutions. Even in 1929 as municipal finances
deteriorated, Max Brauer, the Social Democratic mayor of Altona,
still pointed to the benefits that ambitious government could provide.
"For the development of the great social and cultural tasks," he maintained, "the emphasis lies in the communes."[1]

Recovery as a vehicle for democratizing access to such benefits as
improved housing and leisure offered the promise of reducing social
and political cleavages within the urban population. Observing
shared civic interest in better urban living conditions, municipal
leaders themselves suggested that programs of recovery encouraged
social peace. As Berlin's Mayor Böß told a meeting of municipal
leaders in November 1927, "our hope in the social peace of the German people is founded on the conversion of the social idea into
action by the cities."[2]

How strong a bulwark did the common civic interest in recovery
programs offer against the attacks against municipal activity?
Although the urban population held a common interest in the social
and cultural benefits offered by municipal pursuit of recovery, the
process of organizing municipal programs created multiple disputes
with the potential of weakening civic unity. Drafting and imple-

menting recovery programs, municipal leaders struggled to determine precisely who benefitted from municipal activity. The organization of social provision, in particular, provoked numerous conflicts. In the distribution of public funds, civic leaders found themselves balancing the interests of consumers and producers, and of varied groups of consumers, and having to select appropriate forms of culture created still further conflicts. Drawing attention to the difficulty of defining one single civic public, these varied disputes revealed and created cracks and fissures in the urban population along lines of class, political affiliation, profession, and culture.

City Governments and Rival Networks of Clubs

Under pressure to find solutions to problems of recovery, the rapid expansion of municipal activity of the Weimar period of stabilization fostered disputes over the distribution of public funds. The selection of recipients of municipal assistance could provoke controversy even when sums disposed of by city governments were not vast. Despite the growing appeal of new forms of mass entertainment, the organization of leisure in Weimar Germany still reflected the fragmentation of society into different socio-political milieus. Promotion of sports, to take one example, brought municipal authorities to evaluate requests for assistance from competing networks of clubs and associations. Lacking a single national sports association, Germany instead possessed rival networks of regional and local sports clubs. The Reichsauschuss für Leibesübungen, the largest single sports association, placed clubs under bourgeois leadership, while the Arbeiter Turn- und Sportbund served as the umbrella organization for the workers' sports movement.

Municipal leaders committed to promoting sports struggled to maintain the promise of civic unity despite the rifts between socio-political milieus. Recognizing the risks of becoming ensnared in quarrels over the distribution of funds between clubs affiliated with the rival bourgeois and Social Democratic sports movements, municipal authorities often sought to take a balanced approach to the promotion of sports. Thus, municipal commissions for youth welfare and for the city office for physical exercise in Hanover handed out loans and subsidies in a fairly even-handed manner to both bourgeois and Social Democratic clubs, even though Hanover's city government was dominated by a bourgeois block after 1924. In 1930, Hanover's workers' sports clubs, grouped as the Kartell für

Sport und Körperpflege, received RM 25,700 out of the RM 90,000 dispensed by the city office for physical exercise, a smaller share than the RM 60,500 that went to local bourgeois associations, but not out of line with the workers' sports movement's representation of some 20 percent of all sports club members in the city.[3]

Municipal officials and politicians had reason to seek consensus in the distribution of aid to sports clubs, for arguments about the merits of clubs could split civic leaders along lines of competing social-political milieus. In Frankfurt, for instance, a 1926 proposal to grant RM 1,500 to the local section of the Nature Friends tourist club to pay for a hiking cabin enraged city councilors from Frankfurt's DNVP who charged that any appropriation for the Nature Friends would discriminate against more deserving bourgeois clubs. This dispute pitted champions of a distinct milieu against the ideology of civic unity. Frankfurt's deputy mayor responded to the DNVP's claims of discrimination by pointing to Frankfurt's policy of acting on behalf of a common civic interest by helping all sorts of clubs.[4]

Social Democrats and Communists were, on the whole, more likely than bourgeois municipal leaders to perceive discrimination in municipal treatment of sports clubs. In Gelsenkirchen, a hotbed of soccer fanaticism in the Ruhr, both the KPD and the SPD opposed proposals to subsidize the construction of soccer fields for clubs with ties to business and bourgeois sports associations. The KPD, Gelsenkirchen's largest party of the Left, voted against a 1927 measure to lend RM 20,000 and to grant RM 20,000 to the sports club Union 1910 on the grounds that the club lay under the leadership of United Steel (Vestag), and in 1928, the KPD and the SPD opposed extending a RM 20,000 loan and RM 5,000 subsidy to help pay for the construction of a sports field by the already-legendary soccer club Schalke 04. Calling Schalke 04 a "bourgeois club supported by the Bourgeoisie," a Communist city councilor described its members as "misled workers": Workers belonged in workers' sports clubs not in a "*Klimclub*" (an ascending club).[5]

With the division of the workers' sports movement into rival Social Democratic and Communist organizations, municipal distribution of funds aggravated Communist resentment against the SPD. Communist clubs frequently went without subsidies, a pattern of mistreatment that, as Herbert Dierker shows in the case of Berlin, angered their members. In Düsseldorf, the KPD charged that Social Democratic representatives on the committee for sports worked to exclude Communist clubs from using sports facilities.[6]

Municipal Authorities, Builders, and Architects

While the distribution of small subsidies and loans to sports clubs could provoke charges of discrimination, few municipal duties of the Weimar period of stabilization had more potential to ignite controversy than the promotion of housing construction. With more than 80 percent of all new housing construction reliant on public funds, municipal authorities made decisions that could either aid or injure contractors and building professionals.

Conflicts over the distribution of public funds to finance housing construction took several forms. One possible cause of contention was the division of public funds between different types of sponsors of construction: public authorities, cooperatives, companies with mixed public and private participation, and private contractors. In Altona, for example, bourgeois parties protested the administration's policy of dividing up rent-tax revenues equally between the city itself and building cooperatives, and Kiel's city parliament quarreled about how to distribute rent-tax mortgages between cooperatives, municipal companies, and private construction firms.[7]

Even when, as was often the case, city governments granted funds to both cooperatives and private contractors, municipal guidelines for the use of public funds still held critical importance for building professionals. Efforts by municipal planners to increase housing production and reduce housing costs could shift profit margins for various groups of building professionals. Reserving public funds for the construction of small apartments of two and three rooms reflected widespread demand for accelerated promotion of housing construction, but also threatened to cut the earning of construction firms that could increase their profits by building larger apartments for city governments.

Reaction against plans to encourage construction of small apartments became a major political theme of the bourgeois Right in Düsseldorf when the city's administration decided in 1927 to concentrate public resources on the construction of small apartments. Seeking to amend the administration's housing plan, the Arbeitsgemeinschaft, a short-lived working group of the Wirtschaftsbund, DVP, and DNVP, approved of the administration's proposal to spend RM 14 million in loans on the construction of 4,000 apartments but opposed measures that stipulated the size and rents of all apartments. Hoping to guarantee "a certain freedom for the execution of the housing program," the Arbeitsgemeinschaft moved that the city parliament form a special committee to decide on the distribution of funds between two-, three-, and four-room apartments.[8] The Arbeitsgemeinschaft, in effect, wanted to increase public funding for larger apartments.

Although Düsseldorf's city parliament consented to forming a special housing committee to consider the details of the housing construction program, the outlines of the administration's housing program for 1927 remained generally intact. The proportion of two-room apartments fell from the administration's original estimate of 40 percent to some 29 percent of all new apartments financed with public subsidies, but the proportion of three-room apartments rose to 50 percent. Two-room and three-room apartments therefore accounted for nearly 80 percent of all housing constructed with municipal financial assistance, close to the 85 percent stipulated in the administration's original proposal for 1927.[9]

Critics of Düsseldorf's housing program vented their frustrations in the summer of 1927 as it became clear that the special housing committee had not appreciably altered the administration's housing plan. The Economic Committee of the DNVP, a committee founded in 1925 by councilor Schwietzke, backed the charges by "craftsmen and experts" that certain firms received preferential treatment, but Stadtbaudirektor Meyer reminded the city parliament that "the building program has been approved against the will of certain circles." Meyer won the support of the housing committee, which voted to express full confidence in the administration.[10] Outnumbered on the housing committee, members of the DNVP's Economic Committee and representatives of the Wirtschaftsbund and DVP defiantly maintained that Düsseldorf's distribution of capital discriminated against small contractors.[11]

Municipal strategy to reduce construction costs again raised accusations of discrimination against the city government in 1928 when Düsseldorf's administration unveiled a four-year plan for the construction of 2,800 apartments per year between 1929 and 1932. First approved by the city parliament on 13 November 1928, the four-year plan authorized the city's office building company to sponsor construction of 1,250 apartments per year for the *Minderbemittelte* (those of modest means). To reduce costs for these apartments, the four-year plan assigned larger rent-tax mortgages for apartments sponsored by the city's Office Building Company (Bürohausgesellschaft) than for apartments of equivalent size with other sponsors. Thus, a three-room apartment sponsored by the Office Building Company received a rent-tax mortgage of RM 4,200, while a three-room apartment with a private or even a cooperative sponsor only received a rent-tax mortgage of RM 2,100. A private sponsor therefore had to obtain an additional RM 2,100 at higher interest rates to finance construction of a three-room apartment.[12]

Initial complaints by Düsseldorf's Wirtschaftsbund that the new housing plan discriminated against private building professionals met with a dismissive response from Düsseldorf's municipal officials and most established political parties. A joint declaration of all other parties asserted that the Wirtschaftsbund had misrepresented the administration's treatment of architects. The DNVP called the Wirtschaftsbund "exactly the same on the bourgeois side to what the Bolsheviks are on the Left, namely destructive elements."[13] Denying that the proposed housing construction plan discriminated against private building professionals, Beigeordneter Schilling noted that the Office Building Company employed private architects and craftsmen. The administration's only motive in granting larger rent-tax mortgages to the Office Building Company was to offset the financial risks of building housing for the needy. The city took the "lion's share of the rent tax" so that it could bear the risk of the many rent losses likely from renting to "those of modest means ... and the residents of group quarters."[14]

Such protestations were not entirely convincing to Düsseldorf's architects, professionals who stood to lose income from the administration's decision to reserve comparatively large rent-tax mortgages for housing for the needy. A delegation from the local chapter of the Federation of German Architects (Bund deutsche Architekten) met with the municipal housing committee in December, but the architects and municipal authorities failed to reach any agreement to increase commissions for architects to design housing for the needy.[15]

As controversy over the four-year housing program continued, the administration's refusal to make concessions angered the DVP, which, like the Wirtschaftsbund, criticized provisions that reserved the largest portion of revenues from the rent tax to finance housing for those of modest means. A public letter issued by city councilors of the DVP in early January 1929 disavowed their initial support for the four-year housing program. In a public letter of his own, Düsseldorf's Mayor Lehr countered that neither the local chapter of the Federation of German Architects nor the DVP had advanced any acceptable revision of the housing program.[16]

If merely setting financial guidelines for housing construction exposed municipal authorities to charges of discrimination, the minority of municipal governments that extended promotion of housing construction to cover the selection of construction methods and housing design faced even more potential criticism from contractors and building professionals. This was certainly true in Frankfurt where Ernst May's efforts to cut building costs through the rationalization of construction raised fears that new building techniques might damage existing building trades. Thus, May's wish to substitute concrete panels for bricks caused alarm among defenders of bricks and bricklayers; although, production of concrete panels remained modest.[17]

Whatever the actual impact of the partial introduction of concrete panels on brick makers, the new building style introduced to Frankfurt on a large scale by May altered employment opportunities for architects and roofers. It was not surprising that May, an advocate of the new building style, hired architects who shared his views to help plan the "new Frankfurt," inviting a number of architects from other cities to Frankfurt. He did not exclude Frankfurt architects from municipal planning, but only those described by May as "the most important private Frankfurt architects" were fortunate enough to gain employment on municipal projects.[18]

And what of those architects not deemed "important?" A series of articles by the Frankfurt architect Clemens Musch published in 1929 and 1930 in the newsletter of the Bürgerausschuß (Citizens' Committee), an association with ties to Frankfurt's DVP, gave indication of the feelings of those architects who had been passed over by May. Musch assailed May for, among other things, discriminating against experienced local architects. Combining professional grievances with criticism of May's methods, Musch charged that May had ignored Frankfurt's experienced private architects, choosing instead to assemble a staff of young architects from other parts of Germany and even from foreign countries. Beholden only to May, these architects "unscrupulously joined in the modern *Sachlichkeit* (objectivity) of Mr. May." The result was a housing program dominated by unsound experiments. May and his associates, asserted Musch, "test and learn at the cost of Frankfurt's population."[19]

While May showed little concern for the less adventurous of Frankfurt's architects, he conceded that the new building style injured at least one group of building professionals: roofers. Though he dismissed stylistic and technical objections, May still recognized that roofers felt their existence threatened by the introduction of flat roofs.[20] One of the hallmarks of the new building style, flat roofs capped apartment buildings in Frankfurt's new housing settlements.

The Needs of Consumers

Placed in position of evaluating the conflicting interests of different categories of producers and building professionals, what principles could municipal authorities apply to determine how to organize housing construction? One potential solution for resolving disputes over the distribution of public funds was to place the needs of consumers short of housing above those of producers who might complain of the effects of municipal decisions. Councilor Drösser, the chair of the Center Party in Düsseldorf's city parliament, took this stance in 1927 to try to settle disputes over the details of Düsseldorf's housing policy. Noting that the promotion of housing construction forced municipal authorities to make difficult choices, he conceded that he might be unhappy with the administration's emphasis on small apartments if he adopted the point of view of the construction industry, which "will not profit to the same extent as previously"; however, he advised that the housing program could only be judged accurately by examining "the housing needs of the city population."[21]

Focusing on the needs of consumers provided a benchmark for organizing promotion of housing construction as well as other programs of recovery, though it also raised new questions. Mayors and city councilors spoke with pride of new housing settlements, of sports fields and of cultural offerings, but which urban residents actually gained new apartments and access to these sports facilities and cultural institutions?

Drafting municipal policy with reference to the needs of consumers frequently raised class concerns. Demanding the democratization of access to civic benefits, Social Democrats and Communists active in local politics suspected that workers did not fully share in the benefits of many programs of recovery. Housing construction was one area in which local politicians from the Left were convinced that workers failed to enjoy the gains produced by government spending. Both Social Democrats and Communists asserted that high rents for new apartments prevented most workers from moving into new housing settlements. In a common diagnosis of the impact of high rents, *Die Freiheit*, Düsseldorf's Communist newspaper, noted in 1928 that over 6,000 families still sought apartments and concluded that "the chief source of housing misery lies now not in the lack of housing space, but chiefly in the impossibility of coming up with the high rents, especially for new buildings."[22]

The lack of affordable housing, despite all efforts to lower construction costs, raised Social Democratic dissatisfaction with municipal governments, particularly in cities where Social Democrats remained shut out of decision making. Thus, Hanover's SPD made the high rents of new apartments a centerpiece of its ongoing struggle against municipal government by a bourgeois block. Councilor Westphal, the editor of the SPD's newspaper *Volkswille*, charged in September 1928 that Hanover's housing programs neglected the needs of the working class. The city's new apartments were so expensive, that "someone who works with his hands in factories … cannot pay the rent."[23] Continuing to rebuke the administration for high rents as municipal elections approached in 1929, *Volkswille* recalled that Hanover's SPD had spent years calling for a housing construction program with "affordable new apartment rents for the working population." Not only had the administration failed to meet this goal, but, *Volkswille* claimed rather implausibly, Hanover had the highest rents for new apartments of any city except for Berlin.[24]

High rents, it should be noted, were not exclusively the concern of Communists and Social Democrats. The goal of democratizing access to new housing won broad support within municipal governments. Charging in December 1926 that Frankfurt's housing program benefitted only the wealthy, Konrad Lang, the chair of the KPD in the city parliament, heard his complaints echoed by a member of the Center Party who pointed to the example of a new three-room apartment with a rent of RM 70 a month in order to argue that many could not afford to live in Frankfurt's new apartments. Even three years later in 1929 weekly wages in the metal industry averaged only RM 42.72 for an unskilled worker and RM 55.20 for a skilled worker, and many worker households of the late 1920s in fact spent significantly less than 25 percent of wages on housing.[25]

Municipal planners were themselves dismayed to discover how difficult it was to reduce the rents of new apartments. The head of Hamburg's housing office determined in 1927 that a majority of those seeking housing were unable to afford the rents for new apartments. Altona's City Planner, Gustav Oelsner, regretted in 1928 that "the rents of new apartments are not within the means of most workers in spite of the rent tax and communal sacrifice." In Frankfurt, Ernst May conceded in 1928 that Frankfurt's new apartments, though attractive and well designed, were "still too expensive, measured by the income of the population classes that suffer the most from this fearful housing shortage." Skilled workers occupied 24.5 percent of Frankfurt's new apartments, but unskilled workers occupied only 1.8 percent of new apartments. Some of those too poor to afford new apartments moved into vacated old apartments, but this trend brought little comfort to May. He told the city parliament that "these old apartments are in part ... in such a condition, that it is not responsible to still put families in such apartments today."[26]

While most municipal officials and politicians acknowledged that city governments had not managed to do enough to provide affordable housing for workers, representatives of organized house owners were not above voicing dissent. Düsseldorf's Wirtschaftsbund expressed suspicion of the administration's apparently laudable goal to see that those of modest means received new housing. The featured speaker at an assembly held by the Wirtschaftsbund on 27 November 1928, a local architect named Paetz, questioned the administration's assumption that the shortage of apartments for the "poor" justified setting aside large rent-tax mortgages. "Who are these poor?" asked Paetz. They were workers, he answered, a group which, he claimed, had already received excessive consideration from the municipal government.[27]

Claims that cities had tried to do too much to provide affordable housing for workers constituted a minority position, but workers were not the only group of consumers thought to face trouble finding housing. A broad cross-section of municipal leaders maintained that promotion of housing construction had also neglected the needs of the *Kinderreich*, large families with children. Significant numbers of families with children lived in emergency shelters. In Düsseldorf alone, the administration estimated in 1928 that 400 Kinderreich families urgently required suitable housing. Dismayed by these numbers, councilor Haltenberg of Düsseldorf's DDP observed that an apartment can only be obtained if someone can pay a fee and "has at most one, at best, no children. This state of affairs is a scandal."[28]

The trend towards building small apartments to reduce construction costs and housing rents further troubled municipal leaders who wished to satisfy the needs of families with children. Upon receiving Ernst May's plan to build apartments of 38 square meters as the minimum for living (*Existenzminimum*), a number of Frankfurt's city councilors expressed concern that Frankfurt should not neglect the Kinderreich.[29] Small apartments reduced rents, but the advice of two generations of housing reformers suggested that such apartments were, at best, inappropriate and, at worst, immoral for large families. In Düsseldorf, councilor Liertz, one of the Center Party's most enthusiastic backers of municipal promotion of housing construction, warned that two-room apartments were not "family apartments."[30]

Focusing on the needs of consumers created a new dilemma for municipal planners and politicians. Housing that satisfied a hygiene reformer's or architect's every scruple was too expensive to meet demand for affordable apartments. Responding to criticism of the drawbacks of small apartments, councilor Haltenberg of Düsseldorf's DDP argued that municipal authorities first had to concentrate on supplying affordable housing. He reminded his colleagues of the city government's duty to ensure that the "large masses" of the population obtained housing. Since many residents, unfortunately, could only afford two-room apartments, creating ideal housing for families would have to remain a matter for future action.[31]

Looking for an approach to housing policy that could provide affordable housing in the immediate future while raising housing standards in the long run, municipal politicians and planners devised schemes for building expandable or flexible housing. Two-room apartments intended for either old or young couples, suggested Düsseldorf's SPD, could later be combined into larger apartments.[32] Martin Wagner, Berlin's city planner, refined this housing strategy, drafting plans for flexible housing units in his book, *Das Wachsende Haus*.[33]

Arguments in favor of building small apartments did not fully answer concerns about the apparent neglect of the needs of families. Small apartments might be intended for newly-married couples, but how were such families to obtain larger apartments if they had several children? What reason was there to expect that they would be better placed to pay much higher rents in possibly a few years time? The many city councilors who justified the construction of small apartments by noting the limited means of tenants essentially implied that public authorities could not ensure that new apartments met all of the criteria desirable for family living. Despite concern for the vitality of the work force and even for the health of children, municipal housing policy reflected a curious neglect of the family as a social unit. If, as David Crew and Young-Sun Hong argue, the emerging Weimar social state replaced the family, limited resources constrained the ability of public authorities to pursue a social policy of reconstructing model families.[34]

A major concern in the discussion of housing policy, determination to democratize access to civic benefits was also a recurrent theme in municipal organization of social provision and leisure. Whether the issue at stake was the ability of urban residents to rent new apartments, use sports fields or attend cultural institutions, promises of expanded social provision and leisure heightened scrutiny of any barriers that might prevent consumers from enjoying the full benefits of municipal activity. Just as they demanded that workers gain the opportunity to rent new apartments, Social Democrats supported municipal promotion of culture and leisure on the condition that all subsidized facilities and institutions should be accessible to a broad public audience. As a Social Democratic city councilor in Düsseldorf explained, "My party takes the view that subsidies for the theater and orchestra can only be justified to guarantee broader circles of the people a share of the achievements of culture."[35]

Identifying attendance by workers at civic institutions as a sign of full membership by the working class in civic communities, which had until recently barred most residents from full participation in civic life, municipal politicians from the SPD and KPD were extremely sensitive to any obstacles, real or imagined, to entrance to facilities of leisure and culture. In Frankfurt am Main, for example, Social Democratic city councilors perceived the DVP's opposition to a proposal adding a light and air bath to the city's stadium as evidence of bourgeois desire to limit use of sports facilities. Construing more sinister motives than the DVP's professed desire for thrift, councilor Rebholz of the SPD declared, "Perhaps one still wants to make the stadium into an exclusive bourgeois institution."[36] Social Democratic city councilors worried that Frankfurt's stadium might become exclusive. By 1927 the KPD maintained that it had become a class institution: a Communist city councilor termed the stadium "a privilege for the possessing classes."[37]

Ensuring full participation by workers in civic life seemed to be a simple task if, as many Social Democrats and Communists believed, high entrance prices formed the principle barrier to use of civic facilities. The chair of the KPD in Frankfurt's city parliament claimed that the costs of tickets made the city's stadium a "place of relaxation of the upper ten thousand," and both Social Democrats and Communists argued that high ticket prices hindered the development of a mass audience for theater in Frankfurt. (In 1925 the cheapest seats cost RM 2.20 for the opera and RM 1.70 for the playhouse, though standing places were available for RM 1.70 at the opera and RM 1 at the playhouse.)[38]

In order to remove the economic barriers to access to civic institutions, city councilors from the KPD and the SPD issued a stream of demands for lower admissions prices: Frankfurt's KPD demanded free entrance at all museums and galleries on Sundays; and the SPD called for lower entrance prices to the Palm Garden along with free entrance on Sunday, according to one Social Democrat the only day when workers could manage to go the Garden. In Hanover, Social Democrats sought to reduce entrance prices for public baths and resisted any increase in ticket prices for the Freie Volksbühne (Free Peoples' Theater), an organization which purchased blocks of theater tickets for its members.[39]

For all of their scrutiny regarding the possible obstacles to full participation by workers in civic life, Social Democrats and Communists faced little if any resistance to their calls for extending access to cultural institutions to all social groups. The goal of democratizing cultural life won broad political support. Even Hanover's Heinrich Tramm, a confirmed opponent of Social Democracy, declared in 1925 that "the possibility must be given to the broadest classes of the population ... to visit this institution [Hanover's theater]." Tramm's views in this area corresponded closely to those of many Weimar municipal leaders, including Frankfurt's Mayor Landmann who made the democratization of culture a rationale for theater subsidies. The "justification for the high subsidies," he told city councilors, rested on the city theater's ability to give "large masses the possibility of visiting the theater."[40] Placing a stamp of approval on the goal of democratizing the audience for theater, a subcommittee of the chief committee of Frankfurt's city parliament presented a report in 1928 that recommended the transformation of the municipal theater into a "people's theater."[41]

The financial troubles of theaters reinforced the case for democratizing civic culture. Mayors and city councilors, looking for the causes of rising theater subsidies, found one explanation in the attendance at municipal theaters that ranged from disappointing to dismal. No German municipal theater managed to sell 80 percent of all seats for performances in 1928. Hanover's opera sold 69 percent of all seats, while Frankfurt's opera sold only 60.5 percent of all available seats. Frankfurt's playhouse sold 66.4 percent of seats, a figure that however unsatisfactory, compared favorably with respect to attendance at Hanover's theater (53.6 percent) and the disastrous attendance in Düsseldorf (46.5 percent and 39.7 percent), a poor showing caused in part by Düsseldorf's attempt to operate two stages simultaneously.[42]

Empty seats and persistent deficits at municipally supported theaters raised suspicion that the price of tickets was not the only obstacle to higher attendance. It was by no means clear that the expense of tickets barred urban residents from visiting theaters in greater numbers. At a price of only RM 1.30 in 1925, the cheapest seats available in Hanover did not compare unfavorably with the cost of seeing a film, and Frankfurt's Magistrat reported in 1927 that reducing subscription prices and distributing unsold places to the Bund für Volksbildung had not increased revenues.[43] Perhaps people did not come to theaters in larger numbers because the plays offered did not appeal to them. City councilors and mayors presumed to act in the public interest when they approved of the promotion of theater, other forms of leisure and housing construction, but the question remained: what types of culture, sports, and housing did urban residents want?

Public Taste

The cultural ferment of the Weimar Republic greatly complicated the tasks of determining what varieties of culture complied with public taste. Municipal leaders who wished to cater to public taste found themselves choosing among several varieties of culture. The simplest recipe for democratizing culture was to cultivate public taste for standard works, an approach that called for educating a mass audience in the existing repertory. Voicing optimism in the prospects of molding public taste in this fashion, Frankfurt's Mayor Landmann praised the city's theater for bringing up "the masses to the works of the great."[44] Landmann's expectations were not unreasonable. Enthusiasm for cultural education complied with the views of Social Democrats who had longed wished to make bourgeois culture into workers' culture.[45]

Weimar municipal leaders could not assume that introducing a broad audience to standard cultural works was the only possible aim of municipal promotion of culture, for new styles of culture, including both experiments in political drama and an emerging mass culture, flourished after the First World War. These cultural alternatives met with highly varied responses from municipal politicians. Among them the most enthusiastic proponents of the new political dramas among municipal politicians were members of the parties of the Left. In Frankfurt, Konrad Lang, chair of the KPD in the city parliament, criticized the municipal theater for presenting a program made up of farces, Shakespeare, and light comedies instead of pieces that matched the "psyche of the working population." The theater's program, he maintained, corresponded with the "intellectual views of a decadent upper class." For theater suitable for a mass audience, Frankfurt should look to the work of Erwin Piscator, the noted Berlin director who also won admiration among Frankfurt's Social Democrats.[46] Calling for "more consideration of public taste," the SPD's chair commented favorably on Piscator's experiments with techniques from film.[47]

Where Social Democrats and Communists attributed poor attendance to neglect of new plays, city councilors on the right maintained that public dissatisfaction with theater stemmed precisely from productions of contemporary drama. Councilor Luettke of the DNVP condemned what he called the "new theater," and councilor Lion of the DVP asked for greater consideration for classics.[48] In a most vitriolic attack against contemporary theater, councilor Gemeinder of Frankfurt's small National Socialist splinter party attacked theater and contemporary art as a "discharge of our contemporary time, our present intellectual degeneration."[49]

Plans for rescuing municipal theaters from red ink revealed the pervasive belief of civic leaders in a divided civic public. Municipal leaders based their suggestions for changes to theater programs on their judgments, however misguided, of the presumed preferences of different socio-political milieus. City councilors from all parties wanted theaters to offer programs that would increase attendance, but while Social Democrats and Communists referred to the alleged cultural demands of workers, city councilors from the bourgeois Right looked to what they thought to be the desires of a very different audience.

Weimar disputes over public taste and cultural style reached a fevered pitch with the igniting of theater affairs, controversies that occurred as part of a "sharp cultural backlash" with demonstrations against offending plays and operas.[50] Several theater affairs took place in Frankfurt where the municipal theater, contrary to Communist claims, performed a varied program that included works by Brecht, Kokoschka, Pirandello, Shaw, and Walter Hasenclever among others.[51] The now obscure Hasenclever was one of the more popular playwrights of the Weimar Republic. His comedy, *Ehen werden im Himmel geschlossen* (Marriages Are Celebrated in Heaven), a play in which three actors alternately play God, Saint Peter, and Mary Magdalene in heaven and are participants in love triangles on earth, set off fierce debate in cities including Berlin, Weimar, Vienna, and Frankfurt in 1928 and 1929.[52] While *Ehen werden im Himmel geschlossen* won praise from Frankfurt's SPD, it enraged the city's Center Party and the parties of the bourgeois Right. Angered by Hasenclever's representation of God and of important Christians – St. Peter looked like an old second hand-dealer and God appeared as "a caricature in sports-pants and wearing a monocle" – the Center Party and the DNVP tried to ban the play as an impermissible attack against religion. Councilor Nagel of the DNVP asked if the theater was still a "culture theater." A National Socialist councilor shouted out that it was a "Bordello stall," and the DVP's chair, councilor Landgrebe, thought that the head of the playhouse should pay with his job.[53]

A number of other theater affairs followed in the next several years in Frankfurt. Both the Center Party and the parties of the bourgeois Right objected to the performance in January 1930 of the play *Cyankali*, a piece by Friedrich v. Wolf decrying the effects of laws against abortion. Later in 1930, the performance of Brecht's *The Rise and Fall of the City of Mahagonny* infuriated the bourgeois Right and National Socialists. National Socialist demonstrators threw smoke bombs and fireworks into the audience during the second act of the performance on 19 October 1930. The National Socialist city councilor Kremer's concern for the safety of theatergoers was so great that he asked how the Magistrat intended to protect the public from "systematic attacks on their Christian and German feeling."[54]

Performances of dramas and operas written separately or together by Bert Brecht and Kurt Weill ignited theater affairs in several cities.[55] Hanover's city opera's surprising decision to perform Kurt Weill's *Der Protagonist* in the winter of 1928/29 pleased the theater critic of Hanover's Social Democratic newspaper, but provoked protests from an array of bourgeois and confessional associations offended by Weill's music and by a play-within-a-play pantomime scene involving a monk and a woman. The Evangelical Press Committee warned that a publicly supported theater was obliged "to offer only noble art and to avoid pieces that injured the moral feelings of wide circles of the population," and the German Federation of Women (Deutsche Frauenbund) and the Housewives' Association (Hausfrauverein) signed a joint letter claiming that *Der Protagonist* "injures we German women profoundly and is not consistent with German nature and outlook."[56] Such protests did have effect for the production of the opera was suspended and then canceled in early 1929.[57]

As they debated how municipal theaters could best appeal to public taste, many municipal leaders and theater professionals began to think that it might not matter what types of plays theaters offered so long as new forms of entertainment, film, mass-spectator sports, and radio, enthralled the public. Even as municipal theaters struggled to fill seats, customers flocked to see movies and sporting events. As early as 1922/23, Düsseldorf's Apollo movie theater attracted a total attendance of 600,000 people. Frankfurt, by 1932, had 56 theaters with a total capacity of 26,000 people. Attendance also soared at sporting events. Tens of thousands attended soccer matches, and contests between local favorites drew 30,000 spectators in Frankfurt.[58]

Did the movie and soccer crowds reduce attendance at institutions of bourgeois culture? Theater professionals were divided in their assessments of the threat of mass entertainment. Walter Hasenclever thought that new forms of entertainment posed a challenge to theater, but Max Hochdorf, a theater critic for the Social Democratic newspaper *Vorwärts* asserted that the existence of any competition between film, boxing, six day races, and theater was only an "assumption."[59] Other interested observers were less sanguine. The Directors of Frankfurt's Palm Garden claimed that the botanical garden suffered from competition from "pleasure palaces" and from the "migration of youths devoting themselves more and earlier to sports or to physical culture." A growing number of municipal officials and politicians also concluded that enthusiasm for movies and sports might doom older cultural institutions. "We still do not know," said Max Michel, Frankfurt's Department Head for Theater, "whether the theater will be able to maintain itself as the highly valuable institution of education next to cinema, radio, and sports," and Düsseldorf's administrative report for 1925 to 1927 suggested that the loss of interest in theater was particularly strong among young people attracted by the "growing sports movement."[60]

Whether striving to sustain municipal theaters or promoting popular forms of leisure, municipal leaders struggled to interpret public taste. Mass appeal in itself gave no guarantee that promotion of leisure would serve a useful purpose. There was no cause to doubt public interest in sports; record attendance at soccer matches, flourishing sports clubs, and sports reporting in newspapers were all proof of a growing fascination with sports, but municipal politicians and officials were not certain whether urban residents would make the proper use of sports. Preoccupation with competition and entertainment struck a surprising number of city councilors and sports functionaries as serious drawbacks to the sports boom sweeping Germany during the 1920s. Voicing standard concerns about the form of public enthusiasm for sports, councilor Wilms of Düsseldorf's DVP and a member of the Gesolei's organizing committee cautioned against placing too much weight on records and peak sporting achievements.[61]

Of all of the municipal politicians, Social Democrats and Communists were probably most suspicious of mass-spectator sports.

Members of both the SPD and KPD in Frankfurt disparaged sporting events that catered to crowds of spectators. Councilor Theis of Frankfurt's KPD wished to see the city's new stadium become "a people's park," and set himself against sporting spectacles such as the six-day races that only served "as a tickle for overwrought nerves." Councilor Cremer, the SPD's sports expert, also objected to holding bicycle races in the stadium. Restating reservations about mass-spectator sports, the SPD urged in 1926 that the city's new sports hall should not be used for elite sports events. The SPD's councilor Jourdan expected that the hall would be used to promote health among the "widest circles of the population"; it should not serve "competitive soccer matches and the like."[62]

Alternately encouraged, confused and even dismayed by the trends in public taste for leisure and culture, municipal leaders at least managed to avoid debates over popular views on architecture in those cities that refrained from setting elaborate guidelines for housing design. This was not true, however, in a city like Frankfurt where promotion of housing construction brought innovation in housing design and with it, dispute over public taste in architecture. Frankfurt's residents certainly wanted new apartments, but, local observers asked, did they like the building style of Ernst May's "new Frankfurt?"

While May proclaimed that the "new Frankfurt" would emancipate urban residents, his critics countered that the new building style actually ignored the wishes of Frankfurt's population. Standardization in the "new Frankfurt" struck city councilors from parties of the bourgeois Right as proof of disregard for individual taste.[63] Councilor Landgrebe, the chair of the DVP in the city parliament, predicted that future housing construction would "again have to consider the individual wishes of the individual."[64] Taking a similar stance in February 1927, councilor Dobler of the DNVP asserted that "the art that in the end expresses itself in construction is individual."[65]

Politicians were not the only critics of the new building style; some tenants in Frankfurt were far from satisfied with the design of their new apartments. Frank Herterich aptly notes the unease felt by the "all-too-human" residents of apartments designed for "new people for the new Frankfurt." The *Frankfurter Post*, a newspaper closely associated with the DNVP, acted as an organ for the complaints of the Tenants' Committee of Frankfurt's Riederwald settlement, an organization that found flaws in the design of terraces and even commented unfavorably on the much-lauded Frankfurt kitchen. Whatever its political motivation, the Tenants' Committee displayed impatience with the experimental quality of Frankfurt's housing program, calling on the municipal government to withdraw housing construction from the hands of "theorists."[66]

The charge that Ernst May ignored public taste resurfaced in Frankfurt's municipal election campaign of 1929. *Wie Oberbürgermeister Dr. Landmann regierte*, the most noteworthy piece of political propaganda of the municipal election campaign of 1929, ridiculed Mays's pursuit of innovation. "He came out of Silesia filled with modern ideas," the booklet said of May, "a fanatical follower of the *neuen Sachlichkeit*."[67] The products of May's invention gave ample cause for criticism if not revulsion. They were "plaster board houses, new May Land and new Brestlitowski." The houses and housing settlements incorporated an alien design repugnant to the population. The booklet contended that the population felt the settlements "as foreign bodies, as carnival jokes."[68]

The Fragmentation of Civic Interest

Despite a common civic interest in the pursuit of comprehensive recovery programs, the very process of organizing social provision created political, economic, and cultural lines of division through the civic public. The promotion of sports and culture drew attention to the division of clubs along lines of political affiliation, and class divisions repeatedly resurfaced as municipal leaders discussed social and cultural programs. If such disputes over spending for leisure and culture revealed old political divisions between the Left and the Right, the political Left proved to be less unified than ever as Communists resented the treatment of their organizations by Social Democratic municipal leaders. Efforts to bridge class division by focusing on the shared interests of consumers revealed further cleavages within the civic public. Setting guidelines for the promotion of housing construction showed the difficulty of balancing the interests of consumers and producers. In sum, recurrent disputes over the organization of social provision recast the civic public into such groups as workers, the Kinderreich, consumers, building professionals, and members of Social Democratic, Communist, and bourgeois cultural networks.

Recurrent disputes over the organization of municipal policy might suggest, as economic historians including Knut Borchardt and Harold James argue, that the expansion of state activity embroiled public authorities of the Weimar Republic in new conflicts.[69] In the municipal case, conflicts sparked by the growth of state intervention extended well beyond distributional struggles to encompass debates over public taste and the very structure of the civic public. Were these disputes an inherent product of state expansion? Critics of interventionist states might suggest that any significant phase of state expansion politicizes disputes previously confined to the private realm. However, it must be stressed that Weimar civic leaders believed that the shared benefits of programs of recovery would unite the civic public. The expansion of state activity created both potential shared benefits and possible conflicts over the organization of new forms of intervention. Why, then, in the case of cities of the Weimar Republic, did the strong common civic interest in recovery ultimately fail to close the rifts produced during disputes over the organization of municipal policy?

The multiple cleavages within the civic public reflected both the difficulty of providing shared benefits to urban residents and the persistence of preexisting social and political divisions. The conjunction of significant financial restraints and rapid expansion of state activity limited the ability of city governments to tighten bonds of civic unity by expanding social provision. Despite considerable success in providing social and cultural benefits to urban residents, municipal authorities struggled to meet their own goal of democratizing access to improved living conditions. The constraints facing civic leaders were particularly evident in promotion of housing construction. Municipal officials and politicians could take pride in new housing settlements, yet building officials conceded that new apartments were still comparatively expensive for many urban residents.

Facing obstacles in their efforts of extending social and cultural benefits of recovery to all urban residents, municipal leaders themselves participated in preserving a fractured and fragmented conception of the civic public.[70] Broad support for democratizing access to civic benefits did not bridge the deep divisions between socio-political milieus. Disputes over the distribution of funds to sports clubs revealed persistent rivalry between Social Democratic and bourgeois associations. Political conflicts over guidelines for housing construction often centered on the potential tension between the needs of workers and bourgeois housing professionals. Debates over cultural policy, meanwhile, revealed that many municipal politicians described public taste in terms of the presumed interests of competing socio-political milieus.

The persistent divisions in the civic public created strains in the consensus of recovery as municipal authorities faced charges of discrimination from all sides. City councilors from parties of the Left complained of the neglect of workers' needs, and, at worst, of efforts to exclude workers from full membership in the civic community. Splinter parties, on the other hand, as well as some city councilors from established parties of the bourgeois Right, charged that building professionals and house owners suffered from exaggerated municipal attention to workers. By this calculation, the Mittelstand, not the working class, was truly disadvantaged. Protesting municipal treatment of property owners and building professionals, Düsseldorf's Wirtschaftsbund and other local parties with ties to organized house owners sought to make themselves the champions of the Mittelstand during the period of stabilization.

Further divisions in the civic public sometimes emerged through a series of cultural debates. Promoting culture and leisure during a period of rapid cultural change, municipal leaders struggled to evaluate the new building style, new sports, new theater and other cultural forms which Detlev Peukert has described as "classical modernity." The emerging mass culture captivated, confused and sometimes disturbed mayors and city councilors. The conjunction of high attendance at movies and sporting events with stubborn theater deficits raised concern that mass culture might undermine surviving cultural institutions of the prewar era. Social Democrats and Communists sometimes voiced suspicion of mass-spectator sports, while city councilors from bourgeois parties and the Center Party expressed strong distaste on occasion for experiments in drama and opera. The ensuing theater affairs, though not directly concerned with central programs of recovery, contributed to worsening relations between the Left and the bourgeois Right, and also between Social Democrats and Liberals, on the one hand, and confessional communities, on the other hand.

Debates on defining the needs and desires of the civic public acquired an additional dimension in cities where municipal recovery became closely identified with experiments in cultural modernism. Reaction against cultural modernism was therefore especially strong in Frankfurt where civic leaders promoted innovation in building. While plans to create a "new Frankfurt" through functional planning gained accolades, the administration's pursuit of innovation also produced unease among city councilors on the bourgeois Right during the early years of stabilization, and opposition to the "new Frankfurt" escalated in 1929 and 1930.

If attacks against cultural modernism in the "new Frankfurt" departed from the experience of the many cities that were not centers of innovation, denunciations against Ernst May reflected reaction not simply against cultural modernism, but also against claims of objective expertise made by municipal planners during the period of stabilization. From 1925 to 1928, May's critics had expressed doubts about the effectiveness of rationalization and the advantages of the new building style. In 1929 and 1930, they asserted that they had been right all along to mistrust experimentation.

Notes

1. Oberbürgermeister Brauer, "Die Sozialdemokratie und der Kommunalgroßwahltag unter Berücksichtigung der Wahlen in Preußen" *Die Gemeinde* 6 (1929): 973.

2. BA Potsdam 25:01, deutsches Reichsbank 3360, *Berliner Tageblatt*, 26 November 1927.

3. Zadach-Buchmeier, "Staatliche Jugendpflege in der kommunalen Praxis"; and Hartmut Lohmann, "Organisierter Arbeitersport in Hannover in den 20er Jahren," in *Stadt und Moderne*, ed. von Saldern, pp. 171, 259-60.

4. StVV Frankfurt, 1926, pp. 541-43.

5. *Gelsenkirchner Zeitung*, 22 July 1927; and 2 March 1928; and Siegfried Gehrmann, "Fußball in einer Industrieregion. Das Beispiel F.C. Schalke 04," in *Fabrik Familie Feierabend: Beiträge zur Sozialgeschichte des Alltags im Industriezeitalter*, ed. Jürgen Reulecke and Wolfahrd Weber (Wuppertal, 1978), pp. 382-86.

6. Herbert Dierker, "Arbeitersport im politischen Spannungsfeld der zwanziger Jahre: Sport, Politik, und Alltagserfahrungen," *Stadion* 15 (1989): 92, 96, 98, 104; and StVV Düsseldorf, 1929, p. 119.

7. Timm, *Gustav Oelsner*, p. 147; and Adelheid von Saldern, "Kommunaler Handlungsspielraum in der Wohnungspolitik während der Zeit der Weimarer Republik," in *Stadterneuerung in der Weimarer Republik und im Nationalsozialismus: Beiträge zur stadtbaugeschichtlichen Forschung*, ed. Kopetzki, Lasch, Lüken-Isberner, and Schlier (Kassel, [1987]), p. 244.

8. StVV Düsseldorf, 1927, p. 2.

9. *Statistisches Jahrbuch deutsche Städte* 24 (1929), p. 51.

10. StVV Düsseldorf, 1927, p. 233; and StA Düsseldorf XXIV 1113, *Rheinische Tageszeitung*, 19 August 1927.

11. Hüttenberger, *Die Industrie- und Verwaltungsstadt*, p. 310; and StA Düsseldorf XXIV 1113, *Düsseldorfer Nachrichten*, 19 July 1927; and *Der Führer Düsseldorf*, 13 August 1927.

12. StVV Düsseldorf, 1928, pp. 296-301; StA Düsseldorf XXIV 1113, Wohnungsbauprogramm 1928, and Wohnungsbauprogramm der Stadt Düsseldorf für die Jahre 1929/1932.

13. StA Düsseldorf XXIV 1113, *Düsseldorfer Stadtanzeiger*, 28 November 1928, and *Düsseldorfer Tageblatt*, 30 November 1928; and XXIV 1117, *Düsseldorfer Volkszeitung*, 12 December 1928.

14. StA Düsseldorf XXIV 1113, *Düsseldorfer Nachrichten*, 19 December 1928.

15. Ibid., *Düsseldorfer Nachrichten*, 19 December 1928, and 5 January 1929.

16. StA Düsseldorf XXIV 1113, *Düsseldorfer Nachrichten*, 10 January 1929, and *Düsseldorfer Stadtanzeiger*, 11 January 1929.

17. Andernacht and Kuhn, "Frankfurter Fordismus," pp. 54-55.

18. StVV Frankfurt 1927, p. 132.

19. Clemens Musch, "Die Baupolitik des Frankfurter Hochbauamtes," *Nachrichtenblatt des Bürger-Auschuss* 12 (1930): 30.

20. Ernst May, "Das flache Dach," *Das Neue Frankfurt* 1 (1927): 150.

21. StVV Düsseldorf, 1927, p. 13.

22. StA Düsseldorf XXIV 1112, *Die Freiheit*, 24 July 1928.

23. BVK Hannover, 1928-1929, pp. 61-62.

24. *Volkswille*, 17 November 1929.

25. StVV Frankfurt, 1926, pp. 1079-84; and Andernacht and Kuhn, "Frankfurter Fordismus," pp. 50-51.

26. Hermann Hipp, "Wohnungen für Arbeiter? Zum Wohnungsbau und zur Wohnungsbaupolitik in Hamburg in den 1920er Jahren," in *Arbeiter in Hamburg*, ed., Arno Herzig, Dieter Langewiesche, and Arnold Sywottek (Hamburg: Verlag Erziehung und Wissenschaft, 1983), p. 475; Timm, *Gustav Oelsner*, pp. 139-40; and StVV Frankfurt, 1928, pp. 1018-19.

27. StA Düsseldorf XXIV 1113, *Düsseldorfer Stadtanzeiger*, 28 November 1928.

28. StA Düsseldorf XXIV 1113, Wohnungsbauprogramm 1928; and XXIV 1112, *Düsseldorfer Stadtanzeiger*, 8 August 1928.

29. StVV Frankfurt, 1928, p. 1022.

30. StVV Düsseldorf, 1927, p. 3.

31. Ibid., 1927, 5.

32. Ibid., 1927, pp. 7-8.

33. Martin Wagner, *Das Wachsende Haus: Ein Beitrag zur Lösung der städtischen Wohnungsfrage* (Berlin, 1932).

34. Crew, "German Socialism, the State and Family policy," pp. 241, 258; and Hong, "The Contradictions of Modernization in the German Welfare State: Gender and the Politics of Welfare Reform in First World War Germany," *Social History* 17 (1992): 253-57.

35. StVV Düsseldorf, 1925, pp. 185-86.

36. StVV Frankfurt, 1925, p. 522.

37. Ibid., 1927, p. 1170.

38. Ibid., 1926, pp. 790-91; and 1928, p. 928; and Hugo Lindemann, Otto Most and Albert Sudekum, ed., *Kommunales Jahrbuch*, vol. 1, (Jena, 1927), p. 247.

39. StVV Frankfurt, 1925, p. 381; 1928, pp. 874, 1138, 1323-27; and 1929, p. 762; *Volkswille*, 7 March 1928; StA Hannover Theater Kommission, 13 December 1924, pp. 2-7; Theater Kommission, 26 January 1925, pp. 3-7; and Theater Kommission, 22 August 1925, p. 4.

40. BVK Hannover, 1925-1926, p. 205; and StVV Frankfurt, 1927, p. 1107.

41. StVV Frankfurt, 1928, p. 528.

42. *Statistisches Jahrbuch deutsche Städte* 25 (1930), pp. 43-44.

43. BVK Hannover, 1925-1926, p. 1501; and StVV Frankfurt, 1927, p. 1088.

44. StVV Frankfurt, 1927, p. 1107.

45. Adelheid von Saldern, "Arbeiterkulturbewegung in Deutschland in der Zwischenkriegszeit," in *Arbeiterkulturen zwischen Alltag und Politik: Beiträge zum europäischen Vergleich in der Zwischenkriegszeit,* ed. Friedhelm Boll (Vienna, 1986), pp. 34, 37; and W.L. Guttsman, *Workers' Culture in Weimar Germany: Between Tradition and Commitment* (New York, 1990), pp. 57-58.

46. StVV Frankfurt, 1925, p. 1113; 1926, p. 342; and 1927, pp. 1098, 1253.

47. Ibid., 1928, p. 1553. Note that Piscator in fact stood in the face of bankruptcy when he tried to run his own theater. See Hermand and Trommler, *Die Kultur der Weimarer Republik,* p. 195.

48. StVV Frankfurt, 1926, pp. 787-88; and 1927, p. 1096.

49. Ibid., 1927, p. 1101.

50. Willet, *The Theater of the Weimar Republic,* p. 123.

51. Otfried Buethe, "'Beifall und Skandal' – Beispiele zum Sprechtheater der Frankfurter städtischen Bühnen in den zwanziger Jahren unter Richard Weichert und zu seiner Zusammenarbeit mit dem Bühnenebildner Ludwig Sievert," *Archiv für Frankfurts Geschichte und Kunst* 51 (1968): 152; and *Frankfurter Zeitung,* 19 October 1928.

52. Kurt Pinthus, "Walter Hasenclever Leben und Werk," in *Gedichte, Dramen, Prosa, Walter Hasenclever,* ed., Kurt Pinthus (Hamburg, 1963), pp. 41-44.

53. StVV Frankfurt, 1928, pp. 1443-45, 1452-53.

54. Ibid., 1930, pp. 89, 102, 1031; and *Frankfurter Nachrichten,* 20 October 1930.

55. John Willett, *The Weimar Years: A Culture Cut Short* (New York, 1984), p.144; Willett, *The Theater of the Weimar Republic,* p. 123; and Noakes, *The Nazi Party in Lower Saxony 1921-1933* (Oxford, 1971), p. 135.

56. StA Hannover X C 10 nr. 22, Frauenverbände to the Magistrat, 15 February 1929; *Hannoverscher Volkszeitung,* 14 February 1929; and StA Hannover Theater Kommission, 11 February 1929, pp. 3-6.

57. StA Hannover, Theater Kommission, 11 February 1929, p. 3; and Magistrat, 1929, pp. 556, 613.

58. Lynn Abrams, "From Control to Commercialization: The Triumph of Mass Entertainment in Germany, 1900-1925?" *German History* 8 (1990): 278-82; and James Wickham, "Working-Class Movement and Working-Class Life: Frankfurt am Main during the Weimar Republic," *Social History* 8 (1983): 338.

59. "Die Lebensbedingungen der Schaubühne im Jahre 1927,I," *Die Scene* 17 (1927): 4-6; and "Die Lebensbedingungen der Schaubühne im Jahre 1927, II," *Die Scene* 17 (1927): 34, 38.

60. StA Frankfurt S1723 V, Bericht des Vorstandes der Palmengarten-Gesellschaft über das Geschäftsjahr 1927; StVV Frankfurt, 1927, p. 1095, and 1928, p. 1298; and Verwaltungsbericht der Stadt Düsseldorf, 1 April 1925 bis 31 März 1928, p. 129.

61. Schloßmann, ed., *GE-SO-LEI,* vol. 2, p. 931.

62. StVV Frankfurt, 1925, pp. 307, 422; and 1926, p. 638.

63. Lane, *Architecture and Politics,* p. 103.

64. StVV Frankfurt, 1926, p. 884.

65. Ibid., 1927, p. 124.

66. Frank Herterich, "Neue Menschen für das Neue Frankfurt – oder die Resistenz des Allzu-Menschlichen," in *Ernst May und das Neue Frankfurt,* pp. 85-90; and Andernacht and Kuhn, "Frankfurter Fordismus," p. 61.

67. *Wie Oberbürgermeister Dr. Landmann regierte,* p. 62.

68. Ibid., pp. 62-64.

69. Borchardt, "Wirtschaftliche Ursachen," pp. 187, 189; and James "Economic Reasons for the Collapse of Weimar," p. 32.

70. See also Thomas Childers, "The Social Language of Politics in Germany: The Sociology of Political Discourse in the Weimar Republic," *American Historical Review* 95 (1990): 331-58.

Chapter 7

STATE AND SOCIETY

The Contradictions of Recovery

German mayors, city planners, and other civic leaders of the Weimar Republic made recovery a top priority, but by the late 1920s, municipal officials and politicians found themselves charged with having undermined stabilization. Critics of municipal policy argued that soaring municipal expenditures damaged the economy. Financial authorities and local splinter parties asserted that municipalities squandered large sums on unproductive or useless projects. And while municipal leaders at least promised to provide urban residents with improved living conditions, the organization of programs of recovery revealed and expanded divisions within civic communities.

Growing mistrust of city governments culminated in accusations of municipal scandal and corruption. Charges of municipal corruption became a hallmark of local political activity by National Socialists and organized house owners.[1] Even in cities in which mayors remained unscathed by charges of impropriety, residents had only too look at the front pages of newspapers to learn of scandal elsewhere, most notably in Berlin. The subject of enormous publicity throughout Germany in 1929, the Sklarek scandal was named for the Sklarek Brothers clothing company that bought clothes stockpiled by Berlin during the war, claimed that the clothes were of poor quality, obtained a refund and a monopoly contract on supplying clothing to Berlin, and was then found to have bribed municipal officials and to have sold a coat at far-below market cost to Berlin's Mayor Gustav Böß as a present for his wife.[2] Böß, despite his tangential involvement was vilified and resigned, and the Sklarek scandal became a symbol throughout Germany of municipal corruption.

Amounting to more than a series of isolated scandals and financial and political disputes, the numerous attacks levelled against municipal governments revealed the uneasy relationship between state and society in the Weimar Republic. The growth of government activity during the Weimar Republic made the state, whether national or local, a logical address for directing complaints. As Richard Bessel observes, "the advances of the 1920s ... multiplied the points of conflict between the German State and its citizens."[3] A case can be made for assigning grave consequences to such friction between state and society. The timing of political disintegration in Germany, immediately following a period of extensive state intervention in society, suggests that rapid postwar expansion of all levels of the German State provoked resistance and finally political reaction.

For all of the evidence of mounting antagonism against all levels of government by the late 1920s, the conclusion that the growth of the Weimar State met with a virulent reaction does not fully explain the relationship between state and society during the Weimar Republic. Germans complained about the state for any number of reasons, but most did not wish to be left alone, undisturbed by government. Indeed, many demanded state action and new forms of public intervention to deal with the effects of war and postwar traumas. It was not, then, the uniformity, but the variety of responses to the expansion of the state that fostered political instability during the Weimar Republic.

Contradictory Evaluations of the State

The contradiction between criticism of the Weimar State and demands for state intervention was most severe for politicians from parties of the bourgeois Right. Municipal politicians and officials with ties to established parties of the bourgeois Right mixed demands for savings, a position that logically implied the need to reduce state activity, with pleas for state action to solve problems of recovery. In one particularly striking case in Düsseldorf, councilor Ellenbeck, an influential member of Düsseldorf's DNVP, argued that the consequences of war paradoxically mandated both fiscal caution and government activism. The tremendous cost of war and the added financial burden of reparations compelled thrift, but the damage caused by war made "social, hygienic, and cultural protective measures" necessary. Ellenbeck recognized that his own analysis of social and economic needs yielded contradictory conclusions. "The necessity of simultaneously economizing to be able to get by, and nevertheless paying most serious attention to welfare, in order to secure vitality and capacity for work ..., places extraordinary difficulties before a savings program."[4]

The defense of new forms of state intervention blurred one of the distinctions between established bourgeois parties and the SPD, and even mounting animosity between the political Left and Right did not erase signs of convergence between Social Democratic and bourgeois expectations of the state. Programs for municipal action issued before the communal elections of November 1929 by the DVP and prominent Social Democrats overlapped to a surprising degree. The DVP's municipal political committee promised to combat "luxury expenditures," but, at the same time, suggested that savings should not compromise vital tasks: "a reasonable thrift does not mean abandonment of the fulfillment of essential tasks of cultural and social policy." These tasks included "the physical training of our people." Similar aims for municipal policy received the endorsement of Altona's Mayor Brauer in a speech setting forth a Social Democratic program for the same communal elections of November 1929. Remarking that "man" stood at the center of attention of communal work, Brauer argued that "preserving the health of man, securing the possession of his capacity for work, amounts to the preservation of national and economic strength." Sharing similar goals for municipal policy, both Brauer and the DVP's municipal political committee recommended continued social intervention by the local state. The DVP's committee called for "the fight against the housing shortage," and Brauer praised municipal support for housing construction and physical exercise."[5]

Attempts to resolve the bourgeois Right's contradictory relationship with the state produced an explosive collision between two styles of politics. Local pressure for recovery and desire to improve urban living conditions fostered a consensus in favor of expanding state activity. The political consensus of recovery did not erase distinctions between the political Left and Right but established a broad field of politics, across the center of the political spectrum, in which political rivals accepted the need for increasing state intervention and engaged in debates over the proper boundaries for such state activity.

Recovery created the outlines for a new politics of consensus with a limited ideological terrain for disputing the boundaries of state activity; however, financial, political, and cultural disputes and municipal scandals preserved and even intensified the politics of bitter ideological combat between milieus or political camps. Despite the convergence between expectations of the state in the emerging politics of recovery, the division between Socialists and bourgeois groupings remained salient in the fractured politics of milieus. As reaction against municipal recovery programs gained strength in the late 1920s, criticism of the role of established bourgeois parties extended beyond disputes over the proper boundaries of the state to magnify the force of the collision between the uneasily coexisting forms of politics of Weimar Germany.

Betrayal and Political Mobilization

Sparked by the contradictory attitudes on the bourgeois Right towards the state, the clash between the politics of recovery and the politics of milieus, in turn, fed intense local populist reaction against the established parties of the bourgeois Right. At a time when many of the groupings claiming to speak for bourgeois voters still identified Marxism and Social Democracy as their chief enemies, the partial erosion of distinctions between bourgeois and Social Democratic expectations of the state exposed established bourgeois parties to increasingly bitter attacks from diverse competing splinter parties and local populists of the bourgeois Right. Special-interest lists flourished in towns across Germany by appealing to the resentment of the Mittelstand against established parties. The Economic Party, the most successful of these special interest parties on the national level for much of the 1920s, mobilized resentment against established bourgeois parties in Saxony and in urban regions of the Rhineland. Accusations of betrayal, always a major theme of Weimar politics, proliferated as splinter parties accused their established counterparts of disloyalty. In Lower Saxony, for example, National Socialists active in local politics claimed that the Economic Party, the DVP, and "the other local Mittelstand representatives were failing to assert its [the Mittelstand's] interests."[6]

Few local splinter parties were more successful in capitalizing on resentment against established parties than Düsseldorf's Wirtschaftsbund. After trying to forge a unified bourgeois block during the early years of stabilization, the Wirtschaftsbund began to mobilize opposition against Düsseldorf's Mayor Robert Lehr and the local DNVP.[7] The Wirtschaftsbund and its supporters singled out the city's DNVP for the failure of the Arbeitsgemeinschaft – a short-lived working group of the DNVP, DVP, and Wirtschaftsbund that came into existence in late 1925, but fell apart by 1926. In December 1926, *Haus und Grund*, the newspaper of Düsseldorf's House and Property Owners' Association, was convinced that the DNVP's disloyalty prevented the Arbeitsgemeinschaft from forcing a change in the administration's policies. Disgusted by the DNVP's acceptance of Lehr's explanation for the RM 5 million cost overruns for the permanent exhibition buildings constructed for Düsseldorf's Gesolei exhibition, *Haus und Grund* stated: "Only if the DNVP stands more strongly by the Arbeitsgemeinschaft the Wirtschaftsbund and the DVP, could the situation become a crisis for our city leader." *Haus und Grund* speculated that Lehr's personal dealings with the DNVP crippled the effectiveness of the Arbeitsgemeinschaft. Conversations behind closed doors of the city hall patched up many rips "that threaten to become dangerous clefts."[8]

With the final collapse of the Arbeitsgemeinschaft in 1927, the Wirtschaftsbund and its supporters stepped up attacks against both Mayor Lehr and the city parliament. Lehr, however culpable for the administration's alleged misdeeds, was not the sole author of municipal policy, and the Wirtschaftsbund denounced Düsseldorf's municipal politicians for generally following the mayor's lead. Claiming that craven conduct by city councilors permitted Lehr to carry out unnecessary projects, Dr. Oerding, secretary of the Wirtschaftsbund, asserted that "the parties and the city councilors who have given way to the administration's plans and proposals ... have a good part of the guilt" for the "effects of ... an exaggerated spending policy."[9]

For the Wirtschaftsbund, the failure of established parties to join in a united opposition bourgeois block constituted a betrayal of bourgeois principles. Expecting the worst from Communists and Social Democrats and little better from the Center Party, Düsseldorf's Wirtschaftsbund and its supporters viewed bourgeois cooperation with the administration as treason. Decrying the city parliament's approval in 1928 of new spending for items including land purchases and the construction of a water work and new public baths, *Haus und Grund* stated: "That these expenditures were approved is all the more regrettable, as even bourgeois parties have joined in voting for these expenditures." They had "apparently thrown the old party principles over board."[10]

Haus und Grund predicted that voters betrayed by Düsseldorf's established parties would exact vengeance at the polls. "The rage in the population against this luxurious communal policy has grown so strong," observed the newspaper of the House and Property Owners' Association, "that trust in all parties that have supported the policy of the administration has completely vanished."[11] Taking the fate of French monarchs as a cautionary tale for Düsseldorf's civic leaders, *Haus und Grund* suggested that conspicuous consumption, whether by French kings who "built castles and created a Versailles until their people bled" or by municipal leaders, ultimately provoked political reaction against discredited governments. There could be "parallels," *Haus und Grund* warned, unless Düsseldorf's next communal election brought a change in the city parliament. Luxurious palaces were the downfall of France's monarchs, and Düsseldorf's monuments to waste, most notably the permanent exhibition buildings, could prove to be the undoing of the city's municipal politicians: "The permanent buildings on the Rhine and planetarium are jokingly named the mortuary of the present city councilors and the crematorium of the contemporary city parliament."[12]

In the municipal election of 1929, the Wirtschaftsbund worked to ensure that Düsseldorf's DNVP and DVP paid the full penalty for deviating from what the Wirtschaftsbund claimed to be bourgeois principles of municipal policy. Instructing voters that a record of supporting the administration's excesses demonstrated that the DNVP could no longer be trusted, a campaign advertisement for the Wirtschaftsbund charged that the DNVP members had placed "themselves protectively before the expenditure policy of their party friend Dr. Lehr." Among its sins, the DNVP had approved cost overruns for the permanent exhibition buildings and the purchase of 30 art objects from the Sigmaringen collection.[13]

Even the DVP came in for criticism from the Wirtschaftsbund in the municipal election campaign. Rebuking the DVP for having avoided voting on the motion to authorize funds for the permanent exhibition buildings, the Wirtschaftsbund implied that the DVP could not be relied upon to combat Lehr and the administration. The Wirtschaftsbund reproached the DVP for inconsistency, declaring, "not the words, but the deeds of the DVP are decisive for the electorate."[14]

Attacks by splinter parties against their established counterparts revealed the fragmentation of bourgeois politics during the final years of stabilization, but so too did the ensuing responses by municipal leaders to populist mobilization on the political Right. Rejecting charges of betrayal, municipal leaders associated with established bourgeois parties continued to take contradictory stances towards their own role in shaping programs of recovery.

Under fire from splinter parties, they alternately condemned and defended the recent expansion of municipal activity.

Municipal politics in Düsseldorf furnished striking evidence of both the anger of splinter parties and of the vacillating course of established bourgeois parties. The ambivalence of Düsseldorf's DNVP towards the record of municipal activity surfaced on numerous occasions, including the fall of 1927 when Reichsbank President Schacht's charges of municipal luxury invigorated local critics of municipal policy such as the Wirtschaftsbund. Despite having voted for virtually all major municipal projects, Düsseldorf's DNVP did not join Mayor Lehr in refuting Reichsbank Schacht's charges of municipal "luxury expenditures," but at the same time, the DNVP also declined to pin the label of luxury on any of Düsseldorf's major projects of recovery. The DNVP offered scarcely a hint of disapproval of the sorts of projects that so enraged Schacht and splinter parties. As if at pains to show that Düsseldorf's DNVP opposed some sort of excessive spending, councilor Ellenbeck chided the administration for expenditures on projects including a tool shed in a public garden, examples of wasteful spending that Ellenbeck himself admitted might strike Lehr as "trivialities."[15]

Reluctant to side with Lehr against Schacht in the fall of 1927 at a time when Düsseldorf's administration was pushing for a local tax increase, the DNVP, nevertheless, tired of the Wirtschaftsbund's attempts to identify and prevent municipal extravagance in Düsseldorf. When the Wirtschaftsbund's councilor Schoepwinkel warned in 1929 against traces of luxury in a plan to build a new dormitory for nurses, Ellenbeck replied that critics of municipal policy were far too quick to refer to luxury. "Many things have been described as luxury in public discussion," he said, "that we cannot describe as luxury."[16]

The DNVP was itself divided on the proper response to claims that municipal expenditures had increased to pay for items of questionable utility. To some extent, councilor Schwietzke, the founder of the DNVP's Economic Committee, and councilor Ellenbeck represented different strains within the DNVP. Schwietzke temporarily cooperated with the Wirtschaftsbund in the bourgeois Right's shaky Arbeitsgemeinschaft in 1926 and 1927, while Ellenbeck, a more enthusiastic supporter of Mayor Lehr advocated ambitious programs of urban transformation.

These divisions within the DNVP did not however fully account for the party's contradictory attitude towards municipal policies of recovery, for both wings of the DNVP were inconsistent. Sounding much like a member of the Wirtschaftsbund in March 1928, Schwietzke noted the increasing burden of public spending on the economy, recommended an end to borrowing short-term credit, and called municipal use of foreign loans "a great danger for the entire German economy." Such comments implied that the growth of state activity should be curtailed, yet Schwietzke coupled recommendations for fiscal caution with support for major municipal projects including the construction of a new city hall and the promotion of housing construction. Though displeased by the number of apartments in the city government's possession, he still favored the vigorous promotion of housing construction, describing the "provision of the necessary number of apartments as the most important present cultural task."[17]

No more consistent than Schwietzke, Ellenbeck wrote a series of articles introducing the DNVP's agenda for 1929 in which he simultaneously called for lower taxes and greater savings, and defended ambitious and costly municipal recovery programs. "In no case tax increases," declared Ellenbeck, yet also urged "that now all energy must be exerted" to complete the housing construction program for the those of modest means.[18] Ellenbeck counted promotion of housing construction as one of the chief achievements of five years of municipal activity since the Ruhr struggle. With the four-year housing program, Düsseldorf's municipal government could meet its obligation to ensure that all urban residents enjoyed adequate housing. "Now the poor people for whom the housing program was made," Ellenbeck wrote, "are finally and really helped."[19]

Rejecting the Wirtschaftsbund's account of Düsseldorf's municipal policy as an exercise in squandering funds on luxuries, Ellenbeck defended projects that figured prominently in the Wirtschaftsbund's diatribes against municipal extravagance. One had only to take a trip along the banks of the Rhine to see ample proof of the benefits of Düsseldorf's promotion of culture and leisure. To the north, the new stadium provided "many thousand of city people the possibility for healthy sport." Moving south, Ellenbeck noted the city's new face along the Rhine, particularly the Rhine park where "thousands" walked every day, and the permanent exhibition buildings. If the stylistic interpretation of the museum buildings was a matter of individual taste, the new installations were nonetheless impressive.[20]

Asserting that the DNVP had been correct in supporting projects condemned by the Wirtschaftsbund, Ellenbeck, nonetheless, sensed that his party faced a serious challenge. He urged the DNVP's members "not to allow demagogy to confuse them." Asking for loyalty, he also tried to play on fears of the Left. The Wirtschaftsbund's attacks against the DNVP, he warned, could have the effect of handing power to an alliance anchored by the Left. Overlooking the conservatism of Düsseldorf's Center Party and the animosity between the city's SPD and KPD, he claimed that the majority of the Center Party, SPD, and KPD, that had formed for a single vote on 30 November 1927, might reappear.[21]

TABLE 7.1 Düsseldorf's municipal election of 1929

Party	Percentage of Votes	Seats in City Parliament
KPD	20.1	16
SPD	16.1	13
DDP	2.4	2
Center	27.3	22
Chr. Volksdienst (Christian People's Service)		1
DVP	8.0	6
DNVP	7.7	6
Wirtschaftsbund	13.4	11
NSDAP	2.4	2

Sources: Statistisches Jahrbuch deutscher Städte 28 (1933), 552, 559; and *Dokumentation zur Geschichte der Stadt Düsseldorf während der Weimarer Republik: Quellensammlung,* ed. Pädegogisches Institut der Landeshauptstadt Düsseldorf (Düsseldorf, 1985), p. 102.

Ellenbeck's fears proved prescient. Trying to take both sides in the bitter dispute over municipal programs of recovery, Düsseldorf's DNVP came to lack any clear stance in municipal politics by the end of the period of stabilization. The Wirtschaftsbund, in contrast, gained a strong political profile and had the satisfaction of eclipsing the DNVP as the largest single party on the bourgeois Right in Düsseldorf's municipal election of 1929. While the DNVP suffered disastrous losses falling from 12 to 6 seats in the city parliament, the Wirtschaftsbund won 11 seats – the Center Party and the KPD retained their positions as the two largest parties in the city parliament.[22]

It was not unusual for municipal leaders, whether in Düsseldorf or elsewhere, to adopt a contradictory stance towards municipal policy by the end of the Weimar period of stabilization. The Association of Cities, the chief lobbying organization for Germany's large cities, itself wavered in its defense of the municipal record of recovery. After angrily rejecting Schacht's charges of municipal luxury in the fall of 1927, the Association of Cities adopted an inconsistent approach, combining praise for programs of recovery with stern warnings to member cities to curtail spending. Working to convince national authorities in the winter of 1927/28 that the Advisory Board for Foreign Credit, which had ceased to hold hearings on loans since the fall of 1927, should again begin to process applications for foreign credit, the Association of Cities asked city governments to be on their best financial behavior. The board of the Association of Cities passed a resolution in January 1928 urging municipal administrations to "refrain from every avoidable expenditure"; however this very call for thrift suggested that many social expenditures were not avoidable. The board added that "the alleviation of social need and the overcoming of the housing shortage require, as previously, the utmost use of strength of the cities."[23]

The discrepancy between the Association of Cities' calls for spending cuts and its explanations of the importance of municipal activity became increasingly noticeable during 1928 and 1929 as reaction against municipal policy gathered force throughout Germany. The Finance Committee of the Association of Cities advised in March 1928 that even housing construction would have to take a lower priority, but in September of 1928 the board resolved that "the fight against the housing shortage belongs to the most urgent present tasks and requires the strongest effort of all."[24] Meeting in September 1929, as scandal grasped Berlin and city treasurers across Germany scrambled to cover municipal short-term debt, President Mulert of the Association of Cities spoke of the need for future thrift by municipalities but still called municipal cultural and social tasks "essential for the German people." Pressing needs in the areas of "school construction, housing construction and especially social welfare" had yet to be satisfied.[25]

Fleeing Political Contradictions

Both the Association of Cities and local bourgeois parties found it difficult to resolve the contradiction, created by participation in recovery, between praise for thrift and support for the expansion of state activity. Could municipal leaders associated with established bourgeois parties escape this basic contradiction? Rather than mixing calls for savings with justifications of the growth of state activity, municipal politicians from established bourgeois parties who wished to acquire a clear political identity could pursue an alternative strategy of renouncing municipal actions during the period of stabilization. Taking this course, Frankfurt's DVP performed a dramatic about-face, shifting from cooperation with the administration to complete opposition against Mayor Landmann and his municipal programs. In 1927, at the height of the productivity debate, Frankfurt's DVP had praised the effectiveness of municipal recovery programs in extravagant terms; councilor Landgrebe, chair of the DVP in the city parliament, stated that "the cities have correctly pointed out what important rebuilding work they practice on the German people," but from late 1928 onward, Frankfurt's DVP held municipal leaders and policies largely responsible for the failure of recovery.[26] *Wie Oberbürgermeister Dr. Landmann regierte*, the definitive statement of opposition to Landmann in the municipal election campaign of 1929, asserted that Frankfurt had built up a mountain of debt to pay for projects of questionable utility, all to serve the ambitions of a small clique surrounding Landmann: "One has the feeling in the population that all these buildings that devour huge sums ... comply with the wishes of individual people, who want to dominate everywhere."[27]

TABLE 7.2   Frankfurt's municipal elections of 1928 and 1929

	1928 Percentage of Votes	1928 Seats in City Parliament	1929 Percentage of Votes	1929 Seats in City Parliament
KPD	12.6	11	13.0	11
SPD	32.5	29	27.6	25
DDP	7.9	7	5.5	4
Center	10.8	9	12.2	11
Chr. Volksdienst		1		2
Arbeitnehmer		3		2
DVP	10.3	9	12.9	11
DNVP	8.0	7	4.7	4
Economic Party	5.6	4	6.8	6
NSDAP	4.5	4	9.9	9

Sources: Rebentisch, "Die treusten Söhne," p. 311, Abb. 7; Rebentisch, *Ludwig Landmann*, p. 259; and *Frankfurter Zeitung*, 18 November, 1929.

Charges of corruption, a standard element of reaction against municipal governments in 1929, figured prominently in the DVP's campaign against Landmann in Frankfurt. Councilor Merton, the owner of a metal company and a leader of the DVP in the city parliament for much of 1929, saw evidence of scandal in the discovery of a discrepancy between the balance of Frankfurt's gas company published with the certificate of audit of the accountants Price-Waterhouse & Company and the balance actually given to Price-Waterhouse. Merton wrote a letter on the matter that was first published in the *Deutsche Bergwerkszeitung*, the leading press organ of heavy industry, and Frankfurt's DVP and DNVP took the affair as cause to introduce a motion of no confidence in Landmann and city treasurer Asch on 11 July 1929.[28]

Frankfurt's DVP profited from its campaign against Landmann and municipal policy in the communal election of 1929. While Frankfurt's SPD suffered losses, falling from 29 to 25 seats in the city parliament, the DVP raised its number of city councilors from 9 to 11, but Frankfurt's National Socialists made even greater gains. The NSDAP, in one of its most impressive showings in all of Germany in 1929, more than doubled its number of city councilors from 4 to 9. For all of the DVP's efforts in 1929 to cast itself as the standard-bearer of reaction against Mayor Landmann, the NSDAP already displayed far greater potential to mobilize populist resentment in Frankfurt.

A perceptive, if bitter, analysis of Frankfurt's municipal election of 1929 in the *Frankfurter Zeitung*, a newspaper sympathetic to the DDP, attributed the DVP's gains in the election of 1929 to its adoption of populist radicalism in its campaign against Landmann and his administration. The DVP took advantage of a year's public agitation "against the 'Landmann system'" to make itself the second strongest party in the city parliament. Charging that the DVP's lengthy campaign against the "Landmann system" borrowed a new political style or "clamor" popularized by the KPD and the National Socialists, the *Frankfurter Zeitung* accused the DVP of making radicalism suitable for bourgeois Frankfurt. The DVP "legitimated the red that had been struck by the radical wing parties in years of desolate battle and made it usable for the classes that, in their bourgeois life, otherwise want to know little of that radicalism."[29]

By 1929, the distinction between Frankfurt's DVP and splinter parties of the bourgeois Right had blurred. It was true that National Socialists, who adopted an anti-Semitic line of attack against Landmann and City Treasurer Asch that was absent from the DVP's assault against the municipal administration, were still not entirely suitable for inclusion in a bourgeois block, but the city's Economic Party, long isolated at the margins of municipal politics, became a close ally of the DVP and DNVP, a change in status that did not stem from any shift in the Economic Party's political program.[30] In December 1929, as the city parliament reconvened after the bourgeois Right's electoral gains, the Economic Party joined the DVP and DNVP in submitting a motion of no confidence in Landmann, introduced by a member of the Economic Party with a speech referring to scandals, costly expenditures, and extravagance.[31]

Lending Frankfurt's DVP a clear political profile at a time when many bourgeois municipal leaders struggled to reconcile criticism of public spending with support for municipal activity, the DVP's campaign against Mayor Landmann in Frankfurt created a new political contradiction. As Frankfurt's DDP, Center Party, and SPD pointed out, the city's DVP had itself voted for most of the policies it now described as failures. The *Frankfurter Zeitung* asserted that the DVP "jointly approved and decided all the measures that were afterwards made out to the populace as crimes against the city and its welfare," and the DDP's chair, councilor Korff, estimated in December 1929 that the DVP had supported 90 percent of the Magistrat's motions.[32] Korff reminded the DVP that the city had made real accomplishments: loans had not gone to waste; Frankfurt had invested in housing construction and in utilities; claims of "mismanagement" under these circumstances were "demagogy of the worst sort."[33]

The DVP's abandonment of its own past course angered and surprised city councilors from the DDP and the Center Party. Outraged by the DVP's behavior, the Center Party issued a party declaration in December 1929 objecting to the "continuation of an unobjective and internally untrue election agitation." City councilors from the Center Party were astonished to discover that an established bourgeois party, such as the DVP, could become the companion of extremists. Councilor Scharp of the Center requested that the DVP acknowledge its responsibility for past policies now that it no longer stood to gain immediate electoral benefits from attacks on municipal policy. Scharp suggested that "you only threw off the responsibility that you now do not want to bear, for the special purposes of the election." He personally asked the DVP's chair Landgrebe not to use his modest electoral victory to work with the KPD and NSDAP to carry out destructive policies.[34]

It was precisely such a history of supporting major municipal initiatives that made it extremely difficult for established bourgeois parties to capitalize on resentment against municipal governments. Few established bourgeois parties managed to distance themselves from a past record of participating in recovery. In Berlin for example, the DVP and the DDP attempted to stave off losses in the municipal election of 1929 by campaigning against corruption (exemplified by the Sklarek scandal) and municipal policies of the preceding five years, but Berlin's established bourgeois parties failed to disassociate themselves from the municipal government of the period of stabilization.[35] Instead, the KPD and National Socialists capitalized most effectively on dissatisfaction with municipal affairs in Berlin. Even in Frankfurt, where the DVP displayed unusual strength at a time when established parties suffered from eroding support in much of Germany, the chief benefits of the campaign against Mayor Landmann went to the city's National Socialists.[36]

Attempting to explain the apparent contradiction between its attacks against Mayor Landmann and its prior support for most municipal programs between 1924 and 1928, Frankfurt's DVP blamed a "system" for the city's problems. It was not the DVP, but the "Landmann System" that had led Frankfurt astray. Declaring in October 1930 that "50 percent of the difficulties that we have today in the administration are not inevitable, but the result of a boundless expenditure economy and expansion policy," councilor Landgrebe insisted that the DVP's sharp words of the electoral campaign against the "Landmann system" were still appropriate."[37]

Condemning a "system," Frankfurt's DVP resorted to language common to disaffected political groupings during the latter years of the Weimar Republic. Historians of the Weimar Republic frequently mention the "system" without defining the meaning of "the system" for contemporaries of the Weimar Republic. What was this "system?" Most commonly, historians refer to a "party system" or to the "political system."[38] Thus the Economic Party, notes Martin Schumacher, stood against the "system ... of parliamentarianism and party rule."[39] Such accounts of attacks against "the system" leave the impression that something more than a dislike for parliamentarianism was involved. The "coupling of the parliamentary system with the capitalist system," argues Kurt Sontheimer," was important for the suggestive power" of the term in "National Socialist propaganda."[40] The economic component of anti-system ideology often took the form of complaints about the power of large organized economic interests. In his influential essay on "anti-system politics," Thomas Childers describes the enmity of the NSDAP for "big business, high finance, big agriculture, and organized labor" and attacks by other splinter parties against "big business," "big industry," and "the organized working class."[41]

Anti-system ideology had an elastic quality. The expression, notes Sontheimer, "meant not only the procedures of forming political opinion and distributing political power … but the entire interrelation between political play of forces, poorly functioning parliamentarianism, irresponsible party mastery, weak governments, office patronage, corruption, pacifism, etc."[42] The very flexibility of anti-system ideology made it possible to hold the "system" responsible for any number of ills. National Socialists in Württemberg's Landtag, for example, used the term to "attribute to 'the system' guilt in all crises."[43]

In order to recover the meaning of the expression "the system" during the Weimar Republic, it is useful to ask what institutions or beliefs were not covered by the term. One of the keys to the meaning of the "system" was its odd relationship with the state. Though closely associated with the state, the term, "the system," was not identical to the state. Contemporaries thought of it as a disfiguring growth on the state that could be scraped away to return the state to health. Attacking "the system" resolved a contradiction for politicians who blamed the state for the failures of recovery yet still revered the state, or, rather, a state in principle. Thomas Childers notes that "in spite of their attacks on Weimar's big government, most of the alternative parties envisioned a strong … state."[44]

Just as many critics of the Weimar State condemned "the system," politicians active on the communal or regional level denounced a series of local systems in Frankfurt and elsewhere. National Socialists and established bourgeois parties in Berlin blamed either the "System Böß" of Berlin's Mayor Gustav Böß or the "System" of the Social Democrats for the Sklarek scandal.[45] Nuremberg's National Socialists reviled the "system" of Mayor Hermann Luppe. And Jeremy Noakes notes that the National Socialists in lower Saxony typically sought to discredit the local "system."[46] Attacks against the "system" in general or a particular local "system," though not exclusively the property of any political grouping, marked the fragmentation of bourgeois politics during the transition from stabilization to depression. As in Düsseldorf and Frankfurt, animosity between bourgeois municipal leaders mounted in many other city governments. In Nuremberg, for instance, the National Socialists and the Economic Party campaigned against Mayor Luppe in a communal election in 1929 in which no fewer than ten bourgeois listings ran.[47]

Resisting Fragmentation

Political fragmentation was often the outcome of reaction against the past pursuit of recovery. Under what circumstances, then, if any, could local bourgeois officials and politicians maintain some semblance of unity as charges of failure and betrayal came to dominate municipal politics after 1928? Hanover provides an example of an alternative path from stabilization to depression in which the pressures of recovery did not destroy bourgeois political solidarity. Holding together local bourgeois political forces, Hanover's Mayor Arthur Menge performed a difficult balancing act, promising to fight the influence of party politics, a goal esteemed by municipal leaders of the bourgeois Right, even as he went some way to provide public goods seen as desirable by Social Democrats.

Though Menge did not face a political rebellion from the bourgeois Right, pressures of recovery created tension between the mayor and his ally Heinrich Tramm, the long-time pillar of bourgeois politics in Hanover. Tramm voiced few, if any, objections to his protégé's policies during the early years of stabilization, but Menge's adoption of more aggressive recovery programs, especially after the typhus epidemic of 1926, created friction between the mayor and Tramm. As Menge's administration sought to satisfy public needs identified by his Social Democratic foes, the convergence between the goals and methods championed by Menge and Social Democrats entailed an expansion of municipal spending and responsibilities, which, though judged inadequate by the SPD, went too far in Tramm's view.

Refraining from scornful remarks about luxury of the sort popularized by Schacht, Tramm disputed the need for major municipal projects of recovery, in particular for the continued promotion of housing construction advocated by Menge and Stadtbaurat Elkart. When Elkart calculated in 1929 that Hanover still lacked about 8,800 apartments – not including the dilapidated apartments in the old city and the 3,600 dwellings in barracks and emergency quarters and drafted a program to help finance the construction of 3,500 apartments in 1929 – Tramm countered that the administration wildly overestimated the size of Hanover's housing shortage.[48] Hanover had, after all, helped to fund the construction of 12,000 apartments since 1924, and Tramm doubted whether a real housing shortage still existed. He told a meeting of the Building Commission that 30 percent of those seeking apartments simply wanted to move out of old apartments.[49] Worse yet, unrestrained promotion of housing construction would create an oversupply of apartments, causing owners of old buildings to suffer.[50] It was now time, Tramm argued, to end state interference in the housing market.

As Tramm grew concerned that one-time emergency social measures had become permanent municipal tasks, Menge became convinced of the political value of social spending. Rejecting Tramm's call in 1928 for restricting extraordinary spending, Menge argued that Hanover's administration was obliged to promote housing construction and to control unemployment.[51] The Ordnungsblock of 1924 had identified order with thrift. Menge knew that borrowing brought financial risks, but building housing and new utilities helped to preserve order by providing employment. In a moment of triumph after finally obtaining a long-term American loan in 1929, he admitted that the projects to be paid for with the loan cost "enormous sums" but added that construction was "not only an economic, but also a social question." Taking a position that matched that of the chair of the SPD, Menge noted that construction projects "serve to act against high unemployment."[52]

As the tension between Menge and Tramm indicated, Hanover did not entirely escape the disputes over recovery that drove apart bourgeois municipal leaders in many locales, but bourgeois political unity did not ultimately collapse. The fact that Hanover, unlike most large German cities, had actually been governed at one time by a Social Democrat, albeit a member of the party's conservative wing who lacked a majority in the city parliament, proved of inestimable value in preserving the unity of the bourgeois Ordnungsblock of 1924 and its successor of 1929, the Vereinigte Bürgerschaft. As the municipal election of 1929 would prove, bourgeois municipal leaders had good reason to fear the potential power of Hanover's Social Democrats. The SPD won an absolute majority of 38 out of the 74 seats in Hanover's city parliament, while the Vereinigte Bürgerschaft won only 16 seats, and the dwindling Deutsche Hannoveraner fell to 5 seats in the city parliament.

If Menge's readiness to embark on ambitious projects sometimes worried his oldest ally, he proved resolute in continuing to do all that he could to reduce the opportunities for Social Democrats to exert influence in Hanover's municipal government. Soon after the SPD's victory, Menge moved to reduce the size of the Magistrat, a maneuver that the SPD claimed was designed solely to delay the election of Social Democrats to the Magistrat. Menge, for his part, denied that any political motives could be ascribed to his efforts to reduce the Magistrat, and assured his critics that he was uninterested in part politics. "I personally have absolutely no understanding for party politics," said Menge, insisting that he only wished to achieve savings.[53]

The bourgeois Right and the SPD remained sharply divided in Hanover through the end of the period of stabilization, but Menge's conception of municipal duties overlapped sufficiently with that of Social Democrats to create unexpected opportunities for joint action by Hanover's administration and city parliament. Realizing this potential for consensus, the city parliament approved a plan in 1930 to build a park with extensive facilities for sports and recreation at Hanover's Maschsee wetlands. Both the Vereinigte Bürgerschaft and the SPD enthusiastically backed the plan, going so far as to debate who deserved credit for first making the proposal. The Vereinigte Bürgerschaft wished to begin work on the Maschsee project in order to create a park "for physical recuperation and training ... of our inhabitants" as well as work for the unemployed, goals seen as desirable by Hanover's SPD. Struck by the breadth of support for the plan, Heinrich Tramm declared himself "pleased that no more political conflict exists in this area."[54]

Fending off Hanover's Social Democrats while pushing his own supporters to accept promotion of housing construction and leisure as municipal duties, Arthur Menge carried off a difficult balancing act that stood him well as the Weimar Republic disintegrated under National Socialist pressure. One of the few mayors to retain his office after the National Socialist seizure of power, Menge served out his full term as mayor until 1937. Committed to the reduction of party politics and to well-publicized public works projects, Menge made a smooth transition to National Socialist rule that eliminated the city parliament, permitting him to carry out policies of recovery without political interference from any political party other than the NSDAP.

Accelerating Bourgeois Fragmentation

Providing a context for convergence in policy and, on occasion, for tentative political consensus during the Weimar period of stabilization, pursuit of recovery also created a series of political contradictions that helped to fragment bourgeois politics. Local pressure for recovery and democratization encouraged established bourgeois parties to support much of the expansion of state activity during the Weimar period of stabilization, but an unusual combination of splinter parties and individual branches of established parties simultaneously sought to mobilize populist reaction against the state. Contradictory evaluations of the state and the confrontation between municipal activism and populist reaction produced a rupture that ran directly through the established bourgeois parties. The accelerating fragmentation produced panic, vacillation, and further contradictions as some local parties repudiated their own past records in an attempt to cast themselves as leaders of reaction. The assumption of shared bourgeois interest evident in the proliferating pleas for bourgeois unity could not create unity where none existed. By the end of the period of stabilization, there was no single conception of the approximate boundaries of state activity capable of winning approval from a broad array of bourgeois political groupings. Municipal politicians claiming to represent bourgeois voters decried the growth of state activity, while others, making the same claim, defended the expansion of municipal duties. As bourgeois politics fragmented, party labels became an increasingly inaccurate guide to politicians' ideas about the state's proper obligations to its citizens. Thus, the DNVP suffered losses in Düsseldorf for its defense of much of the Weimar record of recovery, even as Alfred Hugenberg tried to identify the DNVP as a part of reaction against the Weimar State at the national level.

Notes

1. Noakes, *The Nazi Party in Lower Saxony,* pp. 134, 136.
2. Gough, *Die SPD in der Berliner Kommunalpolitik,* pp. 188-208; James, *The German Slump,* pp. 91-2; Lehnert, *Kommunale Politik,* pp. 180-81; Lehnert, "Das 'rote' Berlin,'" pp. 23-24; and Hanschel, *Oberbürgermeister Hermann Luppe,* p. 339.
3. Bessel, "State and Society in Germany in the Aftermath of the First World War," in *The State and Social Change in Germany, 1880-1980,* ed. W.R. Lee and Eve Rosenhaft (New York, 1990), pp. 203-7; and Bessel, "Why did the Weimar Republic Collapse?" in *Weimar: Why did German Democracy Fail?,* ed. Ian Kershaw, p. 134.
4. Ellenbeck, "Sparvorschläge für Großstädte," *Deutsche Gemeinde-Zeitung* 65 (1926): 23.
5. "Deutsche Volkspartei und Kommunalpolitik," *Kommunale Umschau* 5 (1929): 429-30; Brauer, "Die Sozialdemokratie und der Kommunalgroßwahltag"; and *Die Gemeinde* 6 (1929): 976, 978-79.
6. Fritzsche, *Rehearsals for Fascism,* pp. 5, 93, 105-6, 109-11, 117; and Noakes, *The Nazi Party in Lower Saxony,* pp. 134, 136.
7. StVV Düsseldorf, 1925, p. 12.
8. *Haus und Grund,* 4 December 1926.
9. StA Düsseldorf XXIV 1013, *Haus und Grund,* 7 April 1928.
10. *Haus und Grund,* 21 April 1928.

11. Ibid.
12. StA Düsseldorf XXIV 1013, *Haus und Grund*, 29 December 1928.
13. *Düsseldorfer Lokal Zeitung*, 16 November 1929.
14. Ibid.
15. StVV Düsseldorf 1927, pp. 291-92.
16. Ibid., 1929, pp. 242-44.
17. Ibid., 1928, pp. 79-81.
18. StA Düsseldorf XXIV 997, Ellenbeck, "Arbeiten und Pläne der deutschnationalen Fraktion im Stadtparlament," *Der Führer Düsseldorf*, 5 January 1929.
19. Ibid., XXIV 997, Ellenbeck, "Opposition oder Mitarbeit," *Der Führer Düsseldorf*, 12 January 1929.
20. Ibid., Düsseldorf XXIV 997, Ellenbeck "Die deutschnationale Fraktion und die stadtpolitische Arbeit," *Der Führer Düsseldorf*, 15 September 1928.
21. Ibid., XXIV 997, Ellenbeck "Opposition oder Mitarbeit," 12 January 1929.
22. *Düsseldorfer Nachrichten*, 18 November 1928.
23. LA Berlin STA 302, Niederschrift über die Sitzung des Vorstandes, 23January 1928.
24. Ibid., STA 302, Vorbericht für die Vorstandssitzung, 23 March 1928; and STA 538, Niederschrift über die Vorstandssitzung, 24 September 1928.
25. Ibid., STA 603/II, Stenographischer Bericht über die Verhandlungen der Jahresversammlung des deutschen Städtetages, 27 September 1929, pp. 32-33.
26. StVV Frankfurt, 1927, p. 966.
27. *Wie Oberbürgermeister Dr. Landmann regierte*, p. 41.
28. StVV Frankfurt, 1929, pp. 617-25, 629-30, 687-88, 704; Rebentisch, *Ludwig Landmann*, pp. 244-50; and Richard Merton, *Erinnernswertes aus meinem Leben, das über das Personliche hinausgeht* (Frankfurt am Main, 1955), pp. 71-79. Note that a motion of no confidence had no legal authority, even if passed, to force a mayor to resign.
29. *Frankfurter Zeitung*, 18 November 1929.
30. StVV Frankfurt, 1929, p. 1293; and Barbara Köhler, "Die Nationalsozialisten in der Frankfurter Stadtverordneten- versammlung 1929 bis 1933," *Archiv für Frankfurts Geschichte und Kunst* 59 (1985): 443, 447.
31. StVV Frankfurt, 1929, pp. 1284-85.
32. *Frankfurter Zeitung*, 18 November 1929.
33. StVV Frankfurt, 1929, p. 1292.
34. Ibid., 1929, p. 1288.
35. Gough, *Die SPD in der Berliner Kommunalpolitik*, pp. 206-11.
36. For an account of the collapse of the established bourgeois parties in rural areas and in small towns see Fritzsche, *Rehearsals for Fascism*, pp. 190-91.
37. StVV Frankfurt, 1930, p. 990.
38. Jones, *German Liberalism*; Jürgen Bergmann, "'Das Land steht rechts!' Das 'agrarische Milieu,'" in *Politische Identität und nationale Gedenktage: Zur politischen Kultur in der Weimarer Republik*, ed. Lehnert and Megerle (Opladen, 1989), pp. 202-3; and Childers, "Interest and Ideology," p. 7.
39. Martin Schumacher, *Mittelstandsfront und Republik: Die Wirtschaftspartei – Reichspartei des deutschen Mittelstandes 1919-1933* (Düsseldorf, 1972), pp. 56, 116
40. Kurt Sontheimer, *Antidemokratisches Denken in der Weimarer Republik: Die politischen Ideen des deutschen Nationalismus zwischen 1918 und 1933*, 2d ed. (Munich, 1964), pp. 224-25.
41. Childers, "Interest and Ideology," pp. 7, 9-12.

42. Sontheimer, *Antidemokratisches Denken*, pp. 223-24.
43. Benigna Schönhagen, "Zwischen Verweigerung und Agitation: Landtagspolitik der NSDAP in Württemberg 1928/29-1933," in *Die Machtergreifung in Südwestdeutschland: Das Ende der Weimarer Republik in Baden und Württemberg 1928-1933*, ed. Thomas Schnabel (Stuttgart, 1982), p. 137.
44. Childers, "Interest and Ideology," p. 15.
45. Gough, *Die SPD in der Berliner Kommunalpolitik*), pp. 188-208.
46. Ibid., pp. 206, 212; Hanschel, *Oberbürgermeister Hermann Luppe*, p. 340; and Noakes, *The Nazi Party in Lower Saxony*, p. 134.
47. Hanschel, *Oberbürgermeister Hermann Luppe*, pp. 339-42.
48. BVK Hannover, 1928-1929, 31 January 1929, Magistrat Wohnungsbauprogramm 1929.
49. StA Hannover, Baudeputation, 30 January 1929, p. 6.
50. Ibid., Baudeputation, 16 January 1929, pp. 6-7; and Baudeputation, 30 January 1929, pp. 6-9.
51. Ibid., Finanz Kommission, 1927-1928, pp. 102-4.
52. BVK Hannover, 1929-1930, p. 51.
53. BVK Hannover 1929-1930, pp. 158-61, 168-71, 180.
54. Ibid., 1929-1930, 24 March 1930, Anträge zur Haushalt; and 1929-1930, pp. 349, 386-87.

Conclusion

FROM RECOVERY TO DESTABILIZATION

*I*n stressing the fragility of Weimar recovery, historians have been able to place Germany's path from hyperinflation to depression easily into standard narratives of Weimar Republic calamities. Weimar stabilization, however, was no mere illusion, as a close reexamination of the period from the perspective of municipalities shows. The middle years of the Weimar Republic, though not "golden years," did not represent a period of "false" stabilization. Instead, this period of Weimar stabilization was a time in which numerous German institutions, including city governments, undertook a wide range of ambitious and sometimes successful programs in pursuit of recovery.

Municipal history of the Weimar Republic furnishes ample evidence that German city leaders, eager to repair the economic and social damage inflicted by war and inflation, undertook comprehensive, functional programs of recovery in a remarkable display of municipal activism. The pessimism with which historians, knowing of the Weimar Republic's fate, describe Weimar stabilization stands in marked contrast to the optimistic tones adopted by many civic leaders to describe their recovery programs. Until 1928 and 1929, German civic leaders had reason to believe that their work of recovery was headed for success. As late as 1929, political groups of the Left and Right competed to take credit for popular recovery programs in Hanover. Indeed, new housing settlements, sports facilities, utilities, and numerous other projects were the visible achievements of municipal activism in cities across Germany.

In spite of the deep political rifts and persistent feuds over symbolic issues, recovery programs acquired broad political support.

The example of cities suggests that a combination of administrative confidence and democratization, rather than an arrangement between economic blocks of the sort outlined by David Abraham, spurred on these stabilization effort. Even as many mayors built on a prewar record of civic activity to advocate programs of recovery, democratization simultaneously created pressure for municipal leaders across the political spectrum to approve diverse forms of state intervention. Democratization, though not the only historical political cause for the growth of state activity, encouraged a new phase of state expansion at the local level in Weimar Germany, and influenced the specific goals of Weimar municipal policy as civic leaders committed themselves to improving living standards for all urban residents. Along with members of the SPD and KPD, many bourgeois municipal leaders expressed support for democratizing access to cultural and recreational activities, as well as to affordable and attractive housing.

Revealing the strong political appeal and considerable achievements of Weimar stabilization, municipal history also paradoxically shows the simultaneous emergence of reaction against the programs and politics of recovery. The reaction against municipalities was remarkable both for its early timing and for its capacity to unite unlikely allies. Well before the onset of depression or the rise of National Socialism, city governments already faced intense criticism from financial authorities and powerful economic interest groups. Reichsbank President Schacht's 1927 attack against municipal "luxury expenditures," though vigorously rejected by most mayors, placed municipal leaders on the defensive, and Berlin's "Sklarek scandal" of 1929 covered city governments as a group with the taint of corruption. By 1929, established political parties began to suffer from the reaction against municipal governments and policies. Social Democrats lost ground in most cities in 1929, though not, notably, in Hanover, and the established parties of the bourgeois Right faced serious challenges from radical parties to their right. In some locales, established bourgeois parties virtually vanished. It was too soon to speak of a full National Socialist electoral breakthrough in 1929, but election results in cities such as Düsseldorf, Frankfurt, Berlin, and Nuremberg saw a pronounced shift towards the radical Right.

Early reaction against municipalities bridged the gaps between disparate and mutually antagonistic critics of state growth. On the national level, prominent economic and industrial interest groups such as the German Association of Industry charged city governments with much of the blame for leading German recovery astray. Locally, disaffected segments of the old Mittelstand, including organized house owners, engaged in the most vociferous criticism of civic leaders. Reaction against municipal policy provided industry, finance, and interest groups of the old Mittelstand with a common cause even though suspicion of big industry and big capital remained endemic within the old Mittelstand of the Weimar Republic.[1]

In uncovering the simultaneous strength of municipal activism and the vigor and breadth of reaction against recovery programs and politics, municipal history demonstrates the full complexity of Weimar stabilization. While it cannot be explained away as a mirage, discarding interpretations that view stabilization as an illusion does not either justify shifting to the other extreme of proclaiming Weimar stabilization a complete success. Instead, an investigation of Weimar Germany's municipal history raises the following question: Precisely how did impressive and popular recovery programs contribute to the reaction against city governments and the Weimar Republic itself? The attacks – in both their number and their variety – suggest that there were several causes of reaction against municipal pursuit of recovery.

Complying with local demands for recovery, municipal activism provoked broad financial reaction against city governments at the national level. Municipal use of loans to pay for recovery programs brought city governments into intense distributional conflicts with other public institutions and with the private economy. Municipal borrowing produced particular animosity among industrial interest groups and the Reichsbank. As distributional conflict produced sharp reaction against cities at the national level, so too did bitter disputes over the productivity of municipal spending. In an era in which both civic leaders and their critics placed enormous faith in productivity, attacks against the utility of municipal programs posed a serious challenge to the very rationale for much municipal policy.

Distributional conflict and debate over the productivity of municipal spending at the national level, in turn, placed stress on the consensus of recovery at the municipal level. The campaign against cold socialization in 1925/26 did not sweep away support for the communal economy, but encouraged misgivings about ambitious programs of economic promotion. Reichsbank President Schacht's attacks against municipal spending similarly failed to sway most municipal leaders, but reinforced the claims of local critics of municipal spending. Although mayors across Germany deeply resented Schacht's complaints about "luxury expenditures," splinter parties of the bourgeois Right endorsed Schacht's criticism of municipal authorities.

Criticism of municipal finance and complaints of unproductive investment centered not only on municipal spending practices, but also on the effects of democratization. Charging that political parties, parliaments, and electoral competition destroyed thrift, foes of municipal spending made much of the conjunction between democratization and the expansion of state activity. Proposals to limit the spending power of municipal assemblies revealed a strong current of mistrust of democracy among economic interest groups during the late 1920s, and, by the early 1930s, savings commissars reduced the decision-making power of city parliaments in many German municipalities.

The sequence of state expansion, distributional conflict, and criticism of public spending suggests an appealing chain of cause and effect that could explain emerging reaction against German municipalities. However, destabilization in Weimar cities was not simply a financial process. Beginning well before the full onset of depression and focusing on democratic institutions as well as municipal spending, reaction against recovery had political, cultural, and financial causes. The best publicized attacks against municipal finance met with a resolute response from municipal leaders, but the fragmentation of bourgeois politics undermined the politics of recovery several years before the collapse of public finance in Germany.

Even as prominent civic leaders rejected the charges of municipal luxury levelled by Schacht and by splinter parties, contradictory interpretation of state activity by bourgeois parties severely weakened the political consensus of recovery during the Weimar period of stabilization. Although local established bourgeois parties frequently approved of much of the growth of municipal activity, varied splinter groups and populist movements on the bourgeois Right condemned state expansion. Local splinter parties such as Düsseldorf's Wirtschaftsbund positioned themselves as champions of bourgeois politics by charging their established competitors with having betrayed bourgeois values. Facing a barrage of criticism from their closest political rivals, established parties of the bourgeois Right came to adopt an ambiguous and often-contradictory attitude toward their own participation in shaping ambitious programs of recovery. The accelerating fragmentation of bourgeois politics at the local level produced panic, vacillation, and, in extreme cases such as that of Frankfurt's DVP, attempts at complete political reversal.

Few political groups gained from the reaction against municipal recovery. Established parties seldom managed to recast themselves as leaders of opposition to the growth of state activity, but splinter parties struggled to capitalize on the mounting resentment against municipal authorities. The core urban protest voters, pioneers in mobilizing early reaction against stabilization, were not the ultimate winners of reaction against recovery. Vacillation in the face of attacks from splinter parties robbed established bourgeois parties of any clear political identity, but many voters, though disgusted with the "system" did not, in the end, want a sharp reduction of state activity of the magnitude suggested by the propaganda generated by House and Property Owners' Associations. Nothing remotely resembling a government shaped by organized house owners ever emerged in any German-State after 1933. Recognition of the legitimacy of claims of dependency by numerous needy groups, if sometimes grudging, continued to penetrate across much of the political spectrum during the 1920s. Many voters looked to all levels of the state for aid, and attacks against the "system," by targeting all political institutions other than the state, actually shielded the state, leaving open the possibility that a new state could better meet raised expectations for social provision and other forms of government assistance.

Though it is not possible to identify a single cause of reaction against municipal pursuit of recovery, many of the paths to destabilization had common origins in Germany's difficult encounter with modernity, or in what Detlev Peukert termed the crisis "classical modernity." Despite intense criticism, since the 1980s, of the notion of a German Sonderweg of uneven modernization, historians of nineteenth- and twentieth-century Germany have returned with striking regularity to the complex German experience of modernization, and many, along with Peukert, continue to suspect that a problematic encounter with modernization played a major role in the catastrophes of German politics. Some influential historians continue to defend the Sonderweg despite this recent turn of historiography.[2] Historians also continue to find new contradictions of German modernization. Employing a sociology of discourse to recast analysis of German modernization, Thomas Childers finds the survival of "pre-industrial vestiges ... in the political culture of the Weimar Republic."[3]

From multiple perspectives, cities stood at the center of any crisis of modernity in Germany. German cities of the nineteenth and early twentieth century were sites of rapid economic and social change, and cultural innovation. For both admirers and critics, cities served as symbols of modernity. Showplaces for technical progress and new forms of consumption, nineteenth-century German cities struck agrarian romantics as threats to morality and national health.[4] Such dualistic evaluations of the city as the best and worst of modernity survived into the 1920s. Konrad Adenauer, for example, referred to large cities as "in many respects pioneers of progress for the entire country... ," but also conceded that the "damage of the large cities in their present form for the physical and spiritual-intellectual life in the first place for their inhabitants is clearly evident."[5]

Widely identified, for better or for worse, as centers of social, economic, and cultural modernity, cities of the Weimar Republic acquired further modernizing functions through municipal policies. The expansion of the social state, a key characteristic of "classical modernity," took place locally as well as nationally.[6] This expansion of Weimar social policy frequently drew upon the rhetoric of rationalization, a hallmark of modern management in the Weimar Republic.

Of all of the elements central to a definition of German modernity, there is none more likely to excite controversy than democratic politics, but the crises of modern German history cannot be explained without a central focus on Germany's extremely uneven experience with democracy. Critics of the Sonderweg may argue that it understates the pace of politicization and overstates the lingering power of pre-industrial interests; however, the central problem of democracy in the Weimar Republic was not the survival of anti-democratic elites, but the interaction of the politics of milieus with a tentative form of modern democratic politics. Weimar democratization reinforced the emerging trend toward the participation of both the political Right and Left in continuing state expansion. To some degree on the national level but far more clearly locally, democratization blurred boundaries between rival political camps in domestic policy. This convergence created a broad central terrain for political activity in which political competitors accepted the need for numerous forms of state intervention and turned to debate the precise boundaries of state action. In the German context, the extraordinarily broad consensus of recovery marked a partial transition from the politics of hostile political camps to the modern form of democratic politics that only emerged fully after the Second World War in the Federal Republic of Germany.

The emergence of modern forms of culture, policy, and politics produced a series of destabilizing contradictions in Weimar Germany's cities. Although city governments as a group did not establish a clear alliance with any single variety or style of culture, the influence of cultural modernism on building and theater in cities such as Frankfurt produced a cultural backlash toward the end of the period of stabilization. Even if the vast majority of apartments constructed with municipal assistance or of plays produced by municipal theaters did not epitomize experimental cultural trends, cities came to serve as symbols for the ills of cultural modernity in cultural debates of the Weimar Republic.

In cities across Germany, the growth of state activity created a further contradiction of recovery. Criticism of municipal policy suggested that the emerging social state did both too much and too little. While the rapid growth of municipal activity encountered opposition from the Reichsbank, economic interest groups, and sectors of the old Mittelstand, the inability of municipal authorities to meet their own goals disappointed the supporters of programs of recovery. Guidelines for municipal promotion of housing construction, for example, often angered organized house owners and some building professionals while city governments struggled to meet demand for affordable housing with mixed success.

The example of the promotion of housing construction reveals indeed the difficulty of selecting a single standard for judging the effectiveness of Weimar policies of recovery. Dan Silverman, noting that the housing shortage did not end, describes Weimar promotion of housing construction as "a pledge unredeemed, but can the effectiveness of Weimar social policy be measured with an absolute standard? Michael Ruck doubts whether the free economy could have produced more apartments without state intervention, and Peter-Christian Witt argues that the achievements of municipalities in promoting housing construction compared favorably with efforts during both the prewar era and the period of National Socialist rule.[7]

To a certain degree, the choice of a cut-off date can explain the variation in judgements of the effectiveness of Weimar recovery policies. Municipal policy looked more successful in 1928 than in 1930. The results of the 1928 elections suggested significant support for stabilization, at least among supporters of the SPD, which improved its performance in elections to the Reichstag. In Frankfurt, one of the few cities to hold communal elections in 1928, the SPD made significant gains, increasing its percentage of votes from 24.7 percent in 1924 to 32.5 percent in 1928. Even on the bourgeois Right, there was little trace of the animosity against Mayor Ludwig Landmann that would surface by the end of 1928. In 1929, the DVP helped lead the campaign against the "Landmann system," but in the spring of 1928, Frankfurt's parties of the bourgeois Right conducted no full-scale assault against Landmann, and the *Frankfurter Nachrichten*, a newspaper closely associated with the DVP, gave a favorable account of Landmann's performance as mayor.[8]

The contradictions of Weimar municipal recovery extended from policy to politics. Disputes over the growth of state activity brought about a collision between the politics of milieus and the emerging form of modern democratic politics of recovery. Conflict over public spending in the Weimar Republic marked an intensive early debate over the proper limits of the social state, but reaction against recovery policies in the Weimar Republic amounted to far more than a debate over state boundaries. Critiques of municipal policy did not, after all, culminate in calls for thrift, fiscal restraint, and the curtailment of state activity, but in charges of political treason, attacks against democratic institutions, and the fragmentation of bourgeois politics. For champions of the politics of milieus, the tentative participation of established bourgeois parties in the politics of recovery created not only errors of policy, but a record of betrayal of bourgeois politics. Accusing established parties of the Right of treason and condemning them for carrying out policies of the Left, splinter parties signalled their anger at the blurring of the boundaries between political milieus.

The collision between the politics of milieus and the politics of recovery created Weimar Germany's chief political contradiction of "classical modernity" at the municipal level. If democracy, as critics of modernization theory note, is only one form of modern politics, the collision between the politics of recovery and the politics of milieus created only one political contradiction of modernization. However, this clash between competing forms of politics had severe consequences. The interaction between the politics of milieus and the emerging form of modern democratic politics advanced by the politics of recovery helped to destroy consensus at the local level.

Undermining the consensus of recovery, this collision contributed in the short run to the demise of both forms of politics. Splinter parties and local bourgeois populists, fighting to preserve the traditional divisions of prewar politics, placed established bourgeois parties on the defensive. However, the splinter parties' charges that established parties of the Right had betrayed the Mittelstand by adopting politics of the Left failed to produce any new vehicle for bourgeois unity in the politics of milieus, and instead led only to the increasing fragmentation of bourgeois politics. Sweeping away an emerging form of democratic politics for the time being, the collision of politics also discredited the politics of milieus.

Although contradictions of politics, policy, and, to some degree, culture destroyed the consensus of recovery during the Weimar Republic, the pursuit of stabilization revealed the potential for future state expansion. The Weimar Republic did not mark a final end to the growth of the state in Germany. Politicians and officials in the Federal Republic of Germany, though careful to avoid the mistakes of the Weimar Republic, did not hold social provision in dread.[9] If the Weimar experience illustrated some of the pitfalls to be avoided in constructing a social market economy, the convergence between policies advocated by established parties of the Left and the Right during the Weimar period of stabilization also established the possibility of building a broad political consensus in favor of an ambitious social state.

What lessons can be drawn from the reaction against the Weimar growth of state activity? As one episode in the debate over the relationship between state and society, the Weimar Republic suggested the need for a broader consensus on the proper balance between resources and spending. At the same time, the extension of reaction against the Weimar state, far beyond any distributional goals, indicated other requirements for future projects of state expansion.

The destructive collision between the politics of milieus and the politics of recovery suggested that future projects of democratic state expansion could benefit from the further erosion of the politics of milieus. The decline of the politics of milieus would not in and of itself eliminate real differences over the role of the state. Much of the controversy over state expansion in the Weimar Republic, after all, stemmed from disputes over the pace of borrowing and spending, a pattern that has reemerged in other democracies confronting competing demands for resources. Still, an end to the politics of milieus promised to place limits on the extension of distributional conflict. In its absence, bourgeois groups could accept legitimate differences of interest and opinion without resorting as quickly to sweeping charges of betrayal.

As the likelihood of restoring prewar conditions became increasingly remote, future projects of state expansion could also secure a stronger political base. David Harvey notes that disagreements about mapping the future can undermine the political cooperation built on the shared concern for social reproduction. In the case of Weimar cities, disagreement over the ultimate goal of recovery created the potential for conflict even before the full development of reaction against stabilization.[10] Recovery for most Germans required responding to the social and economic problems left by war and inflation. Defining recovery as the repair of damage inflicted by such extraordinary events as the First World War and hyperinflation suggested that the ultimate goal of recovery was recapturing "normal" conditions associated with the prewar era.[11] However, while recovery often meant rebuilding economic and social structures and institutions damaged by catastrophic events, it also encompassed projects that aimed to transform social and cultural conditions left over from the prewar era. The discrepancy between the conception of recovery as a return to past "normality" and the vision of recovery as a program of transformation, as in the New Frankfurt, was never fully resolved during the period of stabilization. A desire to return to the past by restoring order led municipal leaders such as Düsseldorf's Mayor Lehr and Hanover's Mayor Menge to identify themselves with new municipal tasks, a development described by Peter Hüttenberger as "a paradox, civilized progress to 'return home' to the prewar era," but this goal differed markedly from the ideals of the future espoused by municipal leaders like Frankfurt's Mayor Landmann, and city planner Ernst May, and Düsseldorf's councilor Ellenbeck.[12]

Finally, the reaction against Weimar programs of recovery in the end indicated the political limits of the appeal of utility, a highly elusive standard for assessing policy in the absence of a strong solidaristic vision of the purpose of state activity. With the erosion of the productivity consensus in the Weimar period of stabilization, recovery programs lost a unifying ideological core. Municipal leaders presumed that pursuit of recovery provided a common civic and even national interest, but the organization of municipal programs accentuated divisions between the highly fractured communities of the needy. Allegiance to productivity could not indeed reduce these differences.

Notes

1. Childers, "Interest and Ideology," pp. 9-11.
2. See, for example, Feldman, "Hitler's Assumption of Power," p. 96; and Feldman, "The Weimar Republic: A Problem of Modernization?" *Archiv für Sozialgeschichte* 26 (1986): 1-26.
3. Childers, "The Social Language of Politics," p. 357.
4. Peukert, *Die Weimarer Republik*, 181; von Saldern, "Stadt und Moderne"; Peter Fritzsche, *Reading Berlin 1900* (Cambridge, Massachusetts, 1996), pp. 28-47, 189-203; Klaus Bergmann, *Agrarromantik und Großstadtfeindschaft* (Meisenheim, 1970); Lees, *Cities Perceived*; and Fritz Stern, *The Politics of Cultural Despair: A Study in the Rise of the German Ideology* (Berkeley, 1963), p. xxvii.
5. Oberbürgermeister Dr. Adenauer, "Das Großstadt-Problem," *Kommunalpolitische Blätter* 18 (1927): 394. See also Harold Poor, "City Versus Country: Urban Change and Development in the Weimar Republic – a Preliminary Report," in *Industrielles System und politische Entwicklung in der Weimarer Republik*, vol. 1, ed. Hans Mommsen, Dietmar Petzina and Bernd Weisbrod (Düsseldorf, 1974), pp. 119-20.
6. Peukert, *Die Weimarer Republik*, p. 89.
7. Dan Silverman, "A Pledge Unredeemed: The Housing Crisis in Weimar Germany," *Central European History* 3 (1970): 112; Ruck, "Der Wohnungsbau," p. 111; and Witt, "Inflation, Wohnungszwangs, wirtschaft und Hauszinssteuer," pp. 399-403.
8. Rebentisch, *Ludwig Landmann*, p. 222.
9. Ludwig Erhard, *The Economics of Success*, trans. J.A. Arengo-Jones and D.J.S. Thomson. (Princeton, 1963), p. 98.
10. David Harvey, *The Urban Experience* (Baltimore, 1989), p. 150.
11. Bessel, *Germany after the First World War*, p. 141.
12. Hüttenberger, *Die Industrie- und Verwaltungsstadt*, p. 362.

Sources and Select Bibliography

I – Archival Sources

Bundesarchiv Koblenz

R2/2002, R2/2003, R2/2004, R2/2025, R2/2026,
R2/2043, R2/2044, R2/2047, R2/2049, R2/2053,
R2/2067, R2/2074, R2/2084, R2/2126, R2/2127,
R2/2128, R2/2129, R2/2130, R2/2142, R2/4065,
R2/4072

Bundesarchiv Potsdam

25:01 6630, 25:01 3360

Landesarchiv Berlin

STA 27/II, STA 163, STA 177, STA 186/I,
STA 186/II, STA 239, STA 264, STA 302,
STA 387, STA 396, STA 397, STA 398/II,
STA 538, STA 541/I, STA 541/II, STA 467,
STA 603/II, STA 619, STA 634, STA 645,
STA 842/I, STB 1533/I, STB 2784/II,
STB 4721

Stadtarchiv Düsseldorf

Stenographische Verhandlungsberichte der
Stadtverordnetenversammlung Düsseldorf
III 683, III 685, III 11614, III 11637,
III 13854, III 18223, IV 5061, XXIV 982,
XXIV 985, XXIV 997, XXIV 1013, XXIV 1014,
XXIV 1112, XXIV 1113, XXIV 1117
Nachlaß Lehr

Stadtarchiv Frankfurt

Bericht über die Verhandlungen der Stadtverordnetenversammlung
der Stadt Frankfurt am Main nach stenographischer Aufnahme
Akten des Magistrat
S 1723 IV, S 1723 V, S 1723 VI, T862 XIII,
T862 XIV, T862 XV, T862 XVI, T872 I,
T874, T876, T877, T878, T2056 III, T2068 III,
T2073 I, T2073 II, T2085 I, T2085 II, U190 III,
U190 IV, U237, U238, U239, U240, U241, U242,
U243, U244, U245, U246, U504 I, U504 II, U504 III,
U510, U558 III, U748 I, U748 II, U749 I, U750

Stadtkämmerei
53, 116, 144, 145, 150, 170, 176, 694,200,
Akten der StVV
1.593, 1.711, 1.787, 1.793, 1.931

Nordrhein-Westfälisches Haupstaatsarchiv Düsseldorf

Regierung Düsseldorf
31318, 31319, 31320,

Stadtarchiv Hannover

Finanz Kommission Protokolle
Magistrat Protokolle
Magistrat und Bürgervorsteher-Kollegium gemeinschaftliche
    Protokolle
Baukommission Protokolle
Theater Kommission Protokolle

Akten des Magistrat
VII B 2D 116 I, VII B 2D 116 II, VII B 2D 117,
VII B 2D 119, VII B 2D 120, VII B 2D 121,
VII B 2D 124, VII B 2D 127, X C 10 22,
X C 2 14 I 5, X C 2 14 I 6, XX B51,
XXIII D2 6A 1, XXIII D2 6A 2 II,
XXIII D2 6A 2 III, XXIII D2 6A 12,
XXIII D2 6A 13, XXIII D2 6A 13 1,
XIII D2 6A 13 2, XXIII D2 6A 13 3,

Westfälisches Wirtschaftsarchiv

K2 1542, K2 1547

II – Newspapers and Periodicals

Bauamt und Gemeindebau
Deutsche Bergwerkszeitung
Deutsche Gemeinde-Zeitung
Deutsche Hausbesitzer Zeitung
Der deutsche Volkswirt
Düsseldorf Blätter für Wissenschaft Kunst und Bildung
Düsseldorfer Lokal Zeitung
Düsseldorfer-Nachrichten
Frankfurter Nachrichten
Die Gemeinde
Gesolei
Das Grundeigentum
Hannoverscher Anzeiger
Hannoverscher Kurier
Haus und Grund
Kommunalpolitische Blätter
Kommunale Umschau
Die lebendige Stadt: Zweimonatsschrift der Stadt Mannheim
Mitteilungen des Vereins zur Währung der gemeinsamen
wirtschaftlichen Interessen in Rheinland und Westfalen
Nachrichtenblatt des Bürger-Ausschuß (Bürgerrat) E.V. Frankfurt
a.m.
Das Neue Frankfurt: Monatsschrift für die Fragen der Großstadt-
Gestaltung
Die Scene

Selbstverwaltung und Demokratie
Der Städtetag
Das Theater
Die Theaterwelt: Programmheft der Städtischen Theater Düsseldorf
Volksstimme [Frankfurt]
Volkswille [Hanover]
Westfälisches Wohnungsblatt
Die Wohnung
Wirtschaft und Verkehr
Wirtschaftsdienst
Zeitschrift für Kommunalwirtschaft

III – Select General Bibliography

This is a select bibliography. For additional information on specific points consult the notes attached to the discussion in the text.

Abelshauser, Werner. Die Weimarer Republik als Wohlfahrtsstaat: Zum Verhältnis von Wirtschafts- und Sozialpolitik in der Industriegesellschaft. Stuttgart, 1987.

Abraham, David. *The Collapse of the Weimar Republic: Political Economy and Crisis.* 2d ed. New York, 1986.

Abramowski, Günter, ed. *Akten der Reichskanzlei Weimarer Republik: Die Kabinette Marx III und IV.* 2 vols. Boppard am Rhein, 1988.

Abrams, Lynn. "From Control to Commercialization: The Triumph of Mass Entertainment in Germany, 1900-1925?" *German History* 8 (1990): 278-293.

Akademie der Künste. *Martin Wagner, 1885-1957: Wohnungsbau und Weltstadtplanung: Die Rationalisierung des Glücks.* Berlin, 1985.

Albers, Gerd. *Entwicklungslinien im Städtebau: Ideen, Thesen, Aussagen 1875-1945: Texte und Interpretationen.* Düsseldorf, 1975.

Ambrosius, Gerold. *Die öffentliche Wirtschaft in der Weimarer Republik: Kommunale Versorgungsunternehmen als Instrumente der Wirtschaftspolitik.* Baden-Baden, 1984.

Ambrosius, Gerold. "Aspekte kommunaler Unternehmungspolitik in der Weimarer Republik." *Archiv für Kommunalwissenschaften* 9 (1980): 239-61.

Amonn, Alfred. *Die Mietzins- und Wohnungsbaufrage von volkswirtschaftlichen Standpunkt.* Warnsdorff, 1925.

Andernacht, Dietrich, and Gerd Kuhn. "Frankfurter Fordismus." In *Ernst May und das neue Frankfurt 1925-1930*, Deutsches Architekturmuseum, 42-62. Berlin, 1986.

Aschoff, Hans-Georg. *Welfische Bewegung und politischer Katholizismus 1866-1918: Die deutschhannoversche Partei und das Zentrum in der Provinz Hannover während des Kaiserreiches.* Düsseldorf, 1987.

Ausschuß zur Untersuchung der Erzeugungs- und Absatzbedingung der Deutsche Wirtschaft. *Der deutsche Wohnungsbau.* Berlin, 1932.

Bähr, Johannes. *Staatliche Schlichtung in der Weimarer Republik: Tarifpolitik, Korporatismus und industrielle Konflikt zwischen Inflation und Deflation 1919-1932.* Berlin, 1989.

Bangert, Wolfgang. *Baupolitik und Stadtgestaltung in Frankfurt am Main: Ein Beitrag zur Entwicklungsgeschichte des deutschen Städtebaus in den letzten 100 Jahren.* Würzburg, 1936.

Balderston, Theo. *The Origins and Course of the German Economic Crisis 1923-1932.* Berlin, 1993.

Baldwin, Peter. *The Politics of Social Solidarity: Class Bases of the European Welfare State 1875-1975.* Cambridge, 1990.

———, "The Welfare State for Historians: A Review Article." *Comparative Studies in Society and History* 34 (1992): 695- 707.

Beck, Hermann. *The Origins of the Authoritarian Welfare State in Prussia: Conservatives, Bureaucracy, and the Social Question, 1815-70.* Ann Arbor, 1994.

Berger-Thimme, Dorothea. *Wohnungsfrage und Sozialstaat: Untersuchungen zu den Anfängen staatlicher Wohnungspolitik in Deutschland 1873-1918.* Frankfurt, 1976.

Bergmann, Klaus. *Agrarromantik und Großstadtfeindschaft.* Meisenheim am Glan, 1970.

Bericht über die Verwaltung und den Stand der Gemeindeangelegenheiten in Düsseldorf, (1929-1931).

Bessel, Richard. "State and Society in Germany in the Aftermath of the First World War." In *The State and Social Change in Germany, 1880-1980,* edited by W.R. Lee and Eve Rosenhaft, 200-27. New York, 1990.

———, "Die Krise der Weimarer Republik als Erblast des verlorenen Krieges." in *Zivilisation und Barbarei: Die widersprüchlichen Potentiale der Moderne; Detlev Peukert zum Gedenken,* edited by Frank Bajohr, 98-114. Hamburg, 1991.

———, *Germany after the First World War.* Oxford, 1993.

Blackbourn, David, and Geoff Eley. *The Peculiarities of German History: Bourgeois Society and Politics in Nineteenth Century Germany*. Oxford, 1984.

Blankenberg, Heinz. *Politischer Katholizismus in Frankfurt am Main 1918-1933* (Mainz, 1981).

Blotevogel, Hans Heinrich. "Einführung." In *Kommunale Leistungsverwaltung und Stadtentwicklung vom Vormärz bis zur Weimarer Republik*, edited by Hans Heinrich Blotevogel. Cologne, 1990.

Böhret, Carl. *Aktion gegen die 'kalte Sozialisierung,' 1926-1930: Ein Beitrag zum Wirken ökonomischer Einflußverbände in der Weimarer Republik*. Berlin, 1966.

Boll, Friedhelm. *Massenbewegungen in Niedersachsen 1906-1920: Eine sozialgeschichtliche Untersuchung zu den unterschiedlichen Entwicklungstypen Braunschweig und Hannover*. Braunschweig, 1981.

Borchardt, Knut. *Wachstum, Krisen, Handlungsspielräume der Wirtschaftspolitik: Studien zur Wirtschaftsgeschichte des 19. und 20. Jahrhunderts*. Göttingen, 1982.

Borst, Otto. *Stuttgart: Die Geschichte der Stadt*. Stuttgart, 1973.

Böß, Gustav. *Wie helfen wir uns? Wege zum wirtschaftlichen Wiederaufstieg*. Berlin, 1926.

_____, *Die sozialen Aufgaben der Kommunalpolitik*. Berlin, 1928.

Bracher, Karl Dietrich. *Die Auflösung der Weimarer Republik: Eine Studie zum Problem des Machtverfalls in der Demokratie*. Villingen, 1955; 6th edition, Düsseldorf, 1978.

Brennert, Hans, and Erwin Stein, eds. *Probleme der neuen Stadt Berlin: Darstellungen der Zukunftsaufgaben einer Viermillionenstadt*. Berlin-Friedenau, 1926.

Brix, J., ed. *Handwörterbuch der Kommunalwissenschaften: Ergänzungsband H-Z*. Jena, 1927.

Buekschmitt. Justus. *Ernst May*. Stuttgart, 1963,

Büsch, Otto. *Geschichte der Berliner Kommunalwirtschaft in der Weimarer Republik*. Berlin, 1960.

_____, ed. *Berliner Demokratie, 1919-1985*. Berlin, 1987.

Buethe, Otfried. "'Beifall und Skandal' – Beispiele zum Sprechtheater der Frankfurter städtischen Bühnen in den Zwanziger Jahren unter Richard Weichert und zu seiner Zusammenarbeit mit dem Bühnenbildner Ludwig Sievert." *Archiv für Frankfurts Geschichte und Kunst* 51 (1968): 145-201.

Büttner, Ursula. *Hamburg in der Staats- und Wirtschaftskrise 1928-1931*. Hamburg, 1982.

_____, *Politische Gerechtigkeit und sozialer Geist: Hamburg zur Zeit der Weimarer Republik*. Hamburg, 1985.

Bullock, Nicholas. "Housing in Frankfurt 1925 to 1931 and the new *Wohnkultur*." *Architectural Review* 163 (1978): 333-44.

Campbell, Joan. *Joy in Work, German Work: The National Debate, 1800-1945*. Princeton, 1989.

Castells, Manuel. *The Urban Question: A Marxist Approach*. Translated by Alan Sheridan. Cambridge, Massachusetts, 1977.

_____, *The City and the Grassroots: A Cross-Cultural Theory of Urban Social Movements*. Berkeley, 1983.

Childers, Thomas. *The Nazi Voter: The Social Foundation of Fascism in Germany 1919-1933*. Chapel Hill, 1983.

_____, "Interest and Ideology: Anti-System Politics in the Era of Stabilization 1924-1928." In *Die Nachwirkungen der Inflation auf die deutsche Geschichte 1924-1933*, edited by Gerald D. Feldman, 1-20. Munich, 1985.

_____, "The Social Language of Politics in Germany: The Sociology of Political Discourse in the Weimar Republic." *American Historical Review* 95 (1990): 331-58.

Cockburn, Cynthia. *The Local State: Management of Cities and People*. London, 1977.

Comfort, Richard A. *Revolutionary Hamburg: Labor Politics in the early Weimar Republic*. Stanford, 1966.

Connell, R. W. *Which Way is Up? Essays on Sex, Class, and Culture*. Sydney, 1983.

Coyner, Sandra J. "Class Consciousness and Consumption: The New Middle Class during the Weimar Republic." *Journal of Social History* 10 (1977): 310-31.

Crew, David. *Town in the Ruhr: A Social History of Bochum, 1860-1914*. New York, 1979.

_____, "German Socialism, the State and Family Policy, 1918-1933." *Continuity and Change* 1 (1986): 235-63.

_____, "The Pathologies of Modernity: Detlev Peukert on Germany's Twentieth Century." *Social History* 17 (1992): 319- 328.

Croon, Helmuth. "Aufgaben deutscher Städte im ersten Drittel des 20. Jahrhunderts." In *Die Städte Mitteleuropas im 20. Jahrhundert*, edited by Wilhelm Rausch, 41-70. Linz, 1984.

Czock, Karl. "Zur Kommunalpolitik in der deutschen Arbeiterbewegung während der neunziger Jahre des 19. Jahrhunderts." *Jahrbuch für Regionalgeschichte* 7 (1979):67-91.

Damaschke, Adolf. *Aufgaben der Gemeindepolitik*. Jena, 1922.

Diem, Carl. *Die Anlage von Spiel- und Sportplätzen*. Berlin, 1926.

Dierker, Herbert. "Arbeitersport in politischen Spannungsfeld der zwanziger Jahre: Sport, Politik, und Alltagserfahrungen." *Stadion* 15 (1989): 91-110.

Dinghaus, Angela, and Bettina Korff. "Wohlfahrtspflege im Hannover der 20er Jahre – Kontinuitätslinien repressiver Armenpflege und sozialer Disziplinierung." In *Stadt und Moderne*, edited by Adelheid von Saldern, 189-224. Hamburg, 1989.

Deutsches Architekturmuseum, ed. *Ernst May und das neue Frankfurt 1925-1930*. Berlin, 1986.

Ebeling, Martin. *Großstadt-Sozialismus*. Berlin and Leipzig, 1909.

Eley, Geoff. *Reshaping the German Right: Radical Nationalism and Political Change after Bismarck*. New Haven, 1980.

Elsas, Fritz, and Erwin Stein, eds. *Die deutschen Städte: ihre Arbeit von 1918 bis 1928*. Berlin-Friedenau, 1928.

Engeli, Christian. *Gustav Böß: Oberbürgermeister von Berlin 1921 bis 1930*. Stuttgart, 1971.

_____, "Siedlungsstruktur und Verwaltungsgrenzen der Städte in Verstädterungsprozeß." *Zeitschrift für Stadtgeschichte, Stadtsoziologie und Denkmalpflege* 4 (1977): 288-307.

Erhard, Ludwig. *The Economics of Success*. Translated by J.A. Arengo-Jones and D.J.S. Thomson. Princeton, 1963.

Esping-Andersen, Gosta. *The Three Worlds of Welfare Capitalism*. Princeton, 1990.

Evans, Richard J. *Death in Hamburg: Society and Politics in the Cholera Years 1830-1910*. Oxford, 1987.

Evans, Richard J., and Dick Geary. *The German Unemployed: Experiences and Consequences of Mass Unemployment from the Weimar Republic to the Third Reich*. New York, 1987.

Feldman, Gerald D. *Iron and Steel in the German Inflation 1916-1923*. Princeton, 1977.

_____, "The Weimar Republic: A Problem of Modernization?" *Archiv für Sozialgeschichte* 26 (1986): 1-26.

_____, *The Great Disorder: Politics, Economics and Society in the German Inflation, 1914-1924*. New York, 1993.

_____, "Hitler's Assumption of Power and the Political Culture of the Weimar Republic," *German Politics and Society* 14 (1996): 96-110.

Feldman, Gerald D., et al., ed. *The German Inflation Reconsidered: A Preliminary Balance*. Berlin, 1982.

_____, eds. *Die Erfahrung der Inflation im internationalen Zusammenhang und Vergleich*. Berlin, 1984.

_____, eds., *Die Anpassung an die Inflation im internationalen Zusammenhang und Vergleich*. Berlin, 1986.

_____, eds. *Konsequenzen der Inflation*. Berlin, 1989.

Feldman, Gerald D., and Elisabeth Müller-Luckner, eds. *Die Nachwirkungen der Inflation auf die deutsche Geschichte 1924-1933*. Munich, 1985.

Feldmann, Friedrich. *Geschichte des Ortsvereins Hannover der Sozialdemokratischen Partei Deutschlands: vom Gründungsjahre 1864 bis 1933*. Hannover, 1952.

Ferguson, Niall. *Paper & Iron: Hamburg Business and German Politics in the Era of Inflation, 1897-1927*. Cambridge, 1995.

Först, Walter. *Robert Lehr als Oberbürgermeister: Ein Kapitel deutscher Kommunalpolitik*. Düsseldorf, 1962.

Fritzsche, Peter. *Rehearsals for Fascism: Populism and Political Mobilization in Weimar Germany*. New York, 1990.

_____, *Reading Berlin 1900*. Cambridge, Massachusetts, 1996.

Füllberth, Georg. *Konzeption und Praxis sozialdemokratischer Kommunalpolitik 1918-1933: Ein Anfang*. Marburg, 1984.

Gehrmann, Siegfried, "Fußball in einer Industrieregion: Das Beispiel F.C. Schalke 04." In *Fabrik, Familie, Feierabend*, edited by Jürgen Reulecke and Wolfhard Weber, 377-98. Wuppertal, 1978.

Geschichtswerkstatt Hannover. *Alltag zwischen Hindenburg und Haarmann: Ein anderer Stadtführer durch das Hannover der 20er Jahre*. Hannover, 1987.

Geyer, Michael. "Nation, Klasse und Macht. Zur Organisation von Herrschaft in der Weimarer Republik." *Archiv für Sozialgeschichte* 26 (1986): 27-48.

Glaessner Gert-Joachim, Detlef Lehnert, and Klaus Sühl, eds. *Studien zur Arbeiterbewegung und Arbeiterkultur in Berlin*. Berlin, 1987.

Goch, Stefan. *Sozialdemokratische Arbeiterbewegung und Arbeiterkultur im Ruhrgebiet: Eine Untersuchung am Beispiel Gelsenkirchen 1848-1975*. Düsseldorf, 1990.

Gough, Edward. *Die SPD in der Berliner Kommunalpolitik 1925-1933*. Berlin, 1984.

Gruber, Helmut. *Red Vienna: Experiment in Working Class Culture 1919-1934*. New York, 1991.

Gut, Albert, ed. *Der Wohnungsbau in Deutschland nach dem Weltkriege: Seine Entwicklung unter der mittelbaren und unmittelbaren Förderung durch die deutschen Gemeindeverwaltungen*. Munich, 1928.

Guttsmann, W.L. *Workers' Culture in Weimar Germany: Between Tradition and Commitment*. New York, 1990.

Hanschel, Hermann. *Oberbürgermeister Hermann Luppe: Nürnberger Kommunalpolitik in der Weimarer Republik*. Nuremberg, 1977.

Hansmeyer, Karl-Heinrich, ed. *Kommunale Finanzpolitik in der Weimarer Republik*. Stuttgart, 1973.

Harlander, Tilman, and Gerhard Fehl, eds. *Hitlers sozialer Wohnungsbau 1940-1945: Aufsätze und Rechtsgrundlagen zur Wohnungspolitik, Baugestaltung und Siedlungsplanung aus der Zeitschrift `Der Soziale Wohnungsbau in Deutschland'*. Hamburg, 1986.

Hartmann, Kristiana. *Deutsche Gartenstadtbewegung: Kulturpolitik und Gesellschaftsreform*. Munich, 1976.

Harvey, David. *The Urban Experience*. Baltimore, 1989.

Harvey, Elizabeth. *Youth and the Welfare State in Weimar Germany*. Oxford, 1993.

Heffter, Heinrich, *Die deutsche Selbstverwaltung im 19. Jahrhundert: Geschichte der Ideen und Institutionen*. Stuttgart, 1950.

Heimrich, Hermann. *Lebenserinnerungen eines Mannheimer Oberbürgermeisters*, edited by Jörg Schadt. Stuttgart, 1982.

Hentschel, Volker. *Geschichte der deutschen Sozialpolitik 1880-1980: soziale Sicherung und kollektive Arbeitsrecht*. Frankfurt am Main, 1983.

Herlemann, Beatrix. *Kommunalpolitik der KPD im Ruhrgebiet 1924-1933*. Wuppertal, 1977.

Hermand, Jost, and Frank Trommler. *Die Kultur der Weimarer Republik*. Munich, 1978.

Herzfeld, Hans. *Demokratie und Selbstverwaltung in der Weimarer Republik*. Stuttgart, 1957.

Hilberseimer, Ludwig. *Großstadt-Architektur*. Stuttgart, 1927.

_____, *Hallenbauten: Stadt- und Festhallen, Turn- und Sporthallen, Austellungshallen, Austellungsanlagen*. Leipzig, 1931.

_____, *Berliner Architektur der 20er Jahre mit einem Nachwort des Herausgebers*, edited by Hans Wingler. Mainz, 1967.

Hipp, Hermann, "Wohnungen für Arbeiter? Zum Wohnungsbau und zur Wohnungsbaupolitik in Hamburg in den 1920er Jahren." In *Arbeiter in Hamburg: Unterschichten, Arbeit und Arbeiterbewegung seit dem ausgehenden 18.Jahrhundert*, edited by Arno Herzig, Dieter Langewiesche and Arnold Sywottek, 471-82. Hamburg, 1983.

_____, "Nachwort" to *Das Werden einer Wohnstadt: Bilder vom neuen Hamburg*, Fritz Schumacher. Hamburg, 1984.

Hofmann, Wolfgang. *Die Bielefelder Stadtverordneten: Ein Beitrag zu bürgerlicher Selbstverwaltung und sozialem Wandel 1850 bis 1914.* Lubeck, 1964.

_____, *Zwischen Rathaus und Reichskanzlei: Die Oberbürgermeister in der Kommunal- und Staatspolitik des Deutschen Reiches von 1890 bis 1933.* Stuttgart, 1974.

Hoffmann, Paul Th., ed. *Neues Altona 1919-1929: Zehn Jahre Aufbau einer deutschen Großstadt.* 2 vols. Jena, 1929.

Holtfrerich, Carl-Ludwig. "Zu höhe Löhne in der Weimar Republik? Bemerkungen zur Borchardt-These." *Geschichte und Gesellschaft* 10 (1984): 122-41.

Hong Young-Sun. "The Contradictions of Modernization in the German Welfare State: Gender and the Politics of Welfare Reform in First World War Germany." *Social History* 17 (1992): 251-70.

Howe, Frederic. *European Cities at Work.* New York, 1914.

Huck, Gerhard, ed. *Sozialgeschichte der Freizeit: Untersuchungen zum Wandel der Alltagskultur in Deutschland.* Wuppertal, 1980.

Hughes, Michael. *Paying for the German Inflation.* Chapel Hill, 1988.

Hüttenberger, Peter. *Die Industrie- und Verwaltungsstadt (20. Jahrhundert).* Vol. 4 of *Düsseldorf: Geschichte von den Ursprüngen bis ins 20. Jahrhundert,* edited by Hugo Weidenhaupt. Düsseldorf, 1989.

Huse, Norbert. *Neues Bauen 1918 bis 1933: Moderne Architektur in der Weimarer Republik.* Berlin, 1985.

Jahresbericht des Statistischen Amtes der Stadt Düsseldorf

James, Harold. *The German Slump: Politics and Economics 1924-1936.* Oxford, 1986.

_____, "Economic Reasons for the Collapse of Weimar." In *Weimar: Why did German Democracy Fail?*, edited by Ian Kershaw, 30- 57. New York, 1990.

_____, "Municipal Finance in the Weimar Republic." In *The State and Social Change in Germany, 1880-1980,* edited by W.R. Lee and Eve Rosenhaft, 228-253. New York, 1990.

Jeske, Regina. "Kommunale Amtsinhaber und Entscheidungsträger – die politische Elite." In *Stadt und Bürgertum im Übergang von der traditionalen zur modernen Gesellschaft,* edited by Lothar Gall, 273-94. Munich, 1993.

Jones, Larry Eugene. *German Liberalism and the Dissolution of the Weimar Party System, 1918-1933.* Chapel Hill, 1988.

Kähler, Gert. *Wohnung und Stadt Hamburg, Frankfurt, Wien: Modelle sozialen Wohnens in den zwanziger Jahren.* Braunschweig, 1985.

Kershaw, Ian, ed. *Weimar: Why did German Democracy Fail?* New York, 1990.

Koehler, Barbara. "Die Nationalsozialisten in der Frankfurter Stadtverordnetenversammlung von 1927 bis 1933." *Archiv für Frankfurts Geschichte und Kunst* 59 (1985): 439-84.

Kölnische Zeitung, ed. *Kommune und Wirtschaft: Tagesprobleme Westdeutscher Kommunal- und Wirtschaftspolitik.* Cologne: 1929.

Kolb, Eberhard. *The Weimar Republic.* Translated by P.S. Falla. London, 1988.

Koshar, Rudy. *Social Life, Local Politics and Nazism: Marburg, 1880-1933.* Chapel Hill, 1986.

Krabbe, Wolfgang. "Munizipalsozialismus und Interventionsstaat." *Geschichte in Wissenschaft und Unterricht.* 30(1979): 265-83.

_____. *Die deutsche Stadt im 19. und 20. Jahrhundert: Eine Einführung.* Göttingen, 1989.

Kramer, Henriette. "Die Anfänge der sozialen Wohnungsbau in Frankfurt am Main 1860-1914." *Archiv für Frankfurts Geschichte und Kunst* 56 (1978): 123-90.

Kramer, Lore. "Rationalisierung des Haushaltes und Frauenfrage." In *Ernst May und das neue Frankfurt 1925-1930*, Deutsches Architekturmuseum, 77-84. Berlin, 1986.

Kreistmeier, Anneliese. "Zur Entwicklung der Kommunalpolitik der Bayerischen Sozialdemokratie im Kaiserreich und in der Weimarer Republik unter besonderer Berücksichtigung Münchens." *Archiv für Sozialgeschichte* 25 (1985): 103-35.

Kruedener, Jürgen Baron von. ed. *Economic Crisis and Political Collapse: The Weimar Republic 1924-1933.* New York, 1990.

Ladd, Brian. "Public Baths and Civic Improvement in Nineteenth-Century German Cities." *Journal of Urban History* 14 (1988): 372-93.

_____, *Urban Planning and Civic Order in Germany, 1860-1914.* Cambridge, Massachusetts, 1990.

Lane, Barbara Miller. *Architecture and Politics in Germany, 1918-1945.* Cambridge, Massachusetts, 1968.

Langewiesche, Dieter. "Politik-Gesellschaft-Kultur: Zur Problematik von Arbeiterkultur und kulturellen Arbeiterorganisation in Deutschland nach dem Ersten Weltkrieg." *Archiv für Sozialgeschichte* 22 (1982): 359-402.

Lees, Andrew, "Debates about the Big City in Germany, 1890-1914." *Societas* 5 (1975): 31-47.

_____, "Critics of Urban Society in Germany. 1854-1914." *Journal of the History of Ideas* 40 (1979):61-85.

_____, *Cities Perceived: Urban Society in European and American Thought, 1820-1940.* Manchester, 1985.

Lehnert, Detlef. "Das 'rote' Berlin: Hauptstadt der deutschen Arbeiterbewegung?" In *Studien zur Arbeiterbewegung und Arbeiterkultur in Berlin,* edited by Gert-Joachim Glaessner, Detlef Lehnert and Klaus Sühl, 1-35. Berlin, 1989.

_____, *Kommunale Politik, Parteiensystem und Interessenkonflikte in Berlin und Wien 1919-1932: Wohnungs-, Verkehrs- und Finanzpolitik im Spannungsfeld von städtischer Selbstverwaltung und Verbandseinflüssen.* Berlin, 1991.

_____, "Organisierter Hausbesitz und Kommunalpolitik in Wien und Berlin 1890-1933." *Geschichte und Gesellschaft* 20 (1994): 29-56

Lehnert, Detlef, and Klaus Megerle, eds. *Politische Identität und nationale Gedenktage: Zur politischen Kultur in der Weimarer Republik.* Opladen, 1989.

_____, eds. *Politische Teilkulturen zwischen Integration und Polarisierung: Zur politischen Kultur in der Weimarer Republik.* Opladen, 1990.

_____, eds. *Pluralismus als Verfassungs- und Gesellschaftsmodell: Zur politischen Kultur in der Weimarer Republik.* Opladen, 1993.

Lepsius, M. Rainer. "From Fragmented Party Democracy to Government by Emergency Decree and National Socialist Takeover: Germany." In *The Breakdown of Democratic Regimes,* edited by Juan J. Linz and Alfred Stepan, 34-79. Baltimore, 1978.

Lieberman, Ben. "Luxury or Public Investment? Productivity and Planning for Weimar Recovery." *Central European History* 26 (1993): 195-213.

_____, "Testing Peukert's Paradigm: The 'Crisis of Classical Modernity' in the 'New Frankfurt,' 1925-1930." *German Studies Review* 17 (1994): 287-303.

Lösche, Peter and Franz Walter. "Zur Organisationskultur der sozialdemokratische Arbeiterbewegung in der Weimarer Republik: Niedergang der Klassenkultur oder solidargemeinschaftlicher Höhepunkt?" *Geschichte und Gesellschaft* 15 (1989): 511-36.

Lohmann, Hartmut. "Organisierter Arbeitersport in Hannover in den 20er Jahren." In *Stadt und Moderne,* edited by Adelheid von Saldern, 253-84. Hamburg, 1989.

Luppe, Hermann. *Mein Leben.* Nuremberg, 1977.

Luther, Hans. *Politiker ohne Partei: Erinnerungen.* Stuttgart, 1960.

Lyth, Peter J. *Inflation and the Merchant Economy: The Hamburg Mittelstand, 1914-1924*. New York, 1990.

Maier, Charles. *Recasting Bourgeois Europe: Stabilization in France, Germany and Italy in the Decade after World War I*. Princeton, 1975.

Matzerath, Horst. *Urbanisierung in Preußen 1815-1914*. 2 vols. Stuttgart, 1985.

McElligott, Anthony. "Workers' Culture and Workers' Politics on Weimar's New Housing Estates: A Response to Adelheid von Saldern."*Social History* 17 (1992): 101-14.

_____, "Crisis in the Cities: The Collapse of Weimar." *History Today* 43 (1993): 18-24.

McNeil, William. *American Money and the Weimar Republic: Economics and Politics on the Eve of the Great Depression. The Political Economy of International Change*. New York, 1986.

Melling, Joseph, ed. *Housing Social Policy and the State*. London, 1980.

Merton, Richard. *Erinnernswertes aus meinem Leben, das über das Persönliche hinausgeht*. Frankfurt am Main, 1955.

Minuth, Karl-Heinz, ed. *Akten der Reichskanzlei Weimarer Republik: Die Kabinette Luther I und II*. 2 vols. Boppard am Rhein, 1977.

Mommsen, Hans. *Die verspielte Freiheit: der Weg der Republik von Weimar in den Untergang, 1918-1933*. Berlin, 1989.

Mommsen, Hans, Dietmar Petzina, and Bernd Weisbrod, eds. *Industrielles System und politische Entwicklung in der Weimarer Republik* 2 vols. Düsseldorf, 1974.

Nadel, Kurt. *Die deutsche Wohnungspolitik der letzten Jahre und die Bekämpfung des Wohnungsmangels*. Berlin, 1927.

Niehuss, Merith. *Arbeiterschaft In Krieg und Inflation: Soziale Schichtung und Lage der Arbeiter in Augsburg und Linz 1910 bis 1925*. Berlin, 1985.

_____, "Lebensweise und Familie in der Inflationszeit." In *Die Anpassung an die Inflation*, edited by Gerald D. Feldman, 237-77. Berlin, 1986.

Niethammer, Lutz, and Franz-Josef Brüggemeier. "Wie wohnten Arbeiter im Kaiserreich?" *Archiv für Sozialgeschichte* 16 (1976): 61-134.

Noakes, Jeremy. *The Nazi Party in Lower Saxony 1921-1933*. Oxford, 1971.

Nolan, Mary. *Social Democracy and Society: Working Class Radicalism in Düsseldorf, 1890-1920*. New York, 1981.

_____, "The Infatuation with Fordism: Social Democracy and Economic Rationalization in Weimar Germany." In *Chance and Illusion Labor in Retreat: Studies on the Social Crisis in Interwar*

Western Europe, edited by Wolfgang Maderthaner and Helmut Gruber, 151-84. Vienna, 1988.

_____, "Housework Made Easy: The Taylorized Housewife in Weimar Germany's Rationalized Economy." *Feminist Studies* 16 (1990): 558-67.

_____, *Visions of Modernity: American Business and the Modernization of Germany*. New York, 1994.

Novy, Klaus. *Strategien der Sozialisierung: Die Diskussion der Wirtschaftsreform in der Weimarer Republik*. Frankfurt, 1978.

Orlow, Dietrich. *Weimar Prussia, 1918-1925: The Unlikely Rock of Democracy*. Pittsburgh, 1986.

_____, *Weimar Prussia, 1925-1933: The Illusion of Strength*. Pittsburgh, 1991.

Parteitagkomittee Sozialdemokratischer Parteitag Magdeburg. *Die Rote Stadt im Roten Land*. Magdeburg, 1929.

Petzina, Dietmar. *Fahnen, Fäuste, Körper: Symbolik und Kultur der Arbeiterbewegung*. Essen, 1986.

Peukert, Detlev. *Grenzen der Sozialdisziplinierung: Aufstieg und Krise der deutschen Jugendfürsorge von 1878 bis 1932*. Cologne, 1986.

_____, *Die Weimarer Republik: Krisenjahre der klassischen Moderne*. Frankfurt am Main, 1987.

Pierson, Christopher. *Beyond the Welfare State? The New Political Economy of Welfare*. University Park, Pennsylvania, 1991.

Pinthus, Kurt. "Walter Hasenclever Leben und Werk." In *Gedichte, Dramen, Prosa, Walter Hasenclever*, edited by Kurt Pinthus, 6-62. Hamburg, 1963.

Pommer, Richard and Christian F Otto. *Weissenhof 1927 and the Modern Movement in Architecture*. Chicago, 1991.

Preller, Ludwig. *Sozialpolitik in der Weimarer Republik*. Stuttgart, 1949.

Rabinbach, Anson. *The Human Motor: Energy, Fatigue, and the Origins of Modernity*. New York, 1990.

Ranft, Norbert. "Erwerbslosenfürsorge, Ruhrkampf und Kommunen: Die Trendwende in der Sozialpolitik im Jahre 1923." In *Die Anpassung an die Inflation*, edited by Gerald D. Feldman, 163-201, Berlin, 1986.

Reagin, Nancy. *A German Women's Movement: Class and Gender in Hannover, 1880-1933*. Chapel Hill, 1995.

Rebentisch, Dieter. *Ludwig Landmann: Frankfurter Oberbürgermeister der Weimarer Republik*. Wiesbaden, 1975.

_____, "Städte und Monopol. Privatwirtschaftliche Ferngas oder kommunale Verbundwirtschaft in der Weimarer Republik."

Zeitschrift für Stadtgeschichte, Stadtsoziologie und Denkmalpflege 3 (1976): 38-80.

_____, "Die deutsche Sozialdemokratie und die kommunale Selbstverwaltung. Ein Überblick über Programmdiskussion und Organisationsproblematik 1890-1975." *Archiv für Sozialgeschichte* 25 (1981): 1-78.

_____, "Die Selbstverwaltung in der Weimarer Zeit." In *Handbuch der kommunalen Wissenschaft und Praxis*, Band 1, edited by Günter Püttner, 86-100. Berlin, 1981.

_____, "'Die treusten Söhne der deutschen Sozialdemokratie.' Linksopposition und kommunale Reformpolitik in der Frankfurter Sozialdemokratie der Weimarer Epoche." *Archiv für Frankfurts Geschichte und Kunst* 61 (1987): 299-354.

Reichsverband der deutschen Industrie. *Deutsche Wirtschafts- und Finanzpolitik*. Veröffentlichungen des Reichsverbandes der deutschen Industrie, Heft 29. Berlin, 1925.

_____, *Mitglieder-Versammlung des Reichsverbandes der deutschen Industrie am 2. und 3. September 1927 in Frankfurt am Main*. Berlin, 1927.

_____, *Aufstieg oder Niedergang? Deutsche Wirtschafts- und Finanzreform 1929*. Berlin, 1929.

Reulecke, Jürgen. *Die wirtschaftliche Entwicklung der Stadt Barmen von 1910 bis 1925*. Neustadt an der Aisch, 1973.

_____, "Vom blauen Montag zum Arbeiterurlaub: Vorgeschichte und Entstehung des Erholungsurlaubs für Arbeiter vor dem Ersten Weltkrieg." *Archiv für Sozialgeschichte* 16 (1976): 205-48.

_____, "Zur städtischen Finanzlage in den Anfangsjahren der Weimarer Republik." *Archiv für Kommunalwissenschaft* 21 (1982): 199-219.

_____, *Geschichte der Urbanisierung in Deutschland*. Frankfurt am Main, 1985.

_____, "Auswirkungen der Inflation auf die städtischen Finanzen." In *Nachwirkungen der Inflation auf die deutsche Geschichte*, edited by Gerald D. Feldman, 97-116. Munich, 1985.

_____, ed. *Die deutsche Stadt in Industrie-Zeitalter: Beiträge zur modernen deutschen Stadtgeschichte*. Wuppertal, 1978.

Reulecke, Jürgen, and Wolfhard Weber, eds. *Fabrik, Familie, Feierabend: Beitrag zur Sozialgeschichte des Alltags in Industriezeitalter*. Wuppertal, 1978.

Ritter, Gerhard A. *Sozialversicherung in Deutschland und England: Entstehung und Grundzüge im Vergleich*. Munich, 1983.

Rive, Richard Robert. *Lebenserinnerungen eines deutschen Oberbürgermeisters*. Stuttgart, 1960.

Rohe, Karl. *Wahlen und Wählertraditionen in Deutschland: Kulturelle Grundlagen deutscher Parteien und Parteiensysteme im 19. und 20. Jahrhundert*. Frankfurt am Main, 1992.

Röhrbein, Waldemar. *Hannover so wie es war*. Düsseldorf, 1979.

Röhrbein, Waldemar R., and Franz R. Zankl, eds. *Hannover im 20. Jahrhundert: Aspekte der neueren Stadtgeschichte*. Hannover, 1978.

Rodenstein, Marianne. *'Mehr Licht Mehr Luft': Gesundheitskonzepte in Städtebau seit 1750*. Frankfurt am Main, 1988.

Rodriguez-Lores, Juan, and Gerhard Fehl, eds. *Städtebaureform 1865-1900: Von Licht, Luft und Ordnung in der Stadt der Gründerzeit*. 2 vols. Hamburg, 1985.

_____, eds. *Die Kleinwohnungsfrage: Zu den Ursprüngen des sozialen Wohnungsbaus in Europa*. Hamburg, 1988.

Rolling, John. "Liberals, Socialists and City Government in Imperial Germany: the Case of Frankfurt am Main, 1900-1918." Ph.D. dissertation, University of Wisconsin-Madison, 1979.

_____, "Das Problem der 'Politisierung' der kommunalen Selbstverwaltung in Frankfurt am Main 1900-1918." *Archiv für Frankfurts Geschichte und Kunst* 57 (1980): 167-86.

Rublack, Hans-Christoph. "Städtebau und Sozialreform." *Die Alte Stadt* 6 (1979): 136-55.

Ruck, Michael, "Der Wohnungsbau – Schnittpunkt von Sozial- und Wirtschaftspolitik: Probleme der öffentlichen Wohnungspolitik in der Hauszinssteuer Ära 1924/24-1930/31." In *Die Weimarer Republik als Wohlfahrtsstaat*, edited by Werner Abelshauser. Stuttgart, 1987.

_____, "Wohnungsbaufinanzierung in der Weimarer Republik: Zielsetzungen, Ergebnisse, Probleme." In *Massenwohnung und Eigenheim: Wohnungsbau und Wohnen in der Großstadt seit dem Ersten Weltkrieg*, edited by Axel Schildt and Arnold Sywottek, 150-180. Frankfurt am Main, 1988.

Ruehl, Konrad, and Gerhard Weisser. *Das Wohnungswesen der Stadt Magdeburg*. Magdegburg, 1927.

Rürup, Reinhard, ed. *Arbeiter- und Soldatenräte im rheinisch-westfälischen Industriegebiet: Studien zur Geschichte der Revolution 1918/19*. Wuppertal, 1975.

Sachße, Christoph and Florian Tennstedt. *Fürsorge und Wohlfahrtspflege 1871 bis 1929*. Vol. 2 of *Geschichte der Armenfürsorge in Deutschland*. Stuttgart, 1988.

Saldern, Adelheid von. *Vom Einwohner zum Bürger: Zur Emanzipation der städtischen Unterschicht Göttingens 1890-1920. Eine sozial- und kommunalhistorische Untersuchung.* Berlin, 1973.

_____, "Sozialdemokratie und kommunale Wohnungsbaupolitik in den 20er Jahren – am Beispiel von Hamburg und Wien." *Archiv für Sozialgeschichte* 25 (1985): 183-237.

_____, "Arbeiterkulturbewegung in Deutschland in der Zwischenkriegszeit." In *Arbeiterkulturen zwischen Alltag und Politik: Beiträge zum europäischen Vergleich in der Zwischenkriegszeit,* edited by Friedehlm Boll, 29-70. Vienna, 1986.

_____, "Kommunale Verarmung und Armut in der Kommunen während der Grosse Krise (1929-1933)." *Soziale Bewegungen* 3 (1987): 69-109.

_____, "Kommunaler Handlungsspielraum in der Wohnungspolitik während der Zeit der Weimarer Republik." In *Stadterneurung in der Weimarer Republik und im Nationalsozialismus: Beiträge zur stadtbaugeschichtlichen Forschung,* edited by Kopetzki, Lasch, Luken-Isberner and Schlier. Kassel, 1987.

_____, ed. *Stadt und Moderne: Hannover in der Weimarer Republik.* Hamburg, 1989.

Saunders, Peter. *Social Theory and the Urban Question.* London, 1986.

Scarpa, Ludovica. "Martin Wagner oder die Rationalisierung des Glücks." In *Martin Wagner 1885-1957,* Akademie der Künste, 8-23. Berlin, 1985.

Schacht, Hjalmar, *Eigene oder geborgte Währung.* Leipzig, 1927.

Schloßmann, Arthur, ed. *GE-SO-LEI Grosse Ausstellung Düsseldorf 1926.* Düsseldorf, 1927.

Scholz, Robert. "Die Auswirkungen der Inflation auf das Sozial- und Wohlfahrtswesen der neuen Stadtgemeinde Berlin." In *Konsequenzen der Inflation,* edited by Gerald D. Feldman, 45-75. Berlin, 1989.

Schöhnhagen, Benigna. "Zwischen Verweigerung und Agitation: Landtagspolitik der NSDAP in Württemberg 1928/29-1933." In *Die Machtergreifung in Südwestdeutschland: Das Ende der Weimarer Republik in Baden und Württemberg 1928-1933,* edited by Thomas Schnabel, 113-49. Stuttgart, 1982.

Schulze, Hagen. *Weimar Deutschland 1917-1933.* Berlin, 1982.

Schumacher, Martin. *Mittelstandsfront und Republik: Die Wirtschaftspartei – Reichspartei des deutschen Mittelstandes 1919-1933.* Düsseldorf, 1972.

Schwarz, Hans-Peter. *Konrad Adenauer: A German Politician and Statesman in a Period of War, Revolution and Reconstruction.* Vol. 1. Translated by Louise Willmot. Providence, 1995.

Schwarzwalder, Herbert. *Bremen in der Weimarer Republik 1918 1933.* Vol. 3 of *Geschichte der Freien Hansestadt Bremen.* Bremen, 1975-1985.

Sheehan, James. "Liberalism and the City in Nineteenth-Century Germany." *Past and Present* 51 (1971): 116-37.

Sierks, Hans Ludwig. *Wirtschaftlicher Städtebau und angewandete kommunale Verkehrs-Wissenschaft.* Dresden, 1926.

————, *Grundriß der sicheren, reichen, ruhigen Stadt.* Dresden, 1929.

Silverman, Dan. "A Pledge Unredeemed: The Housing Crisis in Weimar Germany." *Central European History* 3 (1970): 112-39.

Simons, Hans, Fritz Jahn, Helga Kluge et al. *Die Körperkultur in Deutschland von 1917 bis 1945.* Vol. 3 of *Geschichte der Körperkultur in Deutschland,* edited by Wolfgang Eichel. 3 vols. Berlin, 1964.

Sontheimer, Kurt. *Antidemokratisches Denken in der Weimarer Republik: Die politischen Ideen des deutschen Nationalismus zwischen 1918 und 1933.* Munich, 1962.

Stachura, Peter, ed. *Unemployment and the Great Depression in Weimar Germany.* New York, 1986.

————, *The Weimar Republic and the Younger Proletariat: An Economic and Social Analysis.* New York, 1989.

Statistisches Jahrbuch deutscher Städte. Leipzig, 1927-1929.

Statistisches Jahrbuch deutscher Städte. Jena, 1930-1933.

Stehkämper, Hugo, ed. *Konrad Adenauer: Oberbürgermeister von Köln.* Cologne, 1976.

Stein, Erwin, ed. *Die Finanzierung des Wohnungsbaus.* Berlin-Friedenau, 1927.

Steinborn, Peter. *Grundlagen und Grundzüge Münchener Kommunalpolitik in den Jahren der Weimarer Republik: Zur Geschichte der bayerischen Landeshauptstadt im 20. Jahrhundert.* Munich, 1968.

Stübling, Rainer. *Kultur und Massen: Das Kulturkartell der modernen Arbeiterbewegung in Frankfurt am Main von 1925 bis 1933.* Offenbach am Main, 1983.

Stürmer, Michael. *Koalition und Opposition in der Weimarer Republik 1924-1928.* Düsseldorf, 1967.

Sutcliffe, Anthony. *Towards the Planned City: Germany, Britain, the United States, and France, 1780-1914.* New York, 1981.

————, ed. *Metropolis 1890-1940.* London, 1984.

Suval, Stanley. *Electoral Politics in Wilhelmine Germany*. Chapel Hill, 1985.

Taut, Bruno. *Die neue Baukunst in Europa und Amerika*. Stuttgart, 1929.

Teuteberg, Hans-Jürgen, ed. *Urbanisierung im 19. und 20. Jahrhundert: Historische und geographische Aspekte*. Cologne, 1983.

_____, ed. *Stadtwachstum, Industrialisierung, sozialer Wandel: Beiträge zur Erforschung der Urbanisierung im 19. und 20. Jahrhundert*. Berlin, 1986.

Thienel, Ingrid. "Verstädterung, städtische Infrastruktur und Stadtplanung: Berlin zwischen 1850-1914." *Zeitschrift für Stadtgeschichte, Stadtsoziologie und Denkmalpflege* 4 (1977):55-84.

Timm, Christoph. *Gustav Oelsner und das Neue Altona: Kommunale Architektur und Stadtplanung in der Weimarer Republik*. Hamburg, 1984.

Torinus, Theodor. *Die deutsche Wohnungspolitik der Nachkriegszeit und ihre Auswirkungen auf das Wohnungswesen in Berlin*. Leipzig, 1930.

Turner, Henry Ashby. *German Big Business and the Rise of Hitler*. New York, 1985.

Überhorst, Horst. *Frisch, Frei, Stark und Treu: Die Arbeitersportbewegung in Deutschland 1893-1933*. Düsseldorf, 1983.

Ungers, Liselotte. *Die Suche nach einer neuen Wohnform: Siedlungen der zwanziger Jahre damals und heute*. Stuttgart, 1983.

Van der Will, Wilfried, and Rob Burns. *Arbeiterkulturbewegung in der Weimarer Republik: Texte, Dokumente, Bilder*. Frankfurt am Main, 1982.

Verwaltungsbericht der Stadt Düsseldorf für den Zeitraum vom 1. April 1925 bis 31 März 1928.

Wagner, Martin. *Das wachsende Haus: Ein Beitrag zur Lösung der städtischen Wohnungsfrage*. Berlin, 1932.

Wall, Richard, and Jay Winter, eds. *The Upheaval of War: Family, Work, and Welfare in Europe, 1914-1918*. Cambridge, 1988.

Walter, Franz "Konfliktreiche Integration: Arbeiterkultur im Kaiserreich und in der Weimarer Republik." *Internationale wissenschaftliche Korrespondenz zur Geschichte der deutschen Arbeiterbewegung* 24 (1988):318

Walter, Friedrich. *Schicksal einer deutschen Stadt: Geschichte Mannheims, 1907-1945*. 2 vols. Frankfurt, 1950.

Weber, Adolf. *Hat Schacht Recht? Die Abhängigkeit der deutschen Volkswirtschaft vom Ausland*. Munich, 1927.

Weiss, Wisso. *Die Sozialisierung des Wohnungswesen unter besonderer Berücksichtigung der Verhältnisse in Deutschland und Oesterreich.* Heidelberg, 1930.

Weitensteiner, Hans Kilian. *Karl Flesch: Kommunale Sozialpolitik in Frankfurt am Main.* Frankfurt am Main, 1976.

Weisbrod, Bernd. *Schwerindustrie in der Weimarer Republik: Interessenpolitik zwischen Stabilisierung und Krise.* Wuppertal, 1978.

Wells, Roger. *German Cities: A Study of Contemporary Municipal Politics and Administration.* Princeton, 1932.

Whalen, Robert Weldon. *Bitter Wounds: German Victims of the Great War, 1914-1939.* Ithaca, 1984.

Wickham, James, "Working-Class Movements and Working-Class Life: Frankfurt am Main during the Weimar Republic." *Social History* 8 (1983): 315-44.

Wie Oberbürgermeister Dr. Landmann regierte: Fünf Jahre Frankfurter Kommunalpolitik. Frankfurt am Main-Süd, 1929.

Wiegand, Heinz. *Entwicklung des Stadtgrüns in Deutschland zwischen 1890 und 1925 am Beispiel der Arbeiten Fritz Enckes.* Berlin, 1982.

Willett, John. *The Weimar Years: A Culture Cut Short.* New York, 1984.

———, *The Theater of the Weimar Republic.* New York, 1988.

Winkler, Heinrich August. *Der Schein der Normalität: Arbeiter und Arbeiterbewegung in der Weimarer Republik, 1924 bis 1930.* Berlin, 1985.

Witt, Peter-Christian. "Inflation, Wohnungszwangswirtschaft und Hauszinssteuer: Zur Regelung von Wohnungsbau und Wohnungsmarkt in der Weimarer Republik." In *Wohnen im Wandel: Beiträge zur Geschichte des Alltags in der bürgerlichen Gesellschaft,* edited by Lutz Niethammer, 385-407. Wuppertal, 1979.

Wunderer, Hartmann. *Arbeitervereine und Arbeiterparteien: Kultur und Massenbewegung in der Arbeiterbewegung (1890-1933).* Frankfurt, 1980.

Zehn Jahre deutsche Geschichte 1918-1928. Berlin, 1928.

Zadach-Buchmeier, Frank. "Staatliche Jugendpflege in der kommunalen Praxis: Das Beispiel Hannover." In *Stadt und Moderne,* edited by Adelheid von Saldern, 155-88. Hamburg, 1989.

Ziebill, Otto. *Geschichte des Deutschen Städtetages: Fünfzig Jahre deutsche Kommunalpolitik.* Stuttgart, 1956.

Zitelmann, Rainer. "Die Totalitäre Seite der Moderne." In *Nationalsozialismus und Modernisierung: Mit einem aktuellen Nachwort zur Neuauflage,* edited by Michael Prinz and Rainer Zitelmann, 1-20. Darmstadt, 1994.

Index